From *Antz* to *Titanic*

From *Antz* to *Titanic*

Reinventing Film Analysis

Martin Barker

with Thomas Austin

Pluto Press

First published 2000 by Pluto Press
345 Archway Road, London N6 5AA
and 22883 Quicksilver Drive, Sterling, VA 20166-2012, USA
www.plutobooks.com

British Library Cataloguing in Publication Data
A catalogue record for this book is available from the British Library

ISBN 0 7453 1584 4 hbk
ISBN 0 7453 1579 8 pbk

Library of Congress Cataloging in Publication Data

Barker, Martin.
    From Antz to Titanic : a student guide to film analysis / Martin Barker, with
Thomas Austin.
        p.   cm.
    Includes bibliographical references.
    ISBN 0–7453–1584–4 (hardbound)
    1. Film criticism. I. Austin, Thomas. II. Title.

PN1995 .B266 2000
791.43′01′5—dc21   00–023268

Designed and produced for Pluto Press by
Chase Production Services, Chadlington, OX7 3LN
Typeset from disk by Marina Typesetting, Minsk, Belarus
Printed in the EU by T. J. International, Padstow

Contents

Acknowledgements

This book owes its existence to a confluence of two things. In spring 1999 I was teaching a course at the University of Sussex. The course, called Visual Media Influence, introduces students to the close examination and analysis of media forms, especially films, and asks them to think reflexively about the theories that lie behind different kinds of analysis. Running the course for the first time, and wanting to make a few changes to it, I went looking, with colleagues, for just *good working examples of analysis*: case studies where an author had taken an individual film and shown *how* to do an analysis. Ideally they should have gone the extra step to reflect on their own procedures and assumptions, but OK, even without that.

Trouble was that three of us could come up with only a very few examples. And those that we could find were frequently troubled by doses of theoretical gastro-enteritis. Walking the library shelves one day, I pulled off yet another book with a title something like *Feminism and Film Theory*, and found that two students had written their anguish into the margins, at the end of the first essay:

> **'I'm a first year (male) student and this essay just seems to me a load of jargon'**
> **'Well I'm a second year (female) student and I agree – this entire book is just pants'**

'Pants', of course, is a 1990s young person's term for something that is bad, awful, rubbish, useless. I sympathised – although the book and that first essay were not the worst of their kind. My first acknowledgement therefore goes to two students who really shouldn't write in the margins of library books – but I do sympathise.

This book also owes much to an endless series of conversations between myself and Thomas Austin, who has of course co-authored one chapter. But the book owes much more than that to him. He has been willing to swap references, argue ideas, look at drafts, and agree to endless reworkings of the finer points of theorising 'special effects'.

Beyond this, I owe two apologies. One, to the students on the Visual Media Analysis course that year, who got too much of an undigested version of what, hopefully, makes a bit more sense now. The notion of the 'implied audience' at least should be clear enough, here on in, for the next generation of you to say 'No!' to. And, an apology to Judith, my wife. I promise not to make you watch any of these films again. I wish I could promise that I won't inflict any more of the worst kind of jokes that the process of writing this book has seemed to pull out of me.

1
Films, Audiences and Analyses

Everybody analyses films. People walking out of cinemas turn to each other and say: 'What did you make of that, then?' And as soon as they go past simply recording likes and dislikes, pleasures and disappointments, their answers start dealing in the coinage of analysis: talking about characters and their motivations, about acting, its convincingness and contribution to the film, about the story (did it make sense? *what* sense did it make? what gaps, puzzling bits, incoherences were experienced?). The more people chat about a film afterwards, the more they make analyses, collaboratively.

Journalists do it, too, and all reviewers. They offer versions of each film they write about. Because they do it within a genre of writing – reviews have a job to do, telling you enough about a film to let you think about whether it is for you, without so telling it that you feel pre-empted – they have developed typical ways of recounting the narrative of movies, but often with a degree of conscious withholding. In this they are helped by the film companies who, in press packs and publicity materials, analyse their own movies.

Really clever reviewers enter a new category, they become film *critics* – people who can place a film in a tradition for you, who will tell you about the director, the cinematography, the special effects. They will point you to continuities, and offer a sense of the significance of a particular film. These people are also analysing films. A number of them make an additional living out of writing books about directors, actors, studios, and the making of particular films.

Politicians, pundits and moral campaigners do it. From time to time, they pick up on a film that affronts them. Affront is more than dislike – it signals that they are *worried* by a film, or – perhaps more often – feel that they *ought to be* worried by it. To give voice to their worries, they search the film for 'messages' which they can see, but others unfortunately won't –

but that will be a mark of their weakness, that they are being corrupted and just don't realise it.

So what is it that *academic* analysts of films can claim to do, that others – all those ordinary viewers, fans, reviewers, critics, politicians, pundits – don't, or can't? What knowledge or understanding can we claim to produce that is different from, or even in some ways superior to, what others produce? This book attempts to answer these questions, and at the same time to challenge some worrying answers that are current, indeed fashionable, within film studies.

Why Bother Analysing Films?

There is an unlimited number of questions you can ask of films, each of which will lead you to investigate and analyse them with different priorities. But if you are doing it properly, of course, the results must be in some broad way compatible with each other. It's a useful imaginative exercise to ask, of any films you are interested in: what questions are worth asking here? And then to follow that with some consequential ones: what kind of interest in the film(s) does each question raise, and what sort of object does it presume the films to be? How would each question lead you to investigate your films, what main characteristics would you have to attend to? And, what would be exemplary cases – which films ought most to command your attention, and test the adequacy of your answers?

Here is a sample list of questions that could in principle be asked of films:
1   How does African cinema differ from American cinema?
2   What is the function of point-of-view shots in films, and what are the main kinds of such shots?
3   What are the common characteristics, and the evolving stylistics, of Paul Verhoeven's films?
4   How have star personae been enacted on screen in different periods?
5   How has 1980s Hollywood reflected (on) American politics?
6   What influences are evident in the construction of underground horror films? How do these relate to subcultural uses of these films?

The first – and not inconsequential – thing to note about all these questions is the way each presumes that there is a coherent object that can indeed be investigated. Is there a meaningful object called 'African cinema'? Why should we presume that point-of-view shots perform a delimited set of jobs? Did Paul Verhoeven have sufficient control over all his films, including his earliest ones, for there to be a thread of continuous style? And so on.

The acceptance that there is an object to be researched is vital, as we will see when we consider the still-dominant 'effects' tradition. What's notable, next, is that all these questions make claims about things external to the films they address. This is obvious in some cases. Question 3 will necessarily involve a consideration of Verhoeven's life, and his relations with those he worked with (producers, scriptwriters, cinematographers) since we will need to know that a particular feature was the result of his influence. Question 5, for instance, presumes a knowledge of 1980s American politics – but then seeks not only to add to that, but perhaps to *amend* it in the light of learning about the ways filmic representations of events may themselves have played a role, for example, in the conduct of political campaigns. Question 6 looks in two directions – at the factors shaping makers of films, and at the users of films. But it offers, potentially, to close the loop by seeing these as a live circuit in which fans of these horror movies follow the cues of the makers, and in turn cue them as to their interests: blurring the lines between makers and audiences. Question 1 involves us in creating categories, whose significances we will then have to explore: is there a *typical kind* of film made in Africa, and America, are there not for example directors who have moved from one continent to the other, and are there implied differences in the *uses* to which cinema is put in the two continents? Once again, we have left the purely cinematic. Question 4 is more complicated, but once we take note of, for instance, Richard Dyer's classic works on stars, we realise that these personae are as much produced off screen as on it,[1] and that an important issue is how these were kept in touch and co-ordinated with each other.

The remaining questions get more complicated, the longer you look at them. Question 2 *sounds* as though it only concerns the mechanics of films – and sometimes authors *write* as if this was the case. But in fact, to explain the function of point-of-view shots in a film, you would inevitably have to deal with such things as how this contributes to the construction of positions from which an audience can participate in a film, who or what is in control of showing us things, and so on – or, what is sometimes called 'extra-diegetic constructs'. And so the 'audience' creeps into our film analyses.

In all six cases, then, the questions lead us to examine the relations between the cinematic and the extra-cinematic. And this is where the trouble starts. For we need a theory of how these are related in general. Question 3, about Verhoeven, for instance: answered from within the approach known as 'auteurism', which puts centre-stage the issue of film-makers' style and associates this with meaning and quality, the approach will be markedly different than if it is answered from within a political economy approach, which stresses the structural conditions within which films are made. Question 2, looked at by someone who believes that films work by creating 'identification', will get quite a different answer than when it is examined by someone like myself, who doubts the case for that concept. Putting this generally, before we can begin to answer questions such as these, there has to be some general idea about how films relate to the world beyond them: the world of politics, the wider world of culture, ideas, ideologies, the films' makers, and their audiences. It is this last which, more than the others, this book is interested in.

For behind these many, and perfectly valid, questions lies one which is harder to answer, but which these particular questions in the end all assume – the question how films *mean*. All these questions presume that a film is, at least potentially, more than a passing of $1\frac{1}{2}$ hours (or however much it happens to be) in front of a large or small screen. Every time films come under scrutiny, for morals, causing crime, being politically-charged or whatever, the first response has commonly been: 'But it's only a piece of entertainment.' The 'only' is a boundary fence, designed to guard against any argument that seeing a film was anything beyond a self-enclosed experience: finished, without connections, implications, consequences. 'Just a piece of fun.' Again, hear that gate shutting. 'Simply a film.' Slam. But every kind of film theory is an attempt to say that something more is at stake. What it is, is – and has to be – argued over.

- It may be that film is significant – 'means' – by virtue of its *educational* capacity.[2] Do films in some way broaden people's ability to perceive and understand their world? Is there a connection between film literacy and other kinds of literacy?
- Films may matter ('mean') by virtue of their ability to deliver *aesthetic* experiences. In that case, some working distinctions between 'quality' and other movies would need to be put in place.
- All the arguments about the possible 'harmfulness' of certain kinds of film, in particular those which presume that *visual* materials have greater inherent persuasiveness, are another kind of implication of 'meaningfulness', where films outrun their experiential immediacy.
- Films may resonate significantly with their social, cultural, political environs. The weakest version of this is the claim that films 'reflect' the world – in which case they are only a kind of second-hand evidence of what is going on elsewhere. But in other versions, films *participate* in the social and political process, and are seen as carriers of ideas and ideologies – in extreme versions counting among the most important carriers in the last century.

• Films may work to produce communities of experience: shared perceptions of the world, a joyous sense of belonging and common culture.

All these and potentially many more are claims about the ways films' meaning-making capacities run beyond, or have consequences beyond, the time of actually watching. And of course a number of them may be true together. What matters here is that each claim is simultaneously a claim about the nature of *films* – their nature, organisation and capacity to do more than be watched; a claim about *how* films can work on and with their context to play their larger role; and also a claim about that context – how *it* works, in its relation to films. The part that interests this book, not because it is the only or most important but because a lot of awful claims are made about it, is that part which considers films in relation to their audiences. How may we understand films' potential to engage their audiences in ideas, understandings, images, ideologies, dreams, fantasies, hopes and fears such that the films make a distinguishable contribution to their wider relations to the world?

The Embedded Audience

Consider the following descriptions of a group of films: 'paranoid, claustrophobic, hopeless, doomed, predetermined by the past, without clear moral or personal identity'. Leave aside for a moment what films this was said to be true of, and by whom. Ask instead: if true, what would this say about the people who chose to see such films? If someone whose judgement we trusted told us that a film we were wondering about seeing was paranoid, claustrophobic, etc., chances are we would stay away – unless of course we were the kind of viewer who is into 'sicko' films. If a film publicised *itself* in these terms, it would surely be regarded as, at least, taking a great risk of alienating audiences. Why would a person ever choose to see a film with such characteristics – or if they found themselves in a cinema showing such a film, why would they not leave or just reject the whole horrible experience?

Why indeed? Yet film analysts frequently make claims of this kind. The above words could have come from any number of moralising analyses of films, worrying about the dangers of 'violent' or 'pornographic' movies and their 'effects' on people. And if asked why people then choose to see such films, the answer, explicitly or implicitly, tends to be of one of these kinds: films like this offer cheap thrills and pleasures, to disguise their rotten messages; these are vulnerable audiences, they do not know what they are doing; the fact that they enjoy these things is evidence of how damaged, or degraded, they already are. Without such additions, the account of the films themselves becomes effectively incomprehensible.

The words are in fact taken from an essay on *film noir* by Janey Place, which argues that *noir* films such as *Double Indemnity* (1944) are an expression of male fantasies, 'as is most of our art'.[3] Why, then, did many women enjoy watching them? Place does offer an explanation. Her argument is that these films have a double trajectory: overall they are patriarchal, in that the women – who have endangered male dominance by asserting themselves socially and sexually – mostly have to die by the end of the film. But the films have an 'excess'. In showing these strong, assertive women, the films outdo themselves, and undo some of their own ideological intentions:

> Visually, film noir is fluid, sensual, extraordinarily expressive, making the sexually expressive woman, which is its dominant usage of women, extremely powerful. It is not their inevitable demise we remember but rather their strong, dangerous, and above all, exciting sexuality. In film noir we observe both the social action of myth which damns the sexual woman and all who become enmeshed by her, and a particularly potent stylistic presentation of the sexual strength of women which man fears. This operation of myth is so highly stylised and conventionalised that the final 'lesson' of the myth often fades into the background and we retain the image of the erotic, strong, unrepressed (if destructive) woman.[4]

I am not concerned here with the correctness of this analysis, but with the way it (necessarily) incorporates and builds upon an image of the audience, their reasons for and the manner of their involvement in the film. Notice the repeated 'we' which Place has to intrude. These have surely to be women, not men, or these films are failing badly in their claimed ideological mission. That mission, as commonly stated by work of this ilk, is to give expression to men's supposed fears of the 'castrating woman' who is then punished for the threat she posed. So, men go to see films of this kind because of an endlessly recurrent lack/need in themselves to deal with a fear they are claimed to have. A film is 'good' if it arouses but then swiftly assuages those fears, by punishing the woman. Thus, a man may *say* that he has gone to see, and enjoyed, such a movie because he likes the director, fancies the star, enjoys a good narrative, was keeping his partner company, etc. But these are discountable explanations. His male 'lack' 'explains' the meaning of the film and its role. But not for women. Women enjoying such a film must either be deeply masochistic (as famously Laura Mulvey claimed, and decried[5]) or they must get something different out of it. Either way, what is crucial is that all such arguments are simultaneously making claims about three things: (1) how films work to make meanings, (2) how they work on their audiences, and thus (3) what an implied audience is doing with the film.

All film analysis makes claims about 'the audience'. Some approaches to analysis admit it and openly declare their premises. Others don't. *Very few* have been willing to take the step and look for evidence, let alone conduct research, to find out the truth or otherwise of their claims. This problem is so endemic it is worth pausing on. Suppose a doctor made claims that a drug which s/he had discovered had special properties – s/he analysed the drug's chemistry, and from the basis of that offered a proposition as to the way it would operate on a human body, and thus asserted on which people it would be effective in which ways (curing this, damaging that, having these side-effects). This is a fair analogy, given the number of accounts of films which use medical metaphors (think how often attacks on the media talk about them as 'drug-like', 'addictive', and so on). What would be the response, if it was discovered that no clinical trials had been conducted, and everything was claimed on the basis of a laboratory analysis?

Take a case in point. Here is Douglas Kellner talking about the film *Top Gun* (1986), a film which he claims to be the arch-embodiment of 'Reaganite fantasies':

> The film opens with titles indicating that in 1969 the Navy Air Corps set up a school to train elite aerial fighters, and in a later training session, it is announced that the US needs to maintain its ratio of expert aerial fighter pilots in the contemporary world. The message is that even in a high-tech, computerized society, individual initiative and skill are crucial, indeed essential, to military survival. At one point Maverick valorizes individual intuitive ability rather than cognitive abilities: 'You don't have time to think up there. If you think, you're dead.' The same anti-intellectual ethos pervaded the *Star Wars* films and inadvertently put on display the anti-intellectualism and thoughtlessness that was an essential part of Reaganism, promoted daily by President Feel-Good and by the commercial media which shared his values and anti-intellectualism (i.e. advertising, for instance, works by addressing and manipulating fears and fantasies, and not by utilizing rational discourse: Reaganism and media culture work, I suggest, in a similar fashion).[6]

Again, not because this is specially wrong, or bad, let us explore what assumptions have to be made for this to hold true. (1) It has to make sense to accumulate, additively, an opening piece of narration that sets the scene for the main narrative, with the comment of a character (whose place within the narrative is not considered). (2) We have to know how to find a 'message' – that is, something which has a propositional content and which thus operates to convince audiences about the world around them – within a story. (3) We have to agree to a generalisation from a *case* where thinking is risky (high-speed flying and thinking are not compatible) to a *rule* (there's too much intellectualising going on in our world – get back to good sense). (4) These allow us to jump genres, and see the cumulative presence of an ideology in *Top Gun* and *Star Wars* – although the latter doesn't *look* anti-intellectual, with its emphasis on opening the mind, expanding horizons, etc. (5) All this is framed by an opposition between 'rational discourse', and 'manipulating fears and fantasies'. This latter now sounds very like Janey Place's account of *film noir*. You may think that you watch and enjoy films because they are funny, or well-made, or informing, or whatever. But actually they are working on your fears and fantasies, ones you didn't even know you had … (6) And thus we arrive at a broad conclusion that media culture and a whole style of politics 'work' in the same way.

The point here is not the acceptability or otherwise of Kellner's account, but that to accept it I have tacitly to agree to so many steps. These are steps which simultaneously tell me how to 'read' a film, and tell me how it works on audiences – as a result of which, Kellner can ask:

> One wonders how many pilots and soldiers who joined the military and fought in the Panama invasion, the Gulf War, and other military escapades of the era were influenced by such cinematic propaganda. Hollywood films, like the Hollywood President, are not innocent entertainment, but lethal weapons in the service of dominant socio-economic forces.[7]

Note the rhetorical force of this: 'wondering' becomes an effective substitute for finding out – or at least, asking how we might know if the speculation is true. Would it be an adequate test to see if a higher proportion of those (mainly young males) signing up had seen the film than hadn't? Or how about, seen it more than once? Should we differentiate signing up for *any* role – after all, Kellner does mention soldiers as well as pilots – or signing up to be pilots specifically? Or could we think of a way to distinguish 'rational' from 'non-rational' enlisting? It hardly matters, since Kellner isn't interested in real tests, only in the rhetoric of claims. This is what concerns me.

All film analyses embed claims about the audience – and I am no different. But the claims are of different kinds, and some come closer than others to admitting tests of their claims. Without trying to be panoptic, let me show three different kinds of claims currently to be found at play.

Professor Browne's Belated Bullet

The most common claims, let us first say, are those which belong to the 'effects' tradition. Given so much is said in advocacy of this approach, I don't intend to spend long setting out its basic ideas. Put crudely, it is that films – and other media, especially visual ones – have the potential to influence people in such a way that their wider views of the world will be shifted, and ultimately that they may copy what they have seen. People working in this tradition dislike it when others put their ideas this way, but it seems to me to remain irreducibly true that this is what they continue to claim. The tradition now makes a great virtue of an advance it believes it has made, from the simple 'Magic Bullet' assumption of early research (which saw things like films injecting messages into the brains of the living – ouch!) to supposedly more complex models. These more complex models still use the same *language* – of 'identification', 'desensitisation', 'harm' – but they now add two components: that not everybody is affected equally, and that social processes can mediate impact. So, nowadays the search is on for what might be called the 'conditions of vulnerability'. Who are the most prone to being influenced? What might protect them from such influences, if they can't be eliminated? But what that influence might be is still virtually unquestioned. Since this is the purpose of this book, I am certainly not going to attempt some thorough overview of this field.[8] I am interested here only in the way they embed claims about the nature of films.

Take a working example. Currently influential in the UK with bodies like the British Board of Film Classification is the work of Kevin Browne, and his Home Office-funded research on video and violent offenders. Recently elevated to professorial status, he summarised his approach in his inaugural lecture. Placing himself firmly within the tradition of research currently typified by American researchers such as Huesmann and Eron, he concludes that '[o]verall, psychological research has concluded that an association exists between aggressive behaviour and viewing violence on the screen'. But his research complicates this by distinguishing two modes of influence: 'Those more predisposed to violence will become active in their violent behaviour as their aggressive thoughts are reinforced and triggered', while '[t]hose less predisposed to violence will become passive in their responses to violence as they become desensitised and habituate to violent imagery'.[9]

This doesn't sound like film analysis, but it is. It is, for instance, when he says, as a hundred such accounts before him have: 'The average American child or teenager has been estimated to view 10,000 murders, rapes and aggravated assaults per year on television alone … and a large proportion of studies support the finding that aggressive or anti-social behaviour can be increased after watching violent films and television.' This is not just a claim about effects, but about the material claimed to have those effects. To arrive at those figures, it has been necessary to count incidents without regard to context, across cartoons, news, documentaries, soap operas, sit-coms, dramas, advertisements, etc. It has been necessary to ignore the differences between *witnessing* them, and having them *implied* or *reported*. And it has been necessary to categorise incidents by classificatory techniques which can treat as equivalent a news scene of police and demonstrators clashing, a fight sequence from an action-adventure film, and an over-the-ball challenge in football. No different in principle than Douglas Kellner, this makes presumptions at all those three levels. It finds 'messages' in incidents, and accumulates them. It models a presumed link between films and audiences ('stimulation' or 'desensitisation'). And thus it gets to claims about the 'audience'. The difference is this: whereas Kellner operates with a relatively sophisticated model of what a film is (it has a story, it is narrated, etc.) and then leaps to putative audience effects, Browne works entirely oppositely. For all his sophisticated research techniques, his argument presupposes an utterly naïve and stupid categorisation of films. Here is his account:

Films in the cinema, on video or transmitted to televisions by cable, satellite and terrestrial channels can be classified, in terms of the violence they may portray, into three broad categories: violent drama films, violent action films and violent horror films ('video nasties'). **Violent Drama films** reflect the impetuous violent nature of people's lives, in the context of human personality. The primary purpose of a violent drama film is to express rather than to cause excitement. The violence portrayed is necessary to tell the story (eg. *Schindler's List*). **Violent Action films** represent violence separated from a context of social responsibility. They trivialise violent interactions by treating them in a mechanical way. The primary purpose is to excite and stimulate the viewer rather than concentrate on the story to be told (eg, *Rambo, Out for Justice*). **Violent Horror films** ('video nasties') celebrate excessive violence which misrepresents individual personalities by portraying them as lacking those altruistic factors which are essential to being human. The primary purpose of these films is for the viewer to share in the degradation, humiliation, physical harm and death of people as a form of entertainment (eg, *Cannibal Holocaust* which has been banned in the UK).[10]

What assumptions are at work here? Frankly, too many – and too foolish – to recount in full here.[11] Let the following short selection serve for the remainder. First, the categories are simply incoherent. What should we make of, for instance, *Natural Born Killers* (1994), *Saving Private Ryan* (1998) or *Rocky* (1976)? According to many, *Natural Born Killers* is, precisely, an examination of the 'impetuous violent nature of people's lives', yet according to others this is a movie which might have 'caused' at least one murder. *Saving Private Ryan* was celebrated and Oscar-nominated for its depiction of the horrors of war – yet it aroused hard-to-handle emotions, in particular among war veterans. *Rocky*, very much the partner to *Rambo* (1982) which does service for Browne as a film that just 'excites and stimulates the viewer', was adjudged by many – including the Oscar voters – as a rich study of a man from the back-streets fighting his way up. 'Violent horror films', doubling as 'video nasties' – a term which only ever served to obfuscate – no doubt include *Driller Killer* (1979). For a long time banned, it has now been re-released and is widely regarded as an interesting film.[12] Browne's categories are simply arbitrary collages which only make sense because they allow him the licence then to label film *audiences*: they are either serious and worthy (watching violence only when it is 'necessary in order to tell the story'), gratuitous but probably a bit dumb (watching violence whose 'primary purpose is to excite and stimulate') and downright dangerous (watching just to 'share in the degradation, humiliation, physical harm and death … as a form of entertainment'). *They* might say it differently, *we* know better.

Browne's research is highly regarded – and that tells us a worrying tale. He has a method for looking at films (count up the bad bits; ignore everything to do with history (filmic or social), stylistics, genre, narrative and narration, etc.; then label by current prejudice). He has a theory of how films work (they 'excite', either for good or ill, that's all that is worth saying). And these warrant his hunt for the 'vulnerable audience'. Browne is sadly typical of this whole way of addressing films. Ignorance and stupidity managing to pass unnoticed.

David Bordwell's Cognitive Correspondent

If I dare mention it in the next breath to such dangerous folly, consider next the classic approach of film historian David Bordwell. For twenty years now, Bordwell has been elaborating a sophisticated and grounded approach to film history, and to the ways films are constructed and work with audiences. His approach, often formulated in argument with work on films with which he disagrees, centres on the ways films 'cue' cognitive operations in their viewers. In his *Narration in the Fiction Film*, he deals directly with the view of the 'spectator' his approach presumes:

> [T]he 'spectator' is not a particular person, not even me. Nor is the spectator an 'ideal reader', which in recent reader response criticism tends to be the most fully equipped receiver the text could imagine. The one most adequate to all the aspects of meaning presented. I adopt the term 'viewer' or 'spectator' to name a hypothetical entity executing the operations relevant to constructing a story out of the film's representation.... Insofar as an empirical viewer makes sense of the story, his or her activities coincide with the process I will be describing.[13]

This approach sees films as making proposals to and demands on an audience – who may or may not be willing or fit to meet them. In *Narration*, Bordwell is particularly concerned with all the ways films give and withhold information, explanation and understanding, and how these encourage or discourage our grasp of the unfolding events. In his extended examination of *Rear Window* (1954), for instance, he is able to argue against those who have seen the film as a validation of (male) voyeurism. The 'spectator' at all times knows *more* than the central character, indeed knows things about him that he couldn't articulate to himself. Of necessity, therefore, the spectator has a *critical* position on L. B. Jeffries' (Jeff's) voyeuristic behaviour.[14] It's an irony that passed Bordwell's feminist critics in that they, in their critique of *Rear Window*, are almost exactly fulfilling the spectator role which his approach predicts!

Bordwell's is a sophisticated approach, with the added advantage of making clear how to carry out actual research on films under its aegis. But still, it consciously limits itself. He says:

> As a perceptual-cognitive account, this theory does not address the affective features of film-viewing. This is not because I think that emotion is irrelevant to our experience of cinematic storytelling – far from it – but ... I am assuming that a spectator's comprehension of the film's narrative is theoretically separable from his or her emotional responses. (I suspect that psychoanalytic models may be well suited for explaining emotional aspects of film viewing.)[15]

This self-limitation means that Bordwell's account becomes in effect an account of the *minimum conditions necessary for making sense of a film*. What cognitive operations do we have to go through, and thus what internalised skills and knowledges must we be able to call upon? Having a method for knowing these is immensely valuable in itself, and I maintain that many claims about films fall just against the test of Bordwell's criterion. But beyond this, I have a number of problems with his approach. First, as in a way this whole book is designed to show, I do not believe a separation of cognition and emotion is possible. This is so for a good many reasons. For a start, it makes a puzzle out of why people go to movies. Take *Rear Window* as an example. What *motives* would people have for involving themselves in all the narrational complexities? Either Bordwell is willing to suspend that question, in the hope that the answer won't interfere with people taking up his 'spectator's' position; or he is really interested in those special (mainly art-house) films where our primary engagement with them is cognitive. And indeed it does often seem that the latter is Bordwell's position. He has a penchant for complex narratives, and regards such films as more worthy of interest and probably of greater 'quality'. (See Chapter 2, for a discussion of Kristin Thompson's attempt to go beyond this.)

The Party of the Unconscious

Without question, one of the main motives for writing this book is my dislike of psychoanalytic modes of film analysis. Partly, this is sympathy for students' frequent sense that to read the stuff is to take forced marches through jungles of jargon, behind whose every frond lurks a phallic snake, biting, accusing. Partly, it is because I share Bordwell's feeling that a great deal of such work is a rhetorical game, imposing arbitrary readings on films whose test of success is as much novelty as anything else.[16] A sort of academic speaking in tongues. But mainly, I reject psychoanalytic accounts because their findings resolutely refuse any kind of empirical verification.

Yet, perhaps more strongly than any other approach, psychoanalytic readings of film contain and imply ideas about the audience. And despite recent revisions, these bear a striking similarity with 'effects' theorising. Although the way it was understood and used differed in important respects, psychoanalytic film theory depended, and depends, heavily on the concept of 'identification'. 'Identification' has long been used to offer a picture of how people become involved in films. And it includes the notion of audiences' *vulnerability* to a film. This was a key idea within the 'effects' tradition: first there is 'violence' in movies, then there are weak-minded people, finally there is 'identification' – put them together, and bang! The psychoanalytic tradition developed a more complex approach which at least addressed the filmicness of films. But these became primarily new vehicles for making all kinds of claims about the audience.

As one example, consider Elizabeth Traube's reading of Steven Spielberg's *Indiana Jones and the Temple of Doom* (1984). She depicts it as a 'nightmarish anxiety dream' about men's encounter with female sexuality. Following a lurid sexualised redescription of the scene in which Jones escapes down a tunnel (a 'toothed vagina', 'moist and dank but teeming with hideous life' leading to a place 'between the legs of the hideous idol [where] a pool of lava with a vortex which opens and chooses to receive and consume its victims' – 'the "Mommy" has indeed become the "mummy"'), Traube concludes her account with this claim: 'There is no adventuresome rhythm to this episode. The viewer is not excited or thrilled but almost unbearably disgusted and repelled by the imagery.'[17] Who exactly is this 'viewer'? How does she know? It seems as if Traube has taken her own reaction to this scene, and imputed it to a 'male' viewer (be he real or positional). Yet it must mean something different there, for presumably Traube doesn't have a nightmare about female sexuality, or find all vaginal metaphors 'hideous'.

How could this have the consequences she supposes? In calling the film 'the reinstitution of the phallocentric Law of the Father, gaily packaged as kids' stuff' and an 'ideological project',[18] she is clearly claiming potential impacts on audiences. But what impact? And on what viewers? Traube stays so resolutely at the level of the text that it is easier to imagine ideology without respondents, projects without participants. Yet buried deep there is an answer. Here is how, still speaking of *Indiana Jones*, she explores a consequence. Jones is getting ready to go into that hideous vaginal tunnel. Willie, the female companion, is furiously signalling her sexual interest in him. He seems more concerned, foolish man, with escape from their prison, and sets about handling all parts of a female statue, in hope of finding a hidden control:

> Within the sequential logic of the plot, what follows is a direct consequence of Jones's having avoided sex with Willie. After all, had he chosen her breasts over the statue's, the passageway would never have opened. At another level, however, what ensues is a fantasy realization of that sexual encounter, expressed as a nightmarish anxiety dream. The fantasy moves from the erotic to the anti-erotic, from distorted desire to the utter negation of desire. Ultimately, this fantasy realization of sex vindicates the avoidance of sex.[19]

Traube states this as a piece of filmic logic, but what about the audience? Presumably all those young males who went with their girlfriends ought to leave that cinema repenting their intentions to seduce their girlfriends. Maybe they even kept their hands to themselves for once – fondled the seat arms instead, much safer … Don't handle even fantasy breasts, or 'Mummy' will come and get you! Avoid sex, or you get stuck in hideous tunnels! If this is unfair – and I am not sure it is – then let us hear clearly what the implications of such claims about *Indiana Jones* are, and how they might be tested.

I am using Traube as an example of a broad tendency within psychoanalytic film analysis. Compared to many, she writes clearly, therefore the implications are relatively available. In other cases, they are buried within the theoretical verbiage. Psychoanalytic film analysis thrives on making assertions about audiences, and absorbedly avoiding empirical checks on them.

It's a Wonderful Assumption ...

A case study. Consider four accounts of Frank Capra's *It's a Wonderful Life* (1946). This famous Capra film opens on the despair of one George Bailey, then – through the eyes of a trainee guardian angel given the task of saving him – back-tracks through his life: a small-town boy then man who inherits a small loans company and nourishes the community against a greedy banker who wants to buy him and the town out. But his work is at a price to himself, and to his dreams of going out into the wider world (dreams made more important to him through an adventurous brother). As his business totters, and feeling that his life has been worthless, he attempts suicide, but is saved by an apprentice angel who proceeds to show him what his town would have been like but for him: a mixture of slums and decay, and his wife Mary unmarried and lonely. Coming home, he is welcomed by family and friends who rescue his business and celebrate him, so that he realises 'it's a wonderful life'.

Said to be Capra's personal favourite among his own films, *IAWL* (as I shall call it henceforth) has been a popular film for analysts to delve into. I have chosen four analyses to represent the array: Kaja Silverman, who finds in the film a demonstration of the failure of paternal authority, which can only maintain itself in the end through acts of pure repression; Robert Ray, who discovers in the film a fraught and desperately maintained version of the 'American Dream'; Leland Poague who, openly debating with both Silverman and Ray, finds a 'feminine principle' at work in the film; and Sam Girgus, who counters to Silverman that, rather, the film affirms and celebrates a democratic heroism, where ordinary people are able to make sacrifices for a perceived common good. All four are long, sophisticated readings.

At the same time as testing how film analyses work, I want to use the opportunity to test some of the claims of a meta-critical approach which I greatly admire. David Bordwell has written the book which, to date, best takes scalpel to the claims of film analysis. His *Making Meaning* demonstrates that many claims arrived at through analyses depend on arbitrary moves, rhetorical figures and unsubstantiated claims.[20] I have both learned a great deal from Bordwell's argument and gained much of the confidence I needed to carry through my own challenge here. But one detail I have come to question. In his opening outline of his approach, Bordwell distinguishes four levels of interpretation of films; the deeper one goes in interpreting a film, the more arbitrary becomes the interpretation.[21] Level one is that amount of interpretation needed to make of a film a 'concrete world' where events hang together and make sense (Referential Meaning) – this level being necessary to any participating viewer. Level two involves specific acts of interpretation which 'spot' that a scene, event, included element has a signal *point* to it (the sight of the Statue of Liberty, for example); this, Bordwell calls Explicit Meaning. Level three involves a search for constructive *themes* or organising principles which could be said to mobilise and shape the film, but which are not present overtly on its 'surface' (Implicit Meaning). And lastly, level four involves looking on a film as *hiding* its operative principles or, in the (Freudian) language in which it is normally put, 'repressing' them (Repressed, or Symptomatic Meaning). Bordwell seems to accept the rightness and inevitability of the first two kinds of interpretation, sees the third as a natural but riskier critical process, but is very suspicious of much of what passes for analysis under the last.

As an analytic distinction – that is, one which enables us to see things that otherwise are hard – I find this an admirable way to proceed. However, I have come to see certain problems and limits in it, partly as a result of an excellent essay by George Wilson.[22] Building from an effective example in *Bigger Than Life* (1956), Wilson shows that our interpretation of characters' behaviour necessarily strays across the borders between the types of analysis; that in fact, in order to arrive at *referential* accounts of characters, we often need to invoke much deeper thematic or *implicit* interpretative structures which relate to the *film as a whole*. I find Wilson's account convincing, but itself also incomplete. In Wilson's own argument a further dimension comes into view: this is the way in which film analyses depend upon claims about what the 'audience' must be doing.[23] 'Audience', 'viewer', 'spectator', 'we', 'they': these are the typical sign-post words for the imported assumptions upon which, I want to show, actual interpretations *have to* depend. They are also the most problematic aspects of film analyses, because they are almost always posed in terms which defy any kind of empirical investigation. They are my main object of attention in what follows.

'You Will Be In-Ter-Pell-Ated', by K. Silverman

Kaja Silverman's account of *IAWL* is in part a debate with early versions of Robert Ray's and Leland Poague's.[24] But mostly, it is an expression of a feminist psychoanalytic approach, so confident of its triumph that she feels no need to argue the case any more. This is a major problem in engaging with her. Her analysis reads like an internal document of a psychoanalytic cabal, such that no gap exists between *description* of elements of the film, and the superimposition of Lacanian interpretations. So, for instance, she writes: 'Despite George's protestations to the contrary, the spectacle of his father's shame clearly precipitates a castration crisis. … At this juncture, George has been successfully interpellated into the position of the castrated father. … At a critical moment in the nightmare sequence George's guardian angel tells him that outside Bedford Falls he has no identity … This form of terrorism proves so effective that George literally begs to be re-interpellated, no matter what the cost.' All this and more is, we are told repeatedly, 'clearly' and 'obviously' so. Absolutely not.

In the same way, elements that suit her account are declared 'significant', although we are not told how or why. And there are elisions within particular arguments, where the justification is far from clear. For instance she writes that 'most importantly' the film is set immediately post World War II:

> That day is also the occasion when George's younger Brother Harry returns from the war with a congressional medal of honor – the occasion when Bedford Falls makes contact with what will remain forever unassimilable in its cozy 'truths'. Moreover, Harry stands in for George in his guise as war hero, not only because George has repeatedly sacrificed himself so that Harry can have a life elsewhere, but because George has for years passionately desired a similar escape. The accelerated montage, by means of which *It's a Wonderful Life* represents World War II *thus* serves less to marginalize than to repress that event.[25]

Why 'thus'? What assumptions are condensed in that bridging word? To marginalise something is to pass it by speedily, as of little importance; I would have no problem with such a *description* of the film. But to 'repress' it, in the language of psychoanalysis, is to make it unavailable to conscious inspection, to make it an object of pre-conscious drives and emotions.

For Silverman, *IAWL* plays out a castration drama. The series of incidents which, to her, demonstrate 'castration' would not convince anyone not already soaked in this language. Among them are: losing his hearing as a result of saving his brother from drowning; seeing his father lose out in a business deal; finding his daughter's favourite flower crushed; getting cut during a bar fight; and having a loose banister knob in the family home. Hmm. 'This, then, is the film's dilemma: Unable to conceal the castrations through which the paternal position is consolidated, *It's a Wonderful Life* is at the same time committed to the preservation of the dominant fiction, and so to the succession of father by son' (pp.96–7). George is emasculated, and with such force and ideological power that he comes to enjoy it. What delivers this force, she claims, is the reference to Christianity: 'it is only by giving Christianity an authoritative position that *It's a Wonderful Life* is able to accommodate the spectacle of George's castration and masochism within an ideological system predicated upon the equation of penis and phallus' (p.102). Since Silverman has made this a specific claim, let us use this as our basis for exploring her analysis. What role *does* Christianity play in *IAWL*?

Her first claim is that the film at its opening works by 'suturing' us celestially into granting an authoritative position to Christianity by an 'implied shot/reverse shot between the roofs of the town's houses and the heavens above' (p.93). The term 'suture' is one further psychoanalytic term, which claims that matched shot and reverse force the viewer to view as naturally linked two components which are otherwise quite discrete; they make us responsible for the link, and thus implicate us in the ideological work of a film. General arguments about this aside, what actually happens in *IAWL*? First, we hear George's friends praying for him, and we see the town from a high angle. Then the camera looks upwards, and in a slow zoom seeks out the stars (where Clarence, apprentice angel, will soon be seen). This is not, then, actually a shot/reverse shot. But just as importantly, in what sense does the showing of winking stars imply 'heaven'? Winking stars are only 'heaven' by virtue of a widely recognised cultural simile, virtually a joke. Heaven is 'up there' – but in a way that makes heaven a thing to smile over, as if it were a fairy tale. The point precisely is that the cultural knowledge of the audience has here to be activated, but in a fashion that undercuts any possibility of 'heaven' providing a serious or authoritative resource in the film.

This problem continues in Silverman's second discussion of Christianity. Her argument is that the Symbolic Father (of Lacanian theory) retains all his force by never being seen, instead by being represented at two removes: by Joseph, who with that name 'represents the actual rather than the symbolic father', and Clarence, trainee angel who takes on the task of saving George from suicide. Setting aside the worrying lack of sense of humour Silverman here demonstrates, let us take her seriously. 'Joseph' was not the 'actual' father. Poor man, he was a cuckold – and had to live with the fact. But more than that, he was *Mary's* husband. If we are to play name-symbolism, and build castles of persuasion on them, then let us complete the process. Joseph sends Clarence down to prevent the suicide of the man who is married to 'his' wife. Who exactly is emasculated here? If Silverman's analysis were not so partial and presuming, she ought to have concluded that Christianity is here diminished and made foolish – a diminution made worse by another feature. Silverman refers to the way Clarence is shown George's life, as in a cinematic reel. But Clarence can't get the thing to focus, requiring Joseph to demonstrate 'perfect control of the screening situation' (p.104) – thus, Silverman says, marking his superior position. But not as powerful as God's, who remains unrepresented, since Joseph can't intervene. What kind of picture of the heavenly setup is this? Dependent on dodgy projectors, sending untrained angels on mercy missions – what if Clarence had failed? What Silverman high-handedly pronounces a sign of mediated power, is as easily – though just as arbitrarily – read as a sign of total weakness.[26]

The final and fatal flaw in Silverman's approach is her conflation of film characters with viewers – a conflation so casually done, it can slip by unnoticed. She writes: 'The chief aim of the nightmare sequence is to reconcile George (and the viewer) to the dominant fiction by proving that there is no life outside its boundaries' (p.102). Poague, also almost in passing, dismisses this on the grounds that this clearly doesn't include Silverman as viewer. In exempting herself, Silverman undermines the supposed necessity of the process. True, but not enough. I believe that her account could not be true of any viewer. Take one other shot-transition which she mentions: linking the moment where George protests that he doesn't want to get married, and the following where we see him descending the stairs after the wedding. What work is required of the audience here, given no convenient 'suture' to do the work for us?

In order for the viewer to straddle this gap, s/he must cope with the total lack of explanation. One moment, George is protesting vehemently that he doesn't want to get married, the next minute he is married – and very happy he looks, too! The audience must therefore supply the motivating link, in a way that recognises that it was presumed so obvious that George *would* get married, that we don't need to be told how it came about. But that is only manageable on premises which wholly defeat Silverman's account. The cut across the marriage emphasises the *irony* of George's character – he protests he won't marry, next moment look how happy he is, married. That is only conceivable if the viewer implicitly recognises that s/he knows George better than he knows himself. He was *bound* to get married. Why? Because the film identifies itself as a particular kind of film: a tragi-comedy, in which the audience follows a man through good times

and bad, confident that all will turn out right. This superiority of knowledge, and generically-shaped participation, makes it *inevitable* that any
participative audience cannot be identical/identified with George. That
doesn't rule out rueful sympathy as he wends his way through a succession of plights. But there is no way that 'the viewer' can be sneaked in as a
bracketed addendum in the way that Silverman tries.

Silverman's account is almost entirely composed of fourth-level Bordwellian propositions, that is, claims about repressed meanings. But these become
active, and of significance, if she is allowed that jump from film as couch-
patient being psychoanalysed, to 'the viewer' assumed to be identical.

'I Have Seen Things ...', by R. Ray

Robert Ray's is a long (36 page) analysis, set within the broader framework
of his book which sees Hollywood as dealing in shifting ways with the
politics of the 'American Dream'.[27] *IAWL* is, for Ray, an ambiguous comment on the 'Andy Hardy' tradition of optimistic small-town middle-class
narratives. His main approach is structural, outlining the working of three
thematic oppositions which, he argues, rescue the film from mawkish sentimentality: adventure versus domesticity; individual versus community;
and worldly success versus ordinary life. These are explored in considerable detail through individual scenes, even showing that in some cases
individual shots contain tensions and aspects of both sides of a pair. Ray's
case is that the 'Dream' seemed to promise that one could have all these,
but George Bailey's life proved that one side is forever pulling against the
possibility of the other. So, George forever wants to be a daring individual
and have adventures, but has to sacrifice them in order to fulfil his domestic
and community responsibilities.

In all this, Ray appears to operate as almost a paradigm case of Bordwell's
third level of analysis (Implicit Meanings). Ray is 'discovering' themes and
explanatory motives embedded within the narrative. To do this, he has to
treat George as someone about whom more can be known than is directly
given by the film. So, we can learn through analysis 'what made George
melancholy' (p.189), and we could therefore impute to him a tension coming from his (never stated, but to us knowable) 'susceptibility to myths of
adventure that had long outlived their usefulness in American culture'
(p.193). This is analysis in the sense of *making deeper sense* of the characters.
But then Ray goes further. In phrases that never quite declare themselves,
he not only claims to discover a connecting sense behind characters' actions,
but also hints at how this must reach out to audiences. So, he writes (p.193)
that *IAWL* 'demonstrated that myths that had outlived their basis could in
fact become pernicious'. To whom? The sentence only makes sense if there

is a possible recipient of this demonstration, other than Ray himself. Or again: introducing his three oppositions, Ray writes (p.183) that 'although Capra obviously intended to demonstrate the illusoriness of these oppositions, the film's emotional weight derived from his own, evidently unconscious, sense of their reality'. So film analysis can reveal something happening against the intentions of the director. It can reveal an 'emotional weight': weighing on whom? Again, weight has to bear down, to have meaning. Or third, in his discussion of the use of devices such as freeze frames (p.204), Ray calls their introduction into the body of a film 'more startling'. Startling to whom? This is not an incidental point, since Ray hangs much on this perception. For it is by being 'startling' that *IAWL* occasions its failure to solve the tensions between individual and community, etc. For Ray, this is the point at which an 'ideology' becomes transparent. At this point the film gives itself away, by making visible its narrative devices.

Curiously, Ray's account never deals much with the narrative process of the film – for example, its lengthy flashbacks, its angelic omniscient overview, its parallel narrative of what might have been. As Poague points out, just about his only comment on this is to classify George's vision as 'the film's greatest trick' (p.200). This trick lets cats out of bags: for example, the 'thinly repressed sexuality' which might otherwise have escaped attention (whose attention? who says it was repressed in the first place?). Ray hangs so much on this 'trick', since for him it achieves an ideological miracle. Capra, he claims, had hoped to demonstrate that the opposition between individual and community was illusory, but the tensions were too great. They burst through the envelope of the movie, and thus gave it its emotional weight. That sounds like a demonstration that the movie *undid* the American Dream, doesn't it? But no:

> [T]he success of *It's a Wonderful Life* depended utterly on George's vision, provided by Clarence: the chance to see what Bedford Falls would have been like if he had never been born. That vision was the movie's great trick. Without it, the film would have been unbearably bleak; with it, the movie managed to reaffirm the American Dream.[28]

Contained here are several steps: the film as a wriggling embodiment of contradictions, and not fully containing them; an audience impelled to seek 'reaffirmation'; and the film 'tricking' them into agreement. Ray seemed to be working only with Implicit Meanings. But his implicit claims are all about suppressed tensions. *Ray* perceives these tensions in the film, and the devices which disguise them, but he denies audiences that perception, instead seeing audiences as driven by lacks which the film deceitfully fulfils. All these claims function at that fourth level of Repressed Meanings. As with Silverman, the manoeuvres in the analysis turn on embedded assertions about the audience.

'What George Wants', by L. Poague

Leland Poague's analysis of *IAWL* (another 36-pager) comes as part of a book reinterpreting the overall work of Frank Capra.[29] The book is both theoretically deft and methodologically alert, debating intensively with other analysts. Poague himself draws on the work of Stanley Cavell who is interested in films as particularly self-conscious myths. Overall, Poague aims to show that Capra has been substantially misunderstood. Far from being simply populist (as many have claimed), he argues Capra's films offer a subtle and self-conscious commentary on the progress of 'America'. He does this as much through film style as through pro-filmic events and plot. Contrary to those who suggest that classical Hollywood tends to make its filmic apparatus invisible, the whole point of Capra's film-making is to render technique visible: 'to read Capra's style as invisible is a grievous perceptual and interpretative error' (p.47). What this allows him to suggest is that, generally, Capra puts femininity at the centre of his films. Despite having male leads in all the films Poague analyses, they can be regarded as centring on the achievement of femininity. To get to this conclusion, Poague carries out a dense symptomatology of each film.

In the case of *IAWL*, he sets his conclusions in direct opposition to Silverman and Ray. Most analysts, he says, see George Bailey as frustrated by his life, but then realising right at the end that what he really wants is the ideal of small-town America. They might disagree about whether this is a real or illusory solution, but they all agree that this is what the film shows George wanting. Poague doesn't agree. He asks: what does George Bailey really want? And then proceeds on a close reading of the textual evidence, in a manner that turns Bailey virtually into a psychiatric patient undergoing in-depth analysis. For example, George Bailey 'feels ghostly, unreal, uncreated, a feeling expressed by his repeated assertions of omnipotence' (p.211). This is imputation on a grand scale – Bailey never actually directly states this, therefore everything Poague says is in reality a *possible account* of a fictional character. This is problem enough, but to stop the criticism there would miss much that is revealing in Poague's account. I am interested, as ever, in the ways in which his account presumes an audience.

Poague discusses what he believes to be George Bailey's fear of/desire for femininity. He lists a series of small incidents which, given a special kind of examination, might count as evidence for this. One is this:

The sense that marriage is emasculating is confirmed in the proposal scene when George tells Mary in an angry voice that he does not want to get married. By the time his resistance collapses, marked by his repeating of Mary's name, getting 'married' and getting 'Maryed' sound strikingly similar.[30]

Let us take this strange proposal seriously. Suppose a watcher misses this tiny element, along with the other equally tiny moments on which Poague builds his interpretation. Presumably s/he will then miss the 'meaning' that Poague has now claimed is the 'meaning' of this film. Suppose that s/he did hear it, but read it as an example, mildly amusing, of Jimmy Stewart's drawl almost interfering with the meaning of the words: in that case, s/he has surely got the *wrong* 'meaning'. Suppose, further, that all watchers other than Poague have missed this. In that case, meaning turns into a kind of coded incunabula, a secret which might never have been found, but for Poague's peculiar skills. This is a very strange view of filmic meaning. But take it further still: suppose a watcher did spot this point, and read it as Poague has – what would s/he have done? Think about the mental activities which we have to impute to such a watcher: s/he has to spot the slippage in the speaking of the words, spot it as a similarity *and* as a difference (it sounds like 'married' but isn't, and that is the point). S/he has then to see this as a punning association, but not one that is intended by George himself. It is a symptom *betraying* George's unconscious desire to become more like a woman. So, such a watcher has to put him/herself in a superior position to George Bailey, who has to be treated, not as a character in a film, but as a mythic representative. What kind of film watcher is this? It is Leland Poague, returning via a squared circle as the only virtuous viewer.

A large part of Poague's chapter on *IAWL* is an exploration of 'what George wants'. His procedure is to take actions and events *as if* they were literal, and then question their coherence *as* literal. So, he examines in detail the incident where George escorts Mary home, but in his fumbling way can't manage a sexual advance. Instead, when she invites one, he turns it aside by proposing they play the game of throwing stones at an old empty house. In the town's mythology, if you manage to break glass, you get a wish. George throws, hits a window, and wishes. Mary asks what he wants. He starts on his usual catalogue of wishes: for adventure, to travel, to do wild things … Mary interrupts this interminable list by herself throwing a stone, breaking glass and making a wish. But she won't tell, because to tell someone your wish undoes it. Now, George has told his wish – so did he really want those things, asks Poague? And given he has known Mary all these years, didn't she know already that that is what he would want? Notice the literalism of the questions posed, and the demands for coherence. Notice the difference that is made if we posit a different kind of viewer than Poague's idealised self-as-analyst. Poague's logical investigator declares that George doesn't really want to go away at all – he is only saying this so that Mary can overwhelm him with what he really wants: which is to become (like) her. It isn't even that he secretly wants to get married, he really wants to get Maryed. Now imagine a different kind of audience: a filmically alert audience who recognise that one of George's characteristics is his difficulty with putting things into words, his shyness, and his social, communicative awkwardness. When, therefore, Mary says that she won't say what *her* wish was, the point is that George can't understand her – but *we* (filmically alert watchers) can. She wants him, but in the filmic code of the time can't say so – she has to catch him on his blind side and make him see it for himself.

With this different viewer, other things that are just contradictory in Poague's account can make sense. Poague presses his point about 'what George wants': 'Further complicating our understanding of what George wants is the almost nightmarish frequency with which George's desires are in fact realised' (p.198). So, he suggests quite bizarrely that, in an early scene, by calling his brother Harry a 'scarebaby' he in effect wishes him to have an accident, become scared and need saving. Or when he and his father are about to move out of their house, George hurries to get away from the 'last meal' and leaves his father, Peter – who dies: 'Any number of critics have noted the sense in which George's departure here is death dealing; it is Peter Bailey who eats his last meal, or 'last supper', not George, as if that were George's desire all along' (p.199). There is a deep-seated paradox here in Poague's whole approach. George does not *will* his brother's accident or his father's death. If, therefore, we posit an audience who perceive this relation between events, they have to be making a very particular kind of reading of the film. In short, they must adopt an orientation to the film whereby apparently separated events are in fact linked by 'magic'. George says something, and the saying in some sense *makes its opposite happen*. To call someone a 'scarebaby' is in effect to jinx them, to make them so foolishly brave that they will have an accident – which is what you wanted all along. To wish to avoid your own 'last meal' only counts as wishing for someone else's 'last supper' (death) if a logic of reversal is superimposed. Such an audience would surely, then, have to see George Bailey as the *villain* of the film. Or if not that, then the resolution of the film – when he settles for ordinary life with Mary – would have to be the *giving up of* all *desires,* lest they magically bring about reversals to the very things that he now most wants.

The problem is caused by Poague's insistence on a literalist analysis of George's 'desires', as if he were a real-world person governed by real-world criteria of coherence. Take that away, and the problem dissolves. Imagine an audience whose orientation to the film is to see it as an ordinary allegory. It is not then George's desires that lead to him being thwarted, but the film. George can't leave Bedford Falls, so the film arranges it so that every time he comes close to getting away, something *must* happen to stop him. The only difficulty is that, to get there, we will have to dump a huge amount of film theory which supposes that films are 'invisible' to audiences. I come to this shortly.

'Ameritherapy', by S. Girgus

Sam Girgus' – the most recent of my four – is another long account of *IAWL*, but elusive because allusive. In fact it was the hardest to penetrate. Girgus buries the premises under his argumentative moves very well. Unpacked eventually, there turn out to be some very troubling assumptions.[31]

Girgus wants to celebrate *IAWL*, almost without reservation. It is for him a 'flawed masterpiece' – the flaws deriving mainly from the mess left behind by a long series of scriptwriters. He opens his account by detailing some of the resultant narrative inconsistencies: for example, over how well George and Mary know each other (she has loved him since they were children, yet they seem to need to be reintroduced), over Uncle Billy's absence from their wedding (which enables him to wreck their honeymoon by triggering a run on George's Building & Loan), and so on. Kaja Silverman would do well to note points like these, since they undo her assumption of a tidy, unified and unidirectional narrative process! But to Girgus, these inconsistencies almost add to the power of the film, since they play up the human processes involved.

A different kind of imperfection does bother him, though. This is what he sees as a tendency to 'mawkish sentimentality', brought to us by the references to Mark Twain's *Tom Sawyer* which Clarence is reading in heaven when sent on his assignment: 'The script obviously evokes Twain and Tom Sawyer to maintain a sentimental feeling and attitude towards the past … This view of the past helps create a feeling of comfort and complacency for readers and moviegoers' (p.89). But this is not the 'real meaning' of *IAWL*. That comes from a darker side of the film, and indeed from Twain: 'The nightmare vision in Twain comes much closer to the inner reality of *A Wonderful Life* than popularized and sanitized readings of Twain.' He dismisses both those who read the film 'comfortably' and also those who are infected with 'fashionable theories' of ideology and psychoanalysis; they are both incapable of reading the film properly. Instead, he claims the film to be for and about the 'common people' (p.93): 'This achievement of common people involves facing and dealing with life's exigencies without denying one's humanity or the democratic institutions that empower people to engage existence to the fullest extent possible.' So, 'ordinary' viewers tend to get it wrong, as do the fashionable intellectuals; but 'common' people will see the film for what it is – an impulse to go on with life, a challenge experienced through the way the film culminates. The fact that George at the end loves his life, for all its difficulties and pains, reveals the proper way to view this film. We have to live through the deep pains with George, and thus experience the moment of transcendence and use that as a model for our own lives. There are people who do this properly, hints Girgus; they are the 'contemporary viewers of it [who] continue to find *It's a Wonderful Life* so relevant to their own experiences' (p.95). This is very arguable. Much of the contemporary fan writing I have seen about *IAWL* has veered strongly towards the sentimental, allied with a dose of Stewart fandom. But I doubt this matters, for it is not actual viewers that Girgus is concerned with, rather a figure of a wished-for viewer.

Girgus wants to claim back *IAWL* as an essentially democratic film, which can galvanise and revolutionise people's motives. Indeed it is even 'prescient', it 'anticipates', 'forecasts' aspects of America's democracy that are incomplete – especially, he claims, its attitude to women. In his route to this surprising conclusion we can see how Girgus' account works. In the middle of his analysis, he devotes three pages to the role within *IAWL* of the elements of self-conscious cinema: the opening 'screening' of George Bailey's life in heaven, for example, and that freeze-frame. Girgus declares that these contribute to the film's 'compelling inevitability'. How? This is the beginning of his answer:

> By freezing the frame so that Clarence can study George's face and talk over the visual scene with Joseph, Capra brings attention directly to film as an art-form and to the director's power to control and alter time and space.[32]

This is not self-evident – not every filmic device generates cinematic self-consciousness, and these two in fact serve clear narrative functions. But suppose Girgus is right: what would warrant that wider conclusion? It seems that he is saying that in *IAWL* these self-conscious techniques collapse the distance between viewers, and one particular character – Mary. His case is complex, and specific to the techniques used in this film. He looks closely at the scene where George, as a young man, takes a beating from the druggist Gower whom he has saved from accidentally poisoning a patient. Mary is in the bar as George is being punished in the back room which, Girgus emphasises, is always filmed in self-conscious style:

> Capra's shooting and editing in effect puts the viewer inside Mary's consciousness as she hears, imagines and envisions George's beating. She seems to share the audience's perception of the action as a movie as witnessed through the frames of Gower's shelves. To represent how the beating scene feels and how it affects George and Mary, Capra organises it as a film. The dramatic intensity of the beating as shown through segmented frames compares to the complexity of the filmic viewing process. The fragmentation of framing fractures vision and experience in a manner that reinforces the crippling punishment of George's pain within the frames. In sum, Capra renders the psychological meaning and impact of the beating scene in the form of a movie that the audience sees and Mary hears and imagines.[33]

This 'move' enables Girgus to get to his conclusion. A large number of steps are squeezed into it which have to be decompressed. Descriptively, he is right to say that Gower's office usually is filmed as through shelves, and that in the beating scene Mary is seen reacting to what she is hearing. One way to interpret this indirect vision of the beating is to see it as a form of self-censorship, pain by implication. But Girgus doesn't choose this route. Rather he sees it doubly, as a means of our accessing Mary's head and, through that, a means whereby she/we experience the partiality of our understanding and the limits of our powers: 'A world of infatuation and wholeness … has been shattered. She now appreciates the difference between the immaturity of believing oneself to be the world and being just a limited part of it' (p.97). This is what impels Mary to 'initiate actions and move aggressively to fulfil her ambitions', while poor George 'will go through life as a perennial moral masochist'. So, fragmentation in the filmic frame becomes, for 'real' viewers, a mark of our incompleteness; no person an island complete unto themself. 'Real' viewers have to give themselves over to the film, and specifically to Mary's position within the film, in order to recover wholeness through the ending. In this way, he can conclude that Mary is effectively the storm-centre of the film, that *IAWL* thus experienced provides a renewing dream. And this dream is real in the sense that 'we' can actually be remade through it. Girgus criticises Robert Ray's pessimistic account of *IAWL* on the grounds that Ray presumes a dichotomy between the American Dream as 'external reality' and as 'belief' and 'myth': 'In contrast to Ray, it can be maintained that *IAWL* actually argues that the American Dream never has been a "given" but has always worked as a creation from the vision of people' (p.104). And this film, for the real 'people', enacts that vision.

We can now see Girgus' logic. *IAWL* is not just a film. In the hands of those to whom it really belongs, it is a virtual therapy session. By viewing it appropriately, they first come to admit their own limits, incompleteness, dependency; then, by staying to the end, they are reassembled, put back together in the experience of the renewed 'democratic dream'. 'Film empowers', Girgus declares. By getting its experience as a 'common person', 'you' can become the stuff of the American Dream. You will have to do this, oddly, via *seeing as Mary*:

> What Mary ... sees in George is a man who will never stop trying to be human in spite of the beating he will receive for it. What audiences, *therefore*, have seen in George is the American – naïve, idealistic, the battler for enduring causes, the believer in himself and in the future.[34]

Let us take a closer look at this crucial step. How could an actual viewer play the part here required of him or her? Girgus' 'common viewer' turns out upon examination to be a very specialised animal. S/he must be able and willing to submit his/her experiences of life to the adjudication of film which will show him or her to be incomplete, inadequate. But a suitable mental submission will eventually be rewarded with a part in 'common heroism'. All this requires the watcher to give themself over, in a consistent and almost devoted manner, to Mary's viewing position – otherwise s/he risks experiencing the virtually enforced fragmentation which temporary association with Mary would bring about, without the ultimate relief of being reassembled in the larger whole of the American democratic project. Ouch. S/he has to care, with Mary, about George's inability to achieve this for himself, and the first sacrifice will be to defer personal desires to help this bumblingly good-natured man to find his salvation.

But here a series of problems in conceiving this viewer-position emerge. Mary doesn't know about Clarence. We do. And, at a certain point, so does George. 'Seeing through Mary' must at least defray into 'seeing *as if* through Mary', or all the scenes with the angel are going to make no sense. So it will have to be Mary's *emotional* position that our 'common viewer' adopts – firmly and committedly, mind, so that s/he achieves the fulfilment. What would this be like?

Being a 'common American' turns out to be tough, and the 'heroism' looks like it begins in the cinema. Perhaps, though, the most complicated thing s/he-as-Mary has to achieve is to combine seeing, and caring about, George as an individual, and experiencing through him the idea of 'democratic heroism'. He must become a symbol even as the heroism he supposedly embodies denies such symbolism; for does not Girgus insist that the 'American Dream' is a virtual opposite of a fascistic 'dream' of the kind he finds in Leni Riefenstahl? George can only be what he is by *refusing* symbolism. Yet our viewer, to get from the film more than just a good story and a good weeping smile, must find in George an emblem of something bigger than George. The perquisites of this 'common viewer' have become exceedingly testing.

Conclusion

These four analyses of the same film arrive at four distinct destinations. My investigations were designed to show how they each managed this feat, and the problems each created along the way. We've seen the way the invoked 'figures' of the audience allow the analyses to jump across Bordwell's levels of analysis. Insofar as these are typical of film analyses generally – and I think they are – they pose a problem: maybe we need a different kind of film analysis, answering different sorts of question.

Perhaps the place to start is in the very problems I have identified. In each case, I have shown the presence of an invoked figure of the audience. If we take seriously the claim that each author makes, we see that the 'viewer' postulated has to have skills and understandings, motives and involvements which are *inconsistent with the claims made in the first place*. Follow the logic of implicit claims, and we can in effect ask: if we have to do/know/feel X, what else has to follow? This is an extension of something I explored, with Kate Brooks, in our study of the audiences of *Judge Dredd* (1996). There, we called this 'practical logics'.[35] My argument is that logic applies as much to the emotions as it does to understanding. This is the point at which I believe we can pass beyond David Bordwell's foundational approach.

Bordwell, rightly, insists that cognition is a process. As we make sense of a film, we accumulate information, encounter and resolve puzzles, form hypotheses, and thus construct an imaginative world through the cues and clues of the particular filmic world. The risk is that separating off emotions and allowing a different kind of explanation of them makes them the creatures of pure theory. Psychoanalytic accounts of emotions veer sharply in the direction of seeing them as pre-formed, originary. That gives preference to the general character of films: a search for common themes, and structures. How many films do *not* conform to the Oedipal structure? How many do *not* operate according to the 'Law' of Patriarchy? The motivational structure is, as it were, given in advance and from outside. Films meet pre-given 'needs' (often 'false' ones, on feminist accounts). That would suggest that films are like tanks of ideological water, filling up the (ever-incomplete) gaps in the personality. We drive in, we identify, we get our needful (or false) confirmation of identity, we reverse back out into our culture. Worried at the mechanistic nature of this account, subsequent feminist revisions have proposed that identification is mobile, transitory, maybe multiple – so lots of identities are possible from a film. In this way they have felt they could defend the integrity of women's pleasures in films that were otherwise proving them masochistic, and wilfully subservient. The trouble with this solution is that it is no solution. In place of a putative structure, it offers a shapeless 'anything is possible'.

Yet occasionally within actual accounts of emotional involvement in films, something else glimmers, an account which – if followed through – would alter much else. Putting it crudely, if you start to take up a position, it has consequences. Take two examples of this. James Kavanagh, writing of *Alien* (1979), explores the emotional logic of the fact that the film does not at first centre on Ripley. Only gradually does the elimination of some putative central characters, and Ripley's own increasing cinematic central-ity, put her centre-stage:

> The film ultimately projects Ripley alone as its running hero, her author-ity now definitely seen by the viewer grounded in intelligence and strength of character ... [T]he viewer registers definite subliminal sur-prise that the woman actually will be the strong centre of the film.[36]

Here, Kavanagh is recognising that our cognitive and emotional involve-ments must go hand in hand. Finding ourselves looking for a central character to 'identify with', then finding that it is a woman, has consequences. And however tricky it might be in practice, there is in theory at least the chance of finding out if he is right. Do viewers register surprise, even subliminally?

A second example: Robert Ray, writing of *Taxi Driver* (1976), is interested in the character of the violence used by Travis Bickle and its meanings for audiences. Ray places the film within what he identifies as a 'Right Cycle' in film-making, a cycle which celebrated the individual and his use of violence against immorality and political corruption. But *Taxi Driver* does not fit tidily, he recognises; here is an example of bleak art-house movie-making, using self-conscious techniques to manipulate audiences. While the film opens, he suggests, by making Travis Bickle a sympathetic figure, in its later stages it changes sharply:

> Subtly warned by ... foreshadowing 'corrections' ... the audience should not have been entirely unprepared when *Taxi Driver* abruptly withdrew

its sympathy for Travis with a single shot. After identification with Travis had peaked with his attempts to 'rescue' Iris, the film shifted to Columbus Circle … Suddenly, the movie confirmed any incipient fears that Travis might represent distorted version of the Right hero. The camera panned slowly the podium through the crowd, moving at knee level, finally stopping on a pair of legs, obviously Travis's, stepping out of a cab. Then very slowly (in a shot whose atomization imitated *Breathless*'s policeman killing), the camera moved up his body, to the waist, then to jacket bulging with guns, and at last to Travis's head, horribly shaved in a Mohawk haircut. The shock was terrific. By following the standard Right pattern, *Taxi Driver* had led its audience into an almost complete identification with a hero now revealed as recognizably insane. Like so many Hitchcock films, *Taxi Driver* had implicated the audience in any resulting violence, for the audience had willed this hero and trusted his impulses.[37]

While Ray uses terms like 'implicating', 'willing' and 'identification' – terms I am unwilling to use – his insight stands. Emotional engagement, like cognitive engagement, is a process. We become involved as a film progresses in ways which condition how we respond to subsequent parts. There is, in short, a logic to emotional responses to films. To understand it, we need the equivalent to Bordwell's 'spectator', who sums up the cognitive operations necessary for understanding. Because I do not believe it can be understood separately from cognition – you cannot be involved if you are not understanding, and you only *want* to understand to the extent that you care – I decline to have a new word for this role, like 'carer'. Instead, as we will see, I propose to expand Bordwell's concept to mean the *involved, motivated spectator*.

In fact, in this book I will attempt to go further than this. Bordwell's vital emphasis on processes of knowing leaves us in a dilemma. Not only does it leave emotions to the sink of the unconscious, it also misses out all the other levels at which films can call forth responses in us: sensual, aesthetic and evaluative. A method of film analysis that has nothing to say about these would be thin indeed. In the next chapter I try to lay out the groundwork of an approach that can deal, together, with cognitions and emotions, and also open the door to other dimensions of response.

2
Formalism and the Implied Audience

This book does not start in a vacuum. Like anybody else's, it stands within traditions of ideas, has learnt from some by at least partial agreement, and from others by seeing such major faults in them that they aggravated me into working out why, and where I would go instead. The tradition to which I owe most is generally known as the Neo-Formalist tradition, best illustrated by the work of David Bordwell and his co-workers Janet Staiger and Kristin Thompson. But although their analyses of films seem to me so obviously superior to others, I have some disagreements with them, which I want to explore here. The disagreements focus on two aspects of their ideas in particular: their treatment of emotions in relation to film, and their account of the audience. Behind these stands an issue about what is the point of analysing films.

The Formalist Tradition

In order to explain what I owe and where I diverge, I want to look in a little detail at one book: Kristin Thompson's *Breaking the Glass Armor*.[1] This book aims to prove in action the power of its approach to films, through closely worked examples. In that sense, my project is very similar to hers: let the analyses be their own justification. And insofar as the analyses go, it seems to me that she makes an unanswerable case. The problem is where she stops. To show how this occurs, I have to address her opening account of her method, which she calls 'Neo-Formalist'.

Thompson situates herself in the tradition of the Russian Formalists, such as Victor Shklovsky and Boris Eikhenbaum, who between 1910–30 formulated a theory of literature which, as Thompson rightly notes, is often confused with the idea of 'art for art's sake'. The Formalists' central claim was that art was time-out from practical activities. To read a work of literature, or to watch a film, is to enter into a world where by agreement normal rules temporarily cease to operate. Actions are not measured by their practical consequences, but by their contribution to the working of the 'whole' that is the work of art. Art, therefore, is a 'world apart', and has first to be investigated from the inside, in order to discover the principles which govern it in general (for instance, how stories work, anywhere) and in particular (for example, how does this particular thriller work?).

I agree completely with this central idea. In any work of art, normal rules of life are set aside and events proceed according to an inner logic which has to be discovered, utilised and responded to by anyone becoming its audience. People can of course fail, refuse, turn away. To that extent they have not become audiences for that work of art. But to this central idea, the Formalists added another: the idea of 'defamiliarisation'. Art is important, they argued, because it has the capacity to undo routinism. Most of our lives we live by established habit and learnt routines. Our ways of thinking and understanding become commonplace to us, and this may make us vulnerable to outdated ideas, or to ideas which may run against our interests (ideological accounts of the world, for instance). The function of art is to make strange, to show us things in such a way, through imaginative structures which make us focus on them, to make us think them afresh.

So, good art is that which refreshes the parts of our mind that blocking routines stop us reaching. That means, first, that there is an emphasis on originality and innovation. No art can remain fresh – repeated encounters, the Formalists felt, blunt its ability to awaken sensibilities. Art must endlessly renew itself, in order to fulfil its human function.

Implications? There are many. First, that film or other kinds of art can't be measured against the real world in some direct fashion. A film can't be 'true' or 'false', or 'distorted', because it does not follow real-world rules. Nor can films produce direct behavioural effects on their audiences. That is to make a category mistake of the same order as a government decreeing the mobilisation of wooden horses – they have missed the point. This doesn't make art irrelevant or ineffectual: to the contrary. As Thompson says: 'This is not to say that films have no effect on us. As with all artworks, they are of vital importance in our lives. The nature of practical perception means that our faculties become skilled by the repetitive and habitual activities inherent in much of daily life' (p.9). And film, like any other form of art, can have cogent effects in disturbing settled thinking.

There are two common accusations against this kind of Formalist account that Thompson wants to counter. One is the inability to deal with emotions. Formalism stresses the development of mental (perceptual and cognitive) skills which any work of art requires. So, the joint theses about cinema of

Bordwell, Thompson and Staiger talk a great deal about films 'cueing' us. This is important since it emphasises the ways we have to attend to a film, the orderly progression and emergence of events through a film, and the way we have to develop interpretative strategies, if we are to make any sense of it. But it does not seem to say anything about the affective aspects of film: desire, fear, caring, emotion, motivation. Bordwell concedes this territory, as we've seen. Thompson does not want to accept this. She insists that her approach emphasises the *active* role of audiences, rather than passive contemplation. Citing Nelson Goodman's account of aesthetic involvement as 'restless, searching, testing', she argues that in her approach '[t]he spectator is involved on the levels of perception, emotion, and cognition, all of which are inextricably bound up together. As Nelson Goodman puts it, "In aesthetic experience *the emotions function cognitively*. The work of art is comprehended through the feelings as well as through the senses." ... [A]rtworks engage us at every level and change our ways of perceiving, feeling, and reasoning' (p.10). This is an important rebuttal to those psychoanalytic approaches which treat emotions such as desire as residues, operating independently of reason and by different rules. If cognition cannot function without feelings, and vice versa, then to search for a principle prior to films is otiose. Still, the question must be: does Thompson deliver on this promise?

She also resists the charge of elitism, in its favouring of 'highly original films that may be inaccessible to mass audiences' (p.32). Her reply is: look at my case-studies. I can deal as well with popular films as I can with art films. Neo-Formalist principles of analysis can deal as well with the generically standard as they can with the exceptional or the difficult. And Thompson is as good as her word. Among the films she analyses are some run-of-the-mill genre numbers, such as *Terror by Night* (1946), a Sherlock Holmes screen adaptation, and *Laura* (1944), an Otto Preminger crime thriller. But does that answer the complaint? I believe that, though in both respects Thompson has rightly identified the *task*, she has failed to carry it through.

Take the issue of emotion first. She is surely right to see emotions as functionally inseparable from knowledge. If in *Titanic* (1997) we do not understand that Jack is the hero, and is dying and leaving his loved one in the middle section of the film, how on earth can we feel any emotion for him? Why do we not weep equally at the deaths of the other thousand passengers whom we see plummeting into the water? Because the film has not *involved us in their fate* – and that means perceiving and knowing *along with* caring, hoping, fearing, predicting, dreading, etc. Equally, if we do not feel with Rose the emotions of loss (over Jack) and betrayal (by Cal), how will we understand and respond to her hiding from Cal after they have been rescued? Knowledge and emotion, then, are necessarily interwoven, as Thompson claims.

The trouble is that her actual accounts of her films rarely say anything at all about feelings. The words I encountered all the way through her book were such as the following: we 'attend to', 'look and listen intensely', 'notice', 'recognise', 'piece together', 'question', 'consider', 'examine', 'conceive', 'grasp', 'understand'. It is hard to find examples of languages of affect (pleasure, pain, desire, discomfort, hope, desire, anger, etc.) within any of her analyses, even at the points when she discusses what is being asked of audiences. Why is this so?

What about that charge of 'elitism'? If it meant simply that there is a preference for analysing one kind of film above another, it would be pretty trivial, and easily remedied – and Thompson goes some way towards the remedy. But I would argue that it means more than that. Formalism requires that to be worthy of the name 'art', things such as films must be original enough to disturb 'conventionalised thinking'. And in Thompson's account, popular films are analysed to see how far they may carry the marks that make art films interesting to her. They are worth analysing to the extent that they lift themselves out of the category of the 'popular' and look like art. This is shown very clearly at the end of her analysis of *Terror by Night*, her exemplar of an 'ordinary film'. She writes:

> We have now found a number of underlying patterns in *Terror by Night* that are quite complex – particularly the differing spatial orientations of the first and second halves of the film. The discovery of such complexities might lead us at first to conclude that the film is a good one. Yet in light of the many narrative problems and conventional devices we have also found, it seems unlikely that anyone would claim it is much better than average. I think we must conclude rather that the Hollywood system is in itself quite complex. Its standardized guidelines would allow a wide range of choices that would create a unique artwork. Yet every work could also borrow some of the complexity of the whole system. Many of the types of motivation we have seen at work in *Terror by Night* would have been virtually automatic to Hollywood filmmakers. (pp.85–6)

Notice the questions and criteria in play here: is it a 'good' film, means, is its complexity interesting, compelling and unusual? Does it lift itself out of automaticity? I certainly do not want to argue that there should not be investigations of 'quality' and the conditions under which it becomes possible – although I would want to introduce arguments such as Bourdieu's about the social distribution of criteria of 'taste'. What interests me more is how this displays an unresolved tension within Formalist theory. 'Defamiliarisation', it seems, has two rather different functions: on the one hand to disturb our thinking – a process which may indeed be quite uncomfortable – in order to free our rational-critical faculties; on the other hand to give us aesthetic experiences of novelty. These are only easily compatible if Formalism is pitched in with a current of elitist politics, where artists 'free the masses' from ideological enslavement by provoking them with superior aesthetic experiences.[2]

There is, then, an incipient politics of film audiences in her account. But it is partly concealed by a limitation Thompson puts on herself. When she discusses audiences, her first position is the Bordwellian one, that audiences are necessarily active, in that to watch *any* film is to play a cognitive role opposite it. But then an inconsistency rears its head. Not all films equally require 'activity', it seems. She separates 'aesthetic films' from 'the use of films for practical purposes (advertising, reportage, rhetorical persuasion, and so on)' (p.21). Thompson needs this distinction, if the Formalist project is to continue unamended. But consider a few examples, and try to say which is 'aesthetic' and which 'practical'. What about *Reds* (1981) which tells the story of two Americans in Russia at the time of the 1917 revolution, and which includes filmed interviews with people who remembered the real historical people who were fictionally portrayed? What about *Schindler's List* (1993) which adapts to screen a fictionalised reconstruction of the life of Oscar Schindler who saved some thousand Jews from the concentration camps? What of *Jurassic Park* (1993), pure entertainment except that it contains advertisements for its own merchandising? What of *Little Big Man* (1970), which told the story of the massacre of the Sioux nation – initially, at least, in a context where native Americans in films had been predominantly savages deserving every bullet they got? What about *The Horse Whisperer* (1998), a film that makes a virtue of combining landscape aestheticism with a nostalgia for a simpler America? In none of these can some easy distinction be maintained between their aesthetic or artistic characteristics, and their practical functions. The need to demarcate a sphere called 'art' is the problem – it doesn't do justice to the complexity of the relations between imaginative forms and practical activities.

Thompson manages this problem by putting a wall around her concept of the audience. She writes:

> [I]n accounting for the effects of films on spectators, critics need not go to the opposite extreme of dealing with reactions of actual people. ... The notion of norms and devices allows critics to make assumptions about how viewers will be likely to understand a given device.[3]

If all this means is that prior to consideration of actual audiences we have to enunciate the audience role demanded by a particular film, this would be fine. But I sense that Thompson is building a wall between the 'spectator' implied by a film, and all *actual* spectators. On that basis, the elitist assumptions which have slid in may well pass muster. Imagine an abstract viewer, lacking social and historical location, having no qualities other than a general ability to follow filmic cues, and – most curiously – seeming to be entirely individualised: such a lonely contemplative creature may be a nice figure for film theory, but if s/he can never connect with the reactions of actual people, s/he is surely a hollow, straw person.

If actual people are not to figure, why do film analysis? Thompson suggests that we should study films which 'intrigue' us (p.4). In one sense, that is a perfectly reasonable proposal: why not study *any* film which seriously interests us? But if it means, as I suspect, that films should be studied because we suspect that they have *depths which need uncovering*, then 'intrigue' becomes another coded term for 'hidden quality'. What if I am intrigued by films which are *totally obvious*? Whose pleasures look simple, direct and have mass appeal? In this book I will argue that we can learn a great deal by taking apart how 'obviousness' is *achieved* in popular films.

Which is why I propose instead the ideas which constitute the heart of this book: films are imaginative universes with organising rules and principles; they generate a role into which audiences may (or may not) enter, which I call the implied audience; and through the intersection of these, they generate proposals for how films might intersect with the rest of their audiences' lives, which I call their modalities of use. And in exploring these, I aim to show that motives and emotions are natural and inevitable parts of the invited processes of engagement.

Expanding from Formalism

Where does this leave me? I will try to gather my argument so far via an example. In his useful, brief introduction to Formalist and Neo-Formalist criticism, Ian Christie emphasises, surely rightly, that for Bordwell and co., one of the prime attractions of this approach is its precise emphasis on audience activity: the calls to engaged understanding that films make on us.[4] The reason for its precision lies in its roots in what Christie calls 'Eikhenbaum's most original contribution':

> his answer to the question: what links film phrases? Or, in Formalist terms, how do transitions appear motivated, rather than arbitrary? He suggests that the viewer is prompted to supply links through internal

speech, by completing or articulating what is implied by the sequence of (silent) screen images. This idea is most easily illustrated by examples of visual metaphor. Eikhenbaum quotes the sailor in *The Devil's Island* (1926), who has decided to stay on shore with his girl, and enters a tavern, where we see a billiard-ball *fall* into a pocket, thus triggering the idea of *his* fall from duty.[5]

Eikhenbaum's question is important, since it directs our attention to the details of film form, but also at once presses us to consider what is required of an audience if they are to make sense of it. The problem is that Christie, in much the same fashion as I have argued with Thompson, doesn't complete the exploration of what *is* required here, but instead covers it with that word 'triggered'.

What are the minimum conditions necessary for making the step which Eikhenbaum identifies? In order that a member of an audience should read the shot of the billiard-ball falling into the pocket as an indication of the sailor's moral lapse, the following conditions have to be met:

1   The watcher has to be sufficiently committed to making sense of the film to *want* to complete the step across the edit. This may seem terribly obvious, but certainly is not, in practice. Our ordinary lives are filled with cases where, confronted with a book, a film, a painting, a poem, or whatever, we decide that we can't be bothered or don't have the energy or don't see the point in spending the effort. But these are the negatives, and there has to be a way of stating what happens when we do agree to, when we want to become involved in something that may make all kinds of demands on us. Some are smooth and easy: sharing laughter, for instance – though that in itself carries many complications (risk management: what can be found funny in which company etc.). Others are chosen for their difficulties: emotional demands, for example (risks, fears, hopes, desires: being shocked or embarrassed, caring, crying, recognising bits of ourselves uneasily). To understand commitments, then, we are already addressing rich repertoires of social engagement and their role in particular groups' social worlds.

2   S/he has to identify that this is indeed *a linked, motivated sequence* of a kind that the second shot needs direct linking with the first. Not every pair of shots is of this kind: shifts of scene, of time and place, or any other kind of purposeful discontinuity would require quite other kinds of interpretative activity from our film-watcher. Many things go into this, but one, clearly, is some emergent sense of the *film as a whole* and the place of a particular pair of shots.

3   S/he has to be motivated to read this sequence *metaphorically*, that is, not operating at the level only of the literal meanings of people, objects and events shown. This is really a qualification of 1 (above), in that it specifies the *kind* of commitment our watcher has to have. S/he must not relate solely or even primarily via involvement with characters, or via fascination with spectacle, or via narrative puzzlement and resolution.

Two things have to co-occur for all these to be possible. (a) A film, by dint of its formal organisation at levels of both its components and its totality, generates a *role*. I will call this the role of the *implied audience*: a sum-total of the requirements for being involved both processually and summatively in the world of the film. (b) Anyone watching that film has to *agree* and *be able* to play that role; s/he has to acquire the combination of skills and knowledges, and at the same time agree to be involved in ways which enable her/him to play that role. The task of this book is to explore the first of these. Important in itself, it is doubly important, I am arguing, because we will not know what to ask of actual audiences if we haven't delineated that role. The final chapter of this book will try to point up some of the lines of investigation into audiences which these film analyses index.

Take three examples: on p.101 I look closely at a short sequence from *Titanic*, a vital scene in several ways in the film's narrative when Jack and Rose kiss for the first time, but from which the film, through voice-over, reintroduces the coming disaster. The sequence involves exactly matched shots between the ship in the past, and the ship in the film's present, underwater, then pulling out to show the face of the elderly Rose. What operations are required for an audience to manage this transition? Cognitively, they have to identify the shift between past and present. They are cued to this by the state of the ship, but also importantly by colour (warm sunset pinks and reds, changing to cold midnight blues) and by the disappearance of the extradiegetic music (richly complementing the mood in the past scene, fading out in synchrony with the very slow dissolve). But notice, therefore, that in identifying how the transition is cued, two other things have already been indicated. First, the film cues the *relation between scenes* by the nature of the dissolve: for lingering seconds, Rose remains like a ghost in the figure of her long white scarf on the drowned ship. And in the way in which the contrast is pointed up, the emotional tone of the two scenes is depicted: from wonder, tenderness and also harmony – between the lovers, the enormous ship and even the weather – to a foretelling of doom.

But even more than this is required for an understanding of the scene. The difficulty I have with Eikhenbaum's example is that it is wrenched from context. As such, the operation can be considered (a) purely cognitively and (b) in isolation. But the scene on *Titanic* only gathers sense because by this point the audience is expected to have seen Rose in terms of possible futures (predictions), and to will a better future for her than that offered by Cal. We have learnt about her sense of despair, we have seen her fiancé's callousness, we have heard Jack offer her knowledge of another world, and a different vision of herself. Up to this point, albeit with lurking reminders of a destiny not to be escaped and a present that will return, the narrative's trajectory has been a story of Rose discovering new possibilities for herself, in a world identified as false and oppressive. This is as much an emotional and motivational account as it is cognitive: we are assumed to be *on Rose's side* in and through our cognitive picture of this fake and divided world. But we also know that this is a film heading for the rocks, or better, the bergs. Therefore when, after that slow dissolve through matched shots, elderly Rose is heard saying: 'That was the last time *Titanic* ever saw daylight', we know this was a breakthrough, never quite to be regained. The scene takes on a significance by virtue of its place in the developing wholeness of the film.

Take a second example: *From Dusk Till Dawn* (1996) follows two murderous brothers following a bank raid that has gone wrong. On the run, they shoot up then blow up a store, then at an overnight motel stop kidnap a preacher and his two children – one, a pubescent girl (played by Juliette Lewis). The younger brother Richie can't keep his eyes off her body. Suddenly she turns to him and says: 'Richie … would you lick my pussy?' Before he can respond, his brother interrupts to tell him not to talk to the hostages. What audience understanding of this 'move' is this inviting? Seen as an isolated pair of shots, it must surely confuse – and perhaps appal. But in a widening circle of contexts, it takes on a determinable meaning. First, Richie has been established as dangerously crazy. He has 'heard' words when we know they are imaginary. He judged a terrified elderly woman to be dangerous, so killed her. The indications are all that what we saw and heard at that moment was *his* fantasy. But an audience can only achieve this if they meet and agree to certain other conditions. They must understand that in a film of this kind, normal rules of cinema may be suspended at any moment – the unexpected can happen, indeed should be expected to happen (an audience untrained in Tarantin-esque cinema will surely have difficulties even grasping what has happened). They must be willing to accept that the point of such suspensions is to subject us to ideas which are in themselves outrageous (an audience unwilling to do this will simply find this distasteful). They must at best find an interesting tension between the possibility that it might have been the girl who said it, and a realisation that this is an imputed fantasy-wish (an audience rejecting altogether the notion of a young girl having such sexual desires will find Richie's character too vile to follow).

So, set in the context of the kind of film this is establishing itself to be; set in the wider context of an audience trained in such late-Hollywood 'movies of excess'; set, also, in a context where cinema is accepted as a site for imagining the extravagantly outrageous: thus set, the scene is comprehensible, contributes importantly to the narrative, and is even funny.

Finally, the third and quite different example. In research recently completed with two colleagues on the responses to David Cronenberg's (1996) *Crash*, we found clear evidence of a difference between the ways of responding to the film by 'positive' and 'negative' audiences. *Crash* opens with three scenes of sexual intercourse: first, an as yet unnamed woman letting herself be penetrated from behind by a man whom she seems not to know, in an aircraft hangar; then a film director fucking a young woman off set; finally the man and woman quietly comparing their experiences on a high balcony until the man, turned on by the woman's account, again enters her from behind. In all three scenes, there is virtual absence of facial expressions, and almost no given understanding of *why* these people are having sex. Those who rejected the film took exactly that; they refused to see connections. The scenes were 'gratuitous', 'pointless', 'one scene after another of sex for its own sake'. By contrast, those who became involved worked with a principle of connection between these scenes: the film was showing us the scenes without explanation or judgement *so* that audiences would have to look inside the characters and examine their motives, their attitudes to sex, their will to explore the potentialities of sexuality. This is a clear example, I would argue, of audiences entering or rejecting the implied audience role. *Crash* called on a range of skills and knowledges, motives and interests in those who went to see it. Some, having those, accepted and played the role the film asked; others refused, or failed (the latter often being signalled by confusion). This is not a moral judgement. Rather it shows that through analysing films in the way I am proposing, we can arrive at matters that go way beyond the individual film: what skills and motives films assume are available in a culture; how films fit with distributed cultural modes of involvement and belonging; therefore, in particular, what a positive engagement with a film can tell us about the broader state of our culture. And it will do this in ways which can, both in principle and in practice, be checked by other kinds of research.[6] But to work with a figure of the audience which cannot ever be linked with actual audiences, as seems to be the case with Kristin Thompson, renders film analysis rather a barren venture.

Reader Response Criticism

As I said before, this book does not start in a vacuum. Another of its sources, and especially for this concept of an 'implied audience', is a body of ideas developed fitfully within literary theory. These come from two courses: American New Criticism and European Reader Response work. The first, curiously, had ambitions quite at odds with those of this book. Its proclaimed goal was to turn attention back to the formal organisation of novels, poems and plays, and set the programme for literary studies as the systematic exploration of how texts work, independent of authors' intentions, readers' responses, and their context of reading. In this way, authoritative readings of texts' 'meanings' could be achieved. But adopting that task led some of its adherents to explore how, in particular, texts may *involve* their readers. What demands might a novel incorporate into its very structure? And from that came a way of attending to novels that half broke free of the programme which inspired them. Wayne Booth, for instance, proposed a series of distinctions whose usefulness outruns their source within the extreme textualism of New Criticism.

Booth argues that we need to attend to the 'rhetoric' of works of fiction, that is, the ways in which they address themselves to possible readers. Many older novels did this with some explicitness, addressing themselves to a 'Dear Reader': not a real person, but a *position* that a real reader must be willing to enter if s/he is to read in comfort. But it does not require that explicitness. Booth gives a telling example:

> 'There was a man in the land of Uz, whose name was Job. And that man was perfect and upright, one that feared God and eschewed evil.' With one stroke the unknown author has given us a kind of information never obtained in real life, even about our most intimate friends. Yet it is information we must accept without question if we are going to grasp the story that is to follow. In life, if a friend confided his view that *his* friend was 'perfect' and 'upright', we would accept the information with qualifications imposed by our knowledge of the speaker's character or the general fallibility of mankind. We would never trust even the most reliable of witnesses as completely as we trust the author of the opening statement about Job.[7]

Booth is stressing here the artificiality of adopting this point of view, yet also its feel of naturalness. This is because of the effective textual work in addressing us authoritatively. We can decline, but there has to be something there that we are declining. There are many difficulties with Booth's overall account, but two linked ones in particular concern me. First, he undermines his own identification of this role of being a reader when he equates it effectively with *actual* readers. His grounding in New Criticism has led him to see texts as, in effect, overpowering readers with their manner of addressing us. This in turn leads him to express a preference for those very literary texts that *declare* their mode of address. Putting it simply, Booth loathes popular novels like the hard-boiled detective fiction of Mickey Spillane, because he sees them as blinding readers to its judgements on people and events. They do this by their authoritative mode of address:

> By giving the impression that judgement is withheld, an author can hide from himself that he is sentimentally involved with his characters, and that he is asking for his reader's sympathies, without providing adequate reasons. … But the modern author can reject the charge of sentimentality by saying, in effect, 'Who, me? Not at all. It is the reader's fault if he feels any excessive or unjustified compassion. I didn't say a word, I'm as tight-lipped and unemotional as the next man'. Such effects are most evident, perhaps in the worst of the tough-guy school of detective fiction. Mickey Spillane's Mike Hammer can in effect do no wrong – for those who can stomach him at all. But many of Spillane's readers would drop him immediately if he intruded to make explicit the vicious morality on which enjoyment of his books is based: 'You may notice, dear reader, that when Mike Hammer beats up an Anglo-Saxon American he is less brutal than when he beats up a Jew, and that when he beats up a Negro he is most brutal of all. In this way our hero discriminates his punishment according to the racial worth of his victims'. It is wise of Spillane to avoid making such things explicit.[8]

The error here is unintentionally exposed by a commentary on Booth which, in discussing the implications of his notion of the 'implied reader', remarks that the implied reader's values and beliefs 'are by definition also those of the implied author'.[9] That is certainly Booth's argument. He thinks that novels, for instance, have a 'value-structure' which audiences are subconsciously adopting, at least for the time of the reading, as they process a narrative. This is a jump far beyond the notions of 'implied author' and 'implied reader'. And the pessimistic conclusion about popular story-telling doesn't follow at all if one thinks of the reader as simultaneously *constructing an understanding* and *learning how to respond* through their engagement with the text. The implied author then becomes one structured resource within the text.

Again, check with an example from *Titanic*. In learning how to engage with the film, among the resources we have are (a) what we are shown, and (b) how information is given to us in voice-over. The elderly Rose provides almost all of the latter. If anyone is a 'narrator', she is. But she is not the implied author, in the sense that although in a broad sense she takes us on the long journey back through her experiences on the boat, she does not direct what we are shown. Indeed, at times things are shown to us which she *could not have known*. We see Jack trying to get to her during the religious service – and we see her not seeing him. We see Cal plotting to plant the diamond on Jack so he can be accused of stealing it – and she is almost taken in by this for a while. We know she ought to trust Jack when he asks her to believe him, but she knows less than us.

Following Booth's initial arguments, a number of other analysts – often themselves dismissive of New Criticism's belief that textual analysis could reveal the meaning of texts – still continued that interest in examining the textual conditions of audience involvement. The distinctions they used became finer and finer; for audiences, for example, they worked variously with 'actual', 'implied', 'authorial', 'ideal' and 'competent', and even combinations of these like 'ideal authorial', plus of course the 'narratee', that person addressed by any text's narrator. Despite a sense of desperately divided hairs in much of this, the ambition remains relevant. And often the most useful contribution comes when analysts demonstrate, in specific cases, what must go on if an audience is to manage to read a particular text.

Take two illustrations of this. Peter Rabinowitz, in an essay examining the significance of literary borrowing, uses the case of Dostoyevsky's *The Possessed*, a novel which borrows in different ways from Pushkin and Turgenev, and assumes that readers will recognise these:

> How could [Dostoyevsky] make such assumptions without knowing his actual readers? The best he could do was, as authors have always done, design his book for a hypothetical audience, which I call the *authorial audience*. Since the structure of any work is designed with the authorial audience in mind, we must – as we read – come to share its characteristics if we are to understand the text. … He too writes for an audience – an imitation audience that I call the *narrative audience*. Anton Levrentevich, the narrator of *The Possessed*, is an imitation historian. As such, he writes for an audience which not only knows (as does the authorial audience) that the serfs were freed in 1861, but which also believes that Stavrogin and Kirilov 'really' existed. To read *The Possessed*, we must not only join Dostoyevsky's authorial audience (which treats the text as *what it is* – a novel), but must at the same time pretend to be members of Anton

Levrentevich's narrative audience (which treats the text as if it were really what it *pretends to be* – a history).[10]

As a second example, consider Jonathan Culler's account of Jonathan Swift's (1729) satirical essay on the famine in Ireland, which – to point up the inhumanity of those who blamed the disaster on the Irish themselves – 'seriously' proposed that Irish parents should be encouraged to eat their own children, thus simultaneously solving food shortages and reducing 'overpopulation':

> Someone who reads Swift's 'A Modest Proposal' as a masterpiece of irony first postulates an audience that the narrator appears to think he is addressing: an audience entertaining specific assumptions, inclined to formulate certain objections, but likely to find the narrator's arguments cogent and compelling. The second role the reader postulates is that of an audience attending to a serious proposal for relieving famine in Ireland but finding the values and assumptions of the proposal (and of the 'ideal narrative audience') singularly skewed. Finally, the reader participates in an audience that reads the work not as a narrator's proposal but as an author's ingenious construction, and appreciates its power and skill. Actual readers will combine the roles of authorial, narrative and ideal narrative audiences in varying proportions. One ought, perhaps, to avoid speaking of the 'implied reader' as a single role that the reader is called upon to play, since the reader's pleasure may well come, as Barthes says, from the interaction of contradictory engagements.[11]

These are effective demonstrations of the complex operations involved in reading these texts. But they are more than that. They bring into clear view the skills and knowledges that a reader must possess in order to manage the reading process. The implications from this approach are large, and (it seems to me) by no means fully explored. They seriously challenge, for instance, many conventional notions of literacy. For my purposes, the important thing they demonstrate is how it is possible to unpack the role of the reader – and that concept points to the second major source for my concept of the 'implied reader', in the work of European literary critics such as Roman Ingarten and, especially, Wolfgang Iser.

Iser's *The Implied Reader* systematically unfolds a phenomenological approach to literary works that insists that texts do not have meanings-in-themselves, but *become* meaningful through the activities of readers interpreting them. Like the Formalists, Iser emphasises the incompleteness of texts, and the implication that readers have to fill in the 'blanks' in, for example, novels:

> The readers of the novel are forced to take an active part in the composition of the novel's meaning, which revolves around a basic divergence from the familiar. This active participation is fundamental to the novel; the title of the present collection sums it up with the term 'implied reader'. This term incorporates both the prestructuring of the potential meaning by the text, and the reader's actualisation of this potential through the reading process. It refers to the active nature of this process – which will vary historically from one age to another – and not to a typology of possible readers.[12]

An example: in *Titanic* again, late on, we see Cal trying to get a space on one of the last lifeboats. We see him turn as he hears an abandoned child crying. He picks her up, and forces his way through the crowd to ask for a place on the boat for the child. Why does he do this? At first, it is a blank. Past experience of him in the film supports a cynical interpretation of his motives – is he about to use the child to beg himself a place on a boat? He could on the other hand have been moved, despite himself – why should that not be possible? An audience has to make some kind of interpretation, in order to make a logic of the events. And each one has consequences. Someone who credits him with a moment of charity might not be surprised when he begs his place on the boat because 'she has no one but me' – though it is a straight lie – but what about when, once on the lifeboat, he unceremoniously dumps the child on another passenger? An audience that has accrued steadily an image of Cal as a callous, arrogant man who thinks his wealth entitles him to whatever he desires will find confirmation of their filling of that blank – and of course more is involved in that than simply intra-filmic knowledge. Iser's approach thus once again presses us to attend to what an audience must possess in the way of skills and interests, to complete the work and make the meaning. Or as another literary theorist puts it, with great clarity:

> [A]t a certain stage in the reading process and more or less consciously, we tend to take far-reaching interpretative decisions, we choose an interpretative standpoint towards which, more or less stubbornly, all our further interpretative activity is oriented. … This structured set of interpretations we should understand as a narrative's work-ideology.[13]

Yet there is a risk in Iser's approach, which – not unlike Booth's forced preferring of highly self-consciously authored works – ushers in an extreme literariness. In calling these pulls to interpretations 'blanks', or 'negations',[14] Iser is privileging a rather distanced puzzling of a self-conscious literary work in which we work at it, for the sake of 'finding its meaning'. Indeed, this shows in his main book on the topic, when he presumes a distinction between novels which for him demand this kind of active participation, and films which don't. What else can he intend than this when he writes, countering another proposal, that '[t]he world ... does not pass before the reader's eyes like a film' (p.277)?

This is the tip of an iceberg of issues, which I can't explore here, but which should be signalled. At the back of almost all literary theoretical work on the 'implied reader' is an image of a virtually disinterested semi-scholar, who reads because the text is 'intriguing' by virtue of having ambivalences, puzzles, self-declared gaps and incompletenesses, and whose goal as a reader is 'understanding the meaning'. This model has at least in part been carried over into much film studies, where the notion of films' 'meaning' is one of the great unexplored Lost Worlds.[15] It is almost wholly unhelpful to what audiences *actually* do with films. Someone watching *Titanic* has as many implicit moves to complete as someone reading James Joyce's *Ulysses*, but they are not *experienced as* blanks. Popular films, like popular novels, call on available cultural competences (why *might* Cal have picked up the child?), emergent understandings (knowing him, he's going to use her) and repertoires of emotional response (rich arrogant swine – I wish it wouldn't work for him). Our mode of participation, I am arguing, is awash with elements of practical reasoning coupled with involvements and commitments. But it is only rarely that we have to worry about a film's 'meaning'. When we do, that is either because the film – like the first I analyse below, *The Usual Suspects* – establishes itself as a puzzler; or because we sense a problem, an inconsistency which is blighting our attention to, and acceptance of, the film's imaginative world.[16] But most of the time, our relations to films are participative, sensory, leisured-imaginative, and narratively processual. It is only the folly of so much theorising that supposes that because someone lets go, and runs with the plot, they are somehow implicated, imbricated, interpellated or just plain inebriated by it, that allows much that passes as 'analysis of filmic meanings' to pass muster.

The position this book takes is that all story-following involves audience responsiveness – because all stories activate us, by the manner of their organisation. As John Berger beautifully put it:

> Every narrative proposes an agreement about the unstated but assumed connections between events. No story is like a wheeled vehicle whose contact with the road is continuous. Stories walk, like animals or people.

And their steps are not only between narrated events but between every sentence, sometimes every word. Every step is a stride over something not said. All stories are discontinuous and are based on a tacit agreement about what is not said, about what connects the discontinuities.[17]

Films are simply a different kind of story-telling. They do not differ in principle from anecdotes, jokes, magazine fiction, comics, television programmes or novels. Nor are popular films in principle different from art films. All proffer to audiences an invitation to play a role in activating their story, to play 'the role assigned to the real reader by the instructions in the text'.[18]

The task this book is setting itself is to show, concretely, how we can get at and spell out *what* that role is: what skills, knowledges, interests and motivations are called upon in particular cases, and what eight particular films do with us through their activation of these capacities.

The Implied Audience – a Formal Definition

The role of the implied audience is one that any actual member of the audience of a film must enter into, to some degree, if s/he is to attain a meaningful encounter with the film. It is constructed through the combination and interaction of the presented world, and the presentational process, of the film. The role is made up of *the sequence and the sum-total of cued responses necessary for participation in the world of the story.*

These cued responses will include:
- guessing ahead, formulating hypotheses about characters, motivations and events;
- taking sides: recognising the moral codings of characters; wanting some things to happen, others not;
- being puzzled, confused, trusting or not trusting elements of what is presented;
- revisiting and reassessing earlier moments if and as conflictual signs emerge;
- responding to aspects of the narrated world physically, sensually, emotionally, aesthetically, intellectually;
- assembling a construct of the *whole film* from which it becomes possible to ask the question: what is this story *about*?

In principle, these questions are all answerable by examination of the *film*. The key to the step from film to audience is recognition that film-watching is a *role which we perform* – and, of course, may fail or refuse to perform. The relation of implied audience to actual audiences' responses requires a different body of theory, and other methodologies of research. I come back to say a little more about this in the final chapter of this book, but from here on, my task is to persuade you of my approach to *films* through offering convincing analyses that do at last answer my opening question: what analysis of films can academics do that others can't?

How This Book Is Organised, Henceforth

Each chapter follows a similar pattern: (1) I first say briefly why each film matters – which can include its box office performance and what might be learnt from stunning success; controversies which surrounded a film, to see what light my kind of analysis can throw on the issues; an unusual formal arrangement in a film; or particular objections to a film, or to the company which made it. (2) I follow this with what I call an 'analytic description' – on which, see below. (3) From this, I gather up a set of patterns and preliminary generalisations from the basis of which I can approach my guiding questions. (4) With preliminary questions and hypotheses to hand, I return to the film to examine one or two short scenes in close detail, to see what they reveal that is pertinent to my issues. (5) Finally, I proffer my conclusions.

Why the quite extensive space given to retelling each film's narrative and process? Given the deliberate choice of popular contemporary films, couldn't I presume that you would know the story of most of these films without a detailed retelling? At the beginning I said that everyone analyses films. I now add that everyone retells films' stories – but with quite different intents and outcomes. Here is a sample of ways of retelling the film I analyse as my first case study: *The Usual Suspects*. It is worth asking, as you read them, what appears to be the purpose of the telling in each case, and what kind of response each is trying to elicit. You may also like to look ahead to Chapter 3, to compare these retellings with mine:

1   *From the publicity information for the film:* 'A boat, believed to have $91 million in cocaine on board, is docked at a pier in San Pedro, just south of LA. Suddenly an enormous explosion rips through the still of the night and you know that whatever or whoever was unlucky enough to be on that boat was blown halfway to hell. Within hours, a charred floating carcass is all that's left. That, and twenty seven dead bodies. Miraculously, there are two survivors: a Hungarian gangster who lies, clinging to life and burnt to a crisp; and Roger 'Verbal' Kint, a crippled con-man from New York.

As U.S. Customs Special Agent David Kujan conducts his grueling inquisition, Kint weaves a tale that begins six weeks earlier, at a police lock-up in New York. Five felons, accused of hijacking a truckload of gun parts in Queens, are brought in for a line-up. The cops don't have much in the way of evidence, so the five are held overnight.

Five criminals. Five criminal minds. One night. One plan. They are suspects. Strangers. With one thing in common: Keyser Soze – a criminal so feared, so fabled, even the icy stares of these cold-blooded killers burn with terror at the mere mention of his name. And now, the only one who can identify Keyser Soze, believed to be at the heart of this dockside massacre, is the hospitalized Hungarian. So while an FBI sketch artist struggles to complete his rendering of Soze before the witness dies, Verbal Kint sits in the D.A.'s office, taking Kujan through the steps that led him there.

The inquisition is arduous. Kujan is relentless. Hour after hour he probes. Kint wavers and, finally, breaks. In the end, a pathetic, low-life con-man is outwitted by a smart, shrewd U.S. government agent.

Or is he?'

2 **From the video box for the film:** '5 criminals brought together in a framed line-up. 27 bodies in Long Beach harbour. One dying, terrified witness. One cop hell-bent on unravelling the truth. Their one connection … Keyser Soze. A mysterious criminal overlord with a reign of terror, or the devil himself? In a world where nothing is what it seems you've got to look beyond … The Usual Suspects.'

3 **From USA Today:** 'When a boat said to carry $91 million in drug money mysteriously goes ka-boom in a San Pedro, California harbour, the 27 fatalities include a bumper crop of well-known hoods and, as it turns out, most of the movie's cast. This would seem to diminish the possibilities, but *Suspects*' nearly 2-hour flashback relegates the rest to that too-familiar screen staple, the bungled-caper postmortem with the mainly male cast. You get Chazz Palmintieri in a real dead-end role as an interrogating cop who thinks he knows more than he does. The lowlife roster includes Gabriel Byrne, Stephen Baldwin, Giancarlo Esposito, and two Kevins – Pollack and Spacey.'

4 **From The Guardian:** 'If *Public Access* undeniably showed promise, *The Usual Suspects* vies to become the widescreen genre thriller of the year as it travels backwards and forwards from a San Pedro dockside where a ship full of contraband drugs is fired and an unseen man shoots Gabriel

Byrne's corrupt cop. Earlier in time, if not in the construction of the film, a police round-up in New York includes the ex-cop and introduces us to several other villains, including a crippled squealer called Verbal (Kevin Spacey) and Stephen Baldwin's bad-tempered McManus.

Verbal is given immunity by the New York policeman in charge (Chazz Palmintieri) in exchange for talking. But back in circulation, the gang of usual suspects pulls off a coup by removing $3 million of emeralds from Paul Bartel's smuggler.

Taking the jewels to a fence in Los Angeles, the men become involved in another heist in which several are killed. The result puts them in thrall to a Mr Big, which sends us back to the dockside conflagration.

On this basic structure, the film constructs an elaborate entertainment with a simple moral – that you can't beat corruption even if you are inclined that way yourself. There is always a more powerful broker somewhere around.'

5 *From a personal review (by 'Justin') lodged on the Internet Movie Database:* 'Kevin Spacey is one of Hollywood's most unique and underrated actors in our time. … He's sometimes creepy, always masterful, and splendidly cool. But if you're looking for his best performance, *The Usual Suspects* seats him in a role that you will be thinking about for weeks. Spacey plays Verbal Kint, a cripple whose forced police confession serves as the narration for the story. *Suspects* starts at the end, then flashes back and forth in time until eventually progressing on a linear course. I wouldn't dream of giving away the plot, since this is one of two movies I've seen in the past few years that I could not predict. I will say that it does involve five criminals that get mixed up with a most ruthless man named Keyser Soze and a plot to earn $81 million. It's not exactly a thriller, not exactly a mystery, but it'll leave you grinnin' ear to ear in awe of its sheer brilliance.'

There are a number of important features differentiating these story retellings. First, the official ones clearly operate as titivations. They pose the problem. They tell you enough hopefully to want to know the rest. The first, however, has a function beyond the come-on. As a component in the film's publicity, issued as part of the Press Pack, it tells enough that a working journalist will hopefully scavenge it at speed for a review. The video cover version, shorter partly for space reasons, functions only as a come-on to be read when someone meets it on a shelf. In both cases they read like headlines catching hold, with almost a touch of poetry, of key components ('Five criminals. Five criminal minds. One night. One plan.'). This becomes a symbolic enactment of the promised mystery and excitement of the film – which of course can't be told, or the point would be lost.

The others may also hold back on the outcomes of the film, but they do it differently. Justin tells you that he won't spoil it for you – and importantly does clearly address 'you'. This is a para-friend, wanting to share his sheer exhilaration at the film. He speaks in a language which assumes a degree of film-literacy: 'serves as the narration … progressing on a linear course … not exactly a thriller, not exactly a mystery'. It has, even in this extract, a sense of its audience – a fact that becomes clearer in other elements of it: '*The Usual Suspects* is not your usual movie. But there is a sufficient amount of action to sate your basic slug of a boy-friend, and smart enough to confound your sorority sisters. … Recommended for: Irritable movie-goers who think they've seen it all. A large group of friends (same gender). Who do you trust?' This is a review written on the assumption of a shared culture-group – young people who go to the cinema regularly, and so are very knowing about what to expect, knowing that films are for talking about afterwards in groups, smilingly aware of each others' different gender-preferences. But the end raises a grinning spectre – why should not trusting each other be an issue? A hint that the film will leave you looking around you, in a wondering way … So here the point of the withholding is to gather in the skeins of promised pleasure, raise a knowing tension.

One important feature of the different kinds of telling is the way they mess with what we know, and what we don't know. All of them do this, even the official versions. In the film itself, we do not know at the outset either that the boat is carrying cocaine (publicity version) or that the arrests are a frame-up (video version). In more complicated ways the press reviews do the same. In *The Guardian* version, you might guess that Kint talks voluntarily about Soze, whereas in the film the information has apparently to be startled out of him.

Finally, what is the point of each retelling? Clearly, the video cover's aim is to persuade you to rent/buy. The publicity version's is to give the material to journalists such that *they* will hopefully persuade you to go see the film. Justin's review is a testimonial among 'friends', an imaginary community of like-interested cinema-goers. The *USA Today*'s review is a short notice, giving their (none too positive) view of the film, in effect saying 'Well, this is what it's worth – thin story, narrow range of characters, all a bit obvious … it's your decision now'. The longer review in *The Guardian* works with a different assumed knowingness among their readers. References to genre, to filmic traditions, are completed in *The Guardian*'s case with a moral: a clever winking question which, if you take it up, gives not just another reason to see the film, but another target in watching it ('How will they manage to embody *that* in the movie we've just described?').

Story retellings fulfil many purposes, and converse in many 'languages' with people in different filmic and cultural communities with different interests. They bend their retellings to the ends of those conversations. It may help if we see them as answering different unspoken *questions*. Most of the time in reviews the question is: what is this film about and is it worth seeing for someone like me? And then the publisher of the review speaks to a 'you' that s/he presumes: sharing certain kinds of filmic knowledge, likely to recognise particular (actors', directors') names, enjoying certain kinds of story, looking for this or that kind of experience. There are plenty of others. It isn't difficult to imagine an attack on the film by moral objectors. Indeed it is interesting to play that game – so that you can, at least in imagination, construct your own, I have put my version of this in a note.[19]

These are all ordinary, everyday purposes, but they are not mine in this book. I am interested in how films *work, formally*. I have tried to retell each film in a particular way. First, is to respect the fact that these are *stories*. That to me carries certain implications:

- Stories necessarily have elements which can be analytically distinguished. There have been two main ways, historically, of doing this. First, the Formalists distinguish what they call, in translation, *story* and *plot*.[20] The plot is the sequence of events as – and how – they are given to us in a film's flow. The story is the construction by a viewer of the implied meaningful sequence of events. The most frequent example to explain the point of this is flashbacks, where events prior to what we are currently watching are intruded into the shown sequence. But there are an unlimited number of other ways in which the plot can veer away from the space-time sequence: gaps in time and space where a film jumps forward, sometimes speeding up, sometimes just skipping over a discontinuity; parallel presentation of two components which presume jumps in space, and so on.

  Another quite distinct set of analytic distinctions derives from the New Critics, who explore the differences between what are variously called 'story' and 'discourse', or 'presented world' and 'presentational process'. Very crudely, this marks the difference between *what* occurs in the space of a story, and *how* that is made available to us.
- Films contain *characters*: characters in films are potentially several things, simultaneously. They clearly have to be characters *within* the film: adequately motivated and appropriately presented to fulfil the role the plot requires of them. But they also have to be recognisable to us. In

that way characters always contain elements of typicality within them: ways in which their appearance, their behaviour, the groups they belong to, their ways of thinking and deciding things enable us to place them as kinds of people. This is representation, in the broadest sense.

- Films have available to them a distinctive set of presentational resources. This is not a complete list of these, but clearly it includes the various components of both the sound (dialogue, voice-over, music, special effects and of course the full array of qualities of sound – closeness versus distance, volume, in/audibility, layerings of sound, point of hearing) and the visual (filmed scenes, titles, intertitles, special effects, and of course the full array of cinematographic devices – from close-up to wide angle, different kinds of focus, point of view, high to low angles of filming, editing speeds and rhythms, lens effects (from naturalistic to various kinds of visual distortion), colour balances (and black and white of course)). How these are assembled into a unified composition is a distinct task of film analysis.

- Stories are *told*: that is, characters and events are revealed to us in definite orders, sometimes with rich descriptions, sometimes explained only by implication, sometimes withheld, even concealed. To analyse a film, as any other form of story, it is necessary to describe it, at least to ourselves, in a way that acknowledges the role that is played by the *manner of the telling*. 'Who' or 'what' seems to be speaking at any point, and to 'whom' they seem to be speaking, about what?

In principle, given the density of all that is implied in these, an analytic description of a film could go on for ever. How to know when to stop, then? That is a mixture of the purely pragmatic and the heavily theoretical. The pragmatic considerations are the amount of space available, time, etc. The theoretical considerations are to do with when you feel that you have achieved two things: the first is that your description contains a sufficient sense of the film as a whole. It is after all not a contingent fact that films start and end, and that within those two poles events are managed with enormous care. The second is that your description should allow you to begin to notice patterned presences: repetitions, sequences, continuities and discontinuities.

My way of retelling films is guided by my general account of what films are and how they work. If you like, my retellings of films are preliminary means to answer the following questions: how does each film proceed with its telling of its story? What world is unfolded to us in the course of the film: that is, how are characters and events shown to be connected in motivated ways, and how are we invited to be involved in them? What knowledges, skills, interests and motives are presumed in someone who becomes a watcher of each film? In the presumptions of these questions are contained the key concepts of this book. These concepts, which I have attempted to introduce and explain, are: the concept of an *imaginative universe*; the concept of the *implied audience*; and the concept of *modality of involvement*. The rest of each analysis is, then, an attempt to move from a usable retelling of each film to a measuring of the film against the questions posed by these concepts. What kind of imaginative universe is on offer in each case? How does it invite and structure our possible involvements? And therefore in what way does it offer itself to the rest of our lives?

With each film that follows my narrative retelling is shaped by the questions I want to be able to go on to ask:

- **What patterns and processes become visible through the analytic description, which indicate the fulfilling of my organising principles: the generation of a rule-governed imaginative universe; the construction of an implied audience role; and the proffering of a modality of participation?**
- **What generalisations and preliminary hypotheses am I thus able to develop and sustain that demonstrate the distinctive ways these are at work within each particular film?**

Framing these as what I hope are clear questions has been a tough enough proposition. What happens hereafter becomes a matter of tactics for showing how we might answer them in all the peculiar complexity of my chosen films. In my final chapter I shall reflect a little on the tactics I have found useful.

3
Usual Suspects, Unusual Devices

The Usual Suspects was the surprise hit of 1995. Costing only $6 million, it grossed over $30 million at the box office, despite getting only a small proportion of the number of screens that a big movie expects. It won two Oscars: for best original screenplay (Chris McQuarrie) and best supporting actor (Kevin Spacey) – the irony of this second award being that the film has an ensemble cast, so it is hard to know who Spacey was supposed to be supporting! The Oscars are not designed for such situations ... With these overt recognitions went other kinds of public acknowledgement. Lines from the film became popular coin of exchange for a time, and its poster – the line-up, with five men slouching against a wall marked with height-lines – was honoured in more than a dozen subsequent posters and advertisements.[1]

It almost didn't get made. Its director Bryan Singer and writer McQuarrie tried 130 film financiers before finally cutting a deal with two European sources. Even then, the deal almost fell apart just days before filming was due to start, when one backer withdrew. Finally, a recut of the distribution and video rights brought in combined finance from Polygram and Spelling International. Launched at the Sundance Festival, where Singer and McQuarrie had first achieved notice with *Public Access*, a film about the problems of a TV company investigating corruption in an American city, the praise *The Usual Suspects* attracted won it a US distribution deal and from there it went on world-wide release. The Sundance Festival is in itself important. Founded in 1980 by Robert Redford, it has become a premier site for independent film-makers to present their work and seek the notice of the big companies.

Here is the absolute antithesis of a big studio picture. Cheap by Hollywood standards (in 1995 studio pictures typically ranged from $30–80 million), in various ways it declared its 'independent' status. The lack of star personae, the incorporation of art-house cinematic techniques, and the convoluted plot all marked it apart, to the extent that, like the film or not, critics had to acknowledge its intelligence. Some went so far as to welcome it as proof that cinema-goers had not become dumbed down as much as the cultural pessimists had warned.[2] McQuarrie himself adds a dimension that marks the film as almost a *comment on* more mainstream filming: 'I like toying with points of view, taking a mainstream genre and bending it a little.'[3] From the same interview, it is possible to see signs of a cynical politics in McQuarrie, coupled with an understanding (from having worked as a cinema usher in a tough area) of what particular audiences desire.

The issue of audiences comes to the surface in one essay on the film. American film critic J. P. Tellotte argues that *The Usual Suspects* depends for its effects on the giving and withdrawing of characters.[4] Normally, he argues, we depend on recognisable and likeable characters for 'points of identification' in a film. *The Usual Suspects* appears to give these – but then they are exposed as criminals, cruel, untrustworthy. Tellotte's interesting argument has two premises in it which I want to challenge. First, he assumes that audiences found the five suspects unattractive – but the evidence from reviews, and from conversations I have had with lovers of the film, simply does not sustain this. But his use of the concept of 'identification' requires him to believe this, in which case we will have to query that concept. Second, he makes 'character' the central feature of the film, and derives its processes from that. I want to show that this misses the most important aspect of the film, that it is an extreme case of what Kristin Thompson calls 'duplicitous narration'.[5] An approach via my concept of the 'implied audience' opens the possibility that audiences loved *The Usual Suspects*, and its characters, *because of* the way they trick, cheat and deceive *us* throughout the film.

In a brilliant analysis of Hitchcock's *Stage Fright* (1950), Thompson explores the ways the audience is deceived by filmic processes. In *Stage Fright*, information is visually given in ways that encourages a conviction in its reliability – which proves subsequently to have been 'planted' by the murderer. Flashbacks, normally a moment of truthful revelation in Hollywood films, are used to mislead – making some reviewers complain about the film. Thompson's interests in this seem to be three-fold. First, to show that this strategy, while taken to an extreme in *Stage Fright*, is actually not unusual in either films or in literature. She further suggests that the capacity to use dreams, memories and flashbacks in cheating ways became thematically more possible as Hollywood took up America's 1950s fascination with psychoanalysis, which foregrounded yet simultaneously queried the truthfulness of these mental processes. Finally, she uses it to buttress her wider argument, made with Bordwell and Staiger, that classical Hollywood had to allow degrees of innovation within the constraints and rules that arose from the studios' production systems. *Stage Fright* becomes, most importantly for her, a demonstration of a general process she is exploring throughout her book, 'defamiliarisation'.

I've stated my general worries about the concept of 'defamiliarisation' in the introductory chapter. Here, I want to point to a specific problem: the danger that Thompson's approach can block us noticing something very important about a film like *The Usual Suspects*. By taking us to levels of *generality* – in her instance, *Stage Fright* as an exemplar of defamiliarisation, typifying classical Hollywood's testing of its boundaries in the 1950s – we pay less attention to the themes being worked on. Audiences seem to have gone to see 'yet another film', rather than *this* film. That certainly wasn't true of *The Usual Suspects*, by all accounts. *The Usual Suspects* might have been made in order to demonstrate the effectiveness of the concept of the 'implied audience'. As I hope I have made clear, it's my case that this concept is important and helps us understand every film, but in the case of *The Usual Suspects* its gains are spectacularly clear.

Analytic Description

Following a dissolve out of an undramatic title and credit sequence (small font display off-centre on a background of water at night, with a shimmer of light and a quiet orchestral accompaniment), an intertitle ('San Pedro, California – last night') ushers in a box of matches flaring into flame, then a night scene on a boat. An unidentified man sits, collapsed, on the deck of a ship, lighting first a cigarette, then a line of spilling fuel. But before it can reach its source and explode, it is stopped by a man urinating on it from above. He descends to deck level and speaks quietly to the first man (now named as 'Keaton'). Keaton recognises the (to us unseen) man, and shakes his head in a gesture of … Keaton tells the man he can't feel his legs and – perhaps an act of mercy? – the unseen man takes a gun into his left hand and shoots him. The camera cuts back as he drops his cigarette into the line of fuel and soon the ship explodes into flames. Now we see a pile of crates and baskets, first in mid-shot, then in close-up, beyond which we can see, maybe, a pair of eyes … watching.

Dissolve to a new figure on some kind of podium, harshly lit, and giving evidence: 'It all began back in New York six weeks ago. A truck loaded with stripped gun parts got 'jacked outside of Queens. The driver didn't see any-body, but somebody fucked up. He heard a voice – sometimes that's all you need …' and (via an intertitle: 'New York – 5 weeks ago') the film shows a series of arrests of 'cool' men being made ('McManus' dragged from his bed, 'Hockney' in his garage, a third in the street – this last introducing a stylistic motif, his arrest is punctuated by drum beats within the music, on each of which there is a small jump cut), including Keaton, being arrested as he entertains potential investors at his restaurant. Taken to the police station, we see them being prepared for a line-up. The camera pans up from crippled and limping feet to show us the podium-figure among those arrested. During this the words continue as voice-over: 'It didn't make any sense that I'd be there. I mean, these guys were hardcore hijackers. But, there I was. At that point I wasn't scared. I knew I hadn't done anything they could pin me for. Besides, it was fun – I got to make like I was notorious.'

We watch the men in the line-up, the fragments of their interrogation – with the police being particularly hard on Keaton, as an ex-cop. The voice-over tells of their sense of losing all their rights, and introduces us to each of the characters in turn: McManus – reliable but mad; Fenster – McManus' partner, smart but capable of playing stupid; Hockney – 'the one guy who didn't give a fuck about anybody'; Keaton – provoking the police by calling them stupid and getting hit for it. Now in the holding cell, they talk – treated as a 'team' by the cops, yet not all even knowing each other. Only at the end of this scene do we get to hear who the last man is. Keaton: 'His name is Verbal – Verbal Kint.' 'Verbal?' 'Roger really – people say I talk too much.'

They begin to hatch a scheme for revenge – if the cops think they are a team, they'll be one, to 'salvage a little dignity' – only Keaton, trying to go straight, is unwilling. Kint (voice-over): 'And that was how it started. The five of us being brought in on a trumped-up charge, to be leaned on by half-wits' (this voice-over punctuates the rest of the film at many points, bridging the plot from scene to scene).

Cut back to the ship, the 'present day' after the explosion. Burnt bodies. An FBI officer gathering information on the dead and survivors. The ship still smoulders. Cut to a plane landing, and a telephone message being left by a 'Dave Kujan' saying he can be reached at the investigation. At the precinct station, Kujan pleads for the chance to interview the 'cripple' – who has already somehow cut a deal, and will walk soon ('I tell you this guy is protected from up on high, by the Prince of Darkness', says the local cop). Kujan's motive: 'I want to know why 27 men died on that pier for $91 million of cocaine that wasn't there … above all, I want to be sure Dean Keaton's dead.' Cut to the hospital: a Hungarian survivor hovering near death, muttering in pain suddenly yells the name 'Keyser Soze!' Our FBI man is *very* interested, sends a message to Kujan. At the precinct: Kujan begins questioning Kint, who tries to turn the talk to irrelevant things like the time he played in a barber's shop quartet in Skokie, Illinois, or the time he picked coffee in Guatemala, anything to turn the conversation. Over many scenes Kujan cajoles and threatens to get him to talk about Keaton. 'I'm not a rat', Kint quietly insists. Kujan: 'What happened after the line-up?'

Cut to this: Keaton's lawyer girlfriend, Edie, has got them bailed. The others are waiting outside to see if Keaton will join them. At Keaton's apartment, Kint manages to persuade him to join in a special 'hit', on 'New York's Finest Taxi Service' – something we do not yet know about, but Keaton does, and at first distrusts. As he finally agrees, a sound-bridge of pulsing music and drums (with those jump cuts) takes us into the heist. A plane landing. Drugs money being laundered as emeralds, with the assistance of corrupt police running a bogus taxi service. Shut down after Internal Affairs started asking questions, it had evaded discovery. Kint in voice-over tells us the story, of a plan concocted to deliver 'a little fuck-you to the NYPD'. Ramming and surrounding the police car, they snatch the money and emeralds, then set the vehicle on fire: 'Keaton made an anonymous phone-call. ... Everybody got it right in the ass from the chief on down. It was beautiful.'

Post-heist, they have to go to California to cash in the emeralds, and a small side-scene shows Keaton wanting to say goodbye to Edie. Cut back to the interrogation: Kujan doesn't believe any of this soft stuff about Keaton having been reformed by love. He tells Kint Keaton's history. 'Dean Keaton was under indictment a total of seven times', Kujan relates, but each time witnesses changed their testimony – or died. When finally convicted, three people died inside. Released, he staged his own death, in a warehouse fire – and all the witnesses died. Cut to the hospital: the Hungarian recounts the events at the ship – it wasn't about drugs, they were smuggling people, witnesses. Then the devil appeared – Keyser Soze – and the killing started. A police artist is called on to turn the description into a portrait before the man dies of his burns. Back at the interrogation Kint, seriously threatened by Kujan, starts to tell more of the story. Of a lawyer called Kobayashi.

His story again becomes the diegesis, as we go to LA, to follow the five 'suspects' through their encounter with 'Redfoot', the fence (voice-over: 'He seemed like a good guy. Still, we should have known better ...') who offers them a second job. But this goes badly awry when the jewellery they agree to snatch turns out to be dope – and they have shot the dealer and his two bodyguards. A stand-off with Redfoot nearly spills over into violence, but as a result they demand to meet Kobayashi, who was behind the operation – only to learn he is wanting to meet them. Cut back to Kujan interrogating Kint. Called away to meet the FBI officer who interviewed the Hungarian, Kujan learns about Keyser Soze. Back to Kint who, confronted with the name, yells 'Oh, fuck!' – and the story jumps back to the five waiting to meet Kobayashi. He appears from nowhere, telling them that he works for Soze, whom each of them has in some serious way offended (stealing money from him, interfering with his operations). It was Soze who got them all arrested in New York, but they were released too soon, before he could get to them there. Now they must make recompense by undertaking one job – or die. The job they are set up to undertake is the job on the ship – to steal $91 million of cocaine from an Argentinian gang, Soze's rivals. Some of them will almost certainly die, but the survivors will be immensely rich – and will be left alone by Soze (and Kobayashi leaves them each with a file detailing their entire criminal history). As the others debate the threat, Kint asks nervously: who is Soze?

Cut back to the interrogation, and Kint tells Kujan what he learnt about Soze: an utterly ruthless Turkish criminal who, finding rivals holding his family hostage, preferred to shoot his own wife and children rather than appear weak. As he tells the story, the film enacts it and Soze appears, like a satanic figure, striding through fire into mythology. 'Nobody ever believed he was real. Nobody ever knew him or saw anybody that worked directly for him. But to hear Kobayashi tell it, anybody could have worked for Soze. You never knew. That was his power. The greatest trick the devil ever pulled was convincing the world he didn't exist.' Does Verbal believe in Soze? 'Keaton always said "I don't believe in god but I'm afraid of him". Well I believe in god and the only thing that scares me is Keyser Soze.' Kujan is stunned, as are the other listening cops – all they have had is rumours. Kujan offers Kint a deal – turn State's evidence against Soze and they will protect him. Kint is not having that. He tells Kujan that Soze surely knows exactly where he is and what he is doing, otherwise where is the pressure for his release coming from? No deal. (At the hospital the police artist continues her work.) Now Kint tells Kujan about Fenster having run from them, fearful of Soze, and how they had received a call from Kobayashi telling them where to find Fenster's body. After they bury him, they round on Kobayashi; but even with a gun at his head, he is ultra-controlled and proves that again he is one step ahead of them – he effectively holds Edie hostage. They have to comply – and the story arrives back at their planning the job on the ship, a 'logistical nightmare', four of them against at least twenty – but against all Kint's feelings, they are going to try it.

Night: the job. We watch the slow build-up. All four in position. Keaton orders Kint to stay out, and go to Edie if it all fails: 'Tell her that … tell her I tried …' It all begins well. Keaton acts as stooge, and covered by an explosion he, McManus and Hockney take out the initial group of guards. A gun battle breaks out as Keaton and McManus get on the boat, and gradually work through it taking out defenders. Outside, Hockney finds a stash of

money in the Hungarians' van, but as he looks at it he is shot from behind –
as he turns, the film bleaching out with his death, he sees … Cut back to
the interrogation, and Kint explaining why he didn't just run. Kujan receives
more information, indicating that Soze and Kobayashi were indeed pulling
strings in getting Argentinian witnesses removed. He confronts Kint with
what he now knows: there was no dope on the boat … back into the battle.
In one cabin, a very frightened man sits. Keaton and McManus are seen
hunting. The frightened man pleads with his guards: 'I'm telling you he's
here – it's Keyser Soze!' In the bowels of the ship the pursuit continues.
Keaton meets McManus and tells him: they've been set up – there is no
cocaine. A brief shot shows Kint hurrying along the keyside, then cut back
to the depths of the ship and the scared man – whose door opens. He pleads
for his life with the unseen man, who shoots him with two single deliberate
shots. Now on the deck, McManus emerges and looks at Keaton. 'The
strangest thing …', he calls out – and falls to the deck, a knife in the back
of his neck. Kint finds Hockney's body beside the van – and in a cutaway
as he looks at the body, the camera takes the point of view of a gun pointed
down at Keaton, kneeling beside McManus. A shot rings out, Keaton falls,
and Kint starts up, turning to see a man coming down the stairs towards
Keaton. Cut back to the interrogation. Kujan: 'That's what you say in your
statement. You saw a man in a suit with a slim build.' Kujan now bullies
Kint to the point where he admits that he was terrified, terrified of Soze, of
shooting and missing the 'devil himself. How do you shoot the devil in
the back? What if you miss?', he pleads – and holds up his crippled left
hand, to explain his meaning.

Cut back to the ship, and we see Kint backing away to hide behind the
boxes we saw at the start, and from that angle now, we see the slim figure
shoot Keaton and drop the cigarette that causes the explosion, before moving away; and a straight re-run of the close-up that at the opening of the
film led into Kint's appearance on the podium. Now we see him drop into
a low seat in Kujan's office, broken. The next scene has Kujan prowling
round him with low angle shots emphasising his power as he presents Kint
with the accumulated evidence that Keaton had manipulated them all (with
small flashbacks of moments of Keaton we had seen before, now given
meaning by Kujan's tale), that if anybody was, Keaton was Keyser Soze, a
man who was brutal enough even to kill his own girlfriend, Edie – at which
point Kint breaks down, crying. [See below, **Zooming In …**, for a closer
examination of this scene.]

Kujan offers protection to Kint – even if Keaton is dead, as Kint insists,
there is someone out there still pulling strings. Kint refuses. Again he insists,
'I'm not a rat'. He limps, still half-crying, out of the office, ready to take his

chances on the streets. Now a collage of small scenes: at the hospital, a page being faxed (from the police artist?); Kint recovering his property from the precinct desk; Kujan talking to another officer about the case, with heavy heart, over a cup of coffee, still wondering if Keaton is alive somewhere. Kint exits to the street, slowly limping. In the interrogation room the two officers now chat about the mess in the room, as they drink coffee. Kujan gazes round the room, the camera watches him ... as he hesitates and starts looking closer – at a maker's sign on the bottom of a board, from Skokie, Illinois; at the name 'Redfoot' on a 'Wanted' list. Fragments of Kint's talk keep running back, along with the words of other characters saying things that now seem wrong. He drops his coffee cup, and it smashes, in slow motion. As he looks down at it, the name 'Kobayashi' starts repeating, as he sees that he was drinking from 'Kobayashi Porcelain' ... Running from the room, he tries to intercept Kint, but he is gone. We see him in the street, limping along as a car pulls alongside him and the camera watches him from there as, in recalled speech, Kujan warns him his life will never be safe on the streets. He's stupid – that's why Keaton could use him. The camera tracks Kint's feet, as he gradually stops limping. He pauses to take out a cigarette, igniting it with a lighter held ... in his left hand, then moves sideways to get into the car, in which we see the figure of ... 'Kobayashi'. Too late, Kujan runs into the street, looking up and down. Over the final shots of a frustrated Kujan, we hear the words we heard before: 'The greatest trick the devil ever pulled was to convince the world he didn't exist ... Then like that, he's gone' – and the screen goes black.

Preliminary Analysis

What aspects of the film are brought into view by this account? Here is a preliminary list of those repetitions, patterns, etc.

- *Time signature:* when is everything? The indications given are not so much confusing as veering between the too-precise and the indefinite. The opening scene is presaged with the caption: 'San Pedro – last night.' This indexical expression only has sense when linked to a *person's* last night, and given we have to meet a character it has to be ours, at least imaginatively. This, though, becomes more general later when a subsequent scene is cued with 'present day'. This is a looser expression, allowing a general present tense, without specific links to you or me.

  But along with these direct time references, the film is replete with flashbacks and narrative moves where we can be moved, perhaps over quite a short but still necessary-to-follow time-shift. And in the final two scenes, first when Kint 'cracks' under Kujan's investigation and 'recalls' in a new light a series of moments of Keaton's behaviour, then when Kujan suddenly sees all Kint's references in a new – and suspicious – light, the time-shifting is carried on at a staggering speed.

- *Cinematic aspects:* the film is anything but big budget. Aside from the ship, all scenes are strictly local, unornamented, with cluttered rather than controlled and designed *mise-en-scène*. Indeed, I would go further and say that *The Usual Suspects* positively *avoids* giving even establishing shots. Scenes are introduced by *details* rather than by context. The opening scene begins with a match striking, and it is only gradually that we are able to place the events on a boat. The initial heist may involve New York police but, apart from a general sense of city streets, no markers of New York are admitted. We may be told that after this they are going to LA, but the shot of a hut where their initial meeting with Redfoot is to take place could be anywhere. Geography is unimportant.

  In addition, the film integrates a series of small moments of art-house technique, which are used to punctuate within scenes or to segue between them. As the drug dealer's plane lands in New York, the shot of the landing plane is brought forward by two jump cuts, accompanied by sharp slamming sounds – as though the plane is being hurried into narrative space, and thus made subject to its intensities. In the other direction, our first meeting with the FBI investigating the explosion at the ship closes with the camera pulling away from their conversation to climb and twist in a complex crane shot, so that we can see the ship's still-smoking carcase. One of the memory flashbacks during Kint's interrogation ends with a long matching dissolve from a porthole, to the shape of a coffee mug. If these are noticed at all – they rarely figure directly in any narrative contribution – their role seems to be to help the flow of the plot, yet at the same time introduce a note of uncertainty, unclarity, a query over how and why things are being shown to us.

- *Representation:* all five suspects are individuated, both via the narration (Kint's account of them) and diegetically. They speak in wholly differentiated ways, have different mannerisms and distinctive personalities. They relate to each other in complex ways: immediately post-heist, as they count their haul, they plan and joke together, they tease, help, negotiate, stand up to and back down from each other.

  The authorities have two faces. On the one hand Dave Kujan: a tough investigator who is determined to break Kint's resistance, nonetheless, he is driven by conviction, of the need to expose Keaton's continuing wickedness. He has moments of kindness, even towards Kint. Yet in the background authority appears shady: the FBI official who countermands hospital rules, to the extent of smoking over a dying man; the New York police, with their corrupt taxi service for laundering dirty money; somewhere never seen, but hinted at, officials who have been bought – by Keyser Soze?

Soze himself is enigmatic. Except in as much as Soze may be Kint's other persona – which is left as an enjoyable best bet at the end – we never know him except through others' accounts of him, and a distorted filmic image. Soze *is* a 'spook story', as Kujan puts it, like an impossibly powerful and manipulative figure out of legend.

- *Thematically*, the film is like a set of ever-deepening glimpses into a murderous world. At the outset, Keaton plus an unknown killer. Then five criminals, forced together and planning a heist. Then the corrupt NYPD. Then the spread of this across America. Add a lawyer working for an unknown master-criminal. Add his story. At each stage add hints of skilful manipulation, tentacles of power reaching out to move pieces and people at will. The final mismatch, between our accumulated image of the mysterious, murderous, manipulative Soze and the mild-mannered, gentle-spoken Roger 'Verbal' Kint, leaves a mass of intriguing questions.

Most important of all is a problem of cinematic deceit and, as this becomes visible, the sheer difficulty of knowing what we can and can't believe. I would put it differently than Kristin Thompson's analysis of *Stage Fright*. A film such as *The Usual Suspects* is essentially an exercise in the cinematic art. It does not so much defamiliarise, as give us an opportunity to test our skills as viewers. How many clues did we pick up? When did we start suspecting Verbal Kint? In retrospect did we get the hints about the left-handed gunman?

Yet at the same time, even an exercise has to have content – and this film is, as Tellotte rightly identifies, related to the genre of neo-noir. Many scenes in *The Usual Suspects* are filmed in darkened, enclosed spaces with angular light. Several key moments are filmed through restrictive spaces – for instance, the execution of the Hungarian witness, heard as a shot but seen only as a sudden spray of blood on the glass of a port-hole. More than this purely visual indication, the film proffers a world without secure handholds, lacking moral direction or purpose. Or, if Dave Kujan is that moral point, then he will end baffled and frustrated, having come close but not close enough to a story that can never be told.

How Is Understanding *The Usual Suspects* Possible?[6]

Conceive for a moment a watcher with a good memory. At the start of the film, s/he records the fact that the unidentified killer is left-handed. With good hearing too, s/he hears the man about to die mutter 'Keyser …', as if finally understanding or acknowledging something. For now, these are uninterpretable fragments – or perhaps puzzles, as they are seen at the outset, and that's what films tend to do. But as the film progresses, they turn from unclear items into significant integers in the filmic series. When Verbal Kint's interrogation begins, he asks for a cigarette, and then a lighter. But when he tries to use the lighter a semi-paralysed left hand fails him. He drops the lighter and looks at Dave Kujan for help. The camera frames the moment for us, neither denying it nor highlighting it with a close-up. Or, at one point when the detectives take time out to discuss the case out of Kint's hearing, Kujan gets information – of which our watcher is given only a part – about a master-criminal. Rejoining Kint, he throws him the question without warning: 'Who's Keyser Soze?' 'Oh, fuck!', yells Kint, caught off-guard. That early mutter now takes on a richer meaning.

The Usual Suspects is littered with elements like this. Puzzles, forebodings, hints, anticipations, partial disclosures. But it has something else, too. The film *cheats*. Right at the beginning, as the ship explodes into flames, there is that shot of a pile of fishing baskets and crates – behind which it seems we can make out a pair of eyes. Someone was watching. Someone perhaps saw what we just saw, the injured man being shot by the left-handed man. Saw the cigarette dropped into the spilled fuel. A witness. And immediately afterwards, a witness is heard, then seen on a stand with microphones and intense lighting, testifying: 'It all started six weeks ago …'. Is this the watcher behind the baskets? That link is brought back into place the second time the film shows us the events on the ship – this time more fully, as Kint is cracking under investigation and his tale is spilling out. As Kint tells the story of the fight on the ship leading up to the explosion, our watcher gets to see it all: Keaton telling Kint to stay back from the ship, to hide so that he can tell Edie what happened if it all goes wrong; Kint watching from afar, then hiding behind the baskets; McManus and Keaton searching the ship – Keaton meeting McManus in the engine room and yelling his realisation at him – 'There's no fucking cocaine on this ship!'; finally, a bewildered McManus dropping dying on the deck in front of Keaton, then a shot, followed by the very scene we saw at the outset – the left-handed man shooting the injured Keaton after that moment of recognition, and the figure – who must be Kint!, our acute watcher now realises – observing from behind the baskets. It was a set-up, a hoax.

But hang on, this is where all died bar Kint, s/he knows that now. And Kint was told by Keaton to stay back, and did. So, just how did he know how they searched the ship, and found no cocaine, and argued about that in the engine-room? And … our watcher being fairly cine-literate, how did the *camera* know these things? 'Who' exactly is directing the filming at this moment. Is it in effect Verbal Kint? To all intents and purposes, s/he has been shown Kint's version of events – which are an impossibility. He couldn't have known. Yet it is all coherent, it all makes good sense. And it's a great story! The story of a heist gone wrong, of treachery and wheels within wheels.

The point of all this is that our hypothetical watcher, with good hearing, close attention and good memory, can make links and begin to grasp the film as an unfolding structure. S/he has to see that first the film hints, then it fills in the meanings of those hints but it also cheats in that very act. And it isn't just the character that does this, the film collaborates with him. Kint takes control of the film's diegesis. The film won't be a 'whole' unless and until the watcher assembles the components *in the necessary manner*. Here a hint, there a clue; whoops, an unreliable bit – so who tricked me? To see the full complexity of this, consider one scene in detail.

Zooming In …

My scene comes close to the end, immediately after Kujan has extracted (and we have heard) Verbal Kint's full account of the fight on the boat, closing with dramatic music showing us (again) the explosion, and the fire lighting up the bales of rope behind which are a pair of eyes. The music cuts hard as we see Kint in the interrogation room suddenly sitting, looking dazed. Kujan restarts his interrogation, in an increasingly domineering way. In order to see how the scene works, read first the dialogue between Kujan and Kint without considering the accompanying visuals or music.

> *Kujan*: 'Arturo Marquez – ever hear of him? [Kint: No.] He was a stool-pigeon for the Justice Department. He swore out a statement to Federal Marshals that he had seen and could positively identify one Keyser Soze. It says right here, "he had intimate knowledge of his businesses, including, but not exclusively, drug trafficking and murder". [I never heard of him.] His own people were selling him to a gang of Hungarians, most likely the same Hungarians that Soze all but wiped out back in Turkey. The Hungarians were going to buy the one guy that could incriminate Keyser. [But I never heard of him.] But Keaton did. Edie Fineran was Marquez' extradition adviser. She knew who he was and what he knew. [I don't un …] There were no drugs on that boat. It was a hit, a suicide mission to knock out the one guy that could finger Keyser Soze. So Soze put some thieves to him, men he knew he could march into certain death. [Are you saying Soze sent us to kill someone?] I'm saying Keaton

did. Verbal, he left you behind for a reason ... If you all knew that Soze
could find you anywhere, why did he give you the money to run? He
could have used you on the boat. [He wanted me to live ...] A one-time
dirty cop without a loyalty in the world finds it in his heart to the save
a worthless rat cripple? No. So, why? [Edie ...] I don't buy that reform
story for a minute. Even if I did, I certainly don't believe he would send
you to protect her! So, why? [(Pleadingly) Because he was my friend ...]
No, Verbal, he wasn't your friend. Keaton didn't have friends ... He saved
you because he wanted it that way. It was his will. *Keaton was Keyser
Soze.* [No!] The kind of man who could rattle the wills of men like
Hockney and McManus, the kind of man who could engineer a police
line-up through all his years of contact with the NYPD, the kind of man
who could *kill Edie Fineran* ... [Shocked silence from Kint.] She was found
yesterday in a hotel in Pennsylvania shot twice in the head.' (2'10')

This scene is crucial. We witness Kint break and cry, we hear the overwhelming and unanswerable arguments from Dave Kujan. It provides a
climax both to the interrogation, and to the overall film – except that the
film continues to undo this climax. The words alone are persuasive. But
every bit as important is what we see, as these words are spoken. In the
course of this two minute sequence, there are 25 inserted flashbacks. They
are moments either already seen (for instance, the shot of the terrified
Argentinian, or the shot of Edie being held by Kobayashi) or implied (after
showing the execution of the Argentinian, a further shot of him falling
dead in a pool of water). They provide a confirming commentary on what
Kujan is saying. But the point is that they are things that *only Kint ever 'wit-
nessed'*. Their rhythm is also important: each time Kint tries to fend off
Kujan's explanation, and Kujan rebuts him, a clip is inserted which appears
to confirm Kujan's objection. For instance, when Kint has protested weakly
'Because he was my friend', the visuals double Kujan's riposte with shots
of Keaton hitting Kint and throwing him against the wall – things that only
Kint could be recalling. His memories refute his own protestations. So, the
rapid-fire inserted flashbacks give us the evidence that Kint is realising
how wrong he is. His own memories turn against him and prove Kujan
right, and *we witness it happening*. There is even, for the really attentive, a
momentary glimpse under the hat of the killer on the boat, revealing him
to be ... Keaton (though how *anybody* could have seen this does not bear
asking ...). Finally the music, lurking gravely behind the scene for most of
the time, rises and clamours to a stop at the gun-shot marking Keaton's
supposed shooting of Edie; its drama is the final confirmation that Kint is
indeed a broken man.

The problem is that by the end of the film we come to realise that this is yet another bluff, only this time there is no question but that it is *us* who are bluffed, for Kujan can see none of these 'memories'. So, what mental operations are required of a person who now either reflects back over this scene, or rewatches the film, knowing that this is a deceit? A viewer who agrees to play opposite the film at this point has to do all of the following:

- S/he has to follow the narrative sufficiently closely to find Kint's confusion and breakdown convincing.
- S/he must read the inserted flashbacks as a demonstration of the internal processes he is going through.
- At the same time s/he must now recognise these as deceitful, untrue, a ruse.

To enjoy such a ruse on oneself, whether retrospectively or in rewatching (and I have an unconfirmed sense that *The Usual Suspects* was watched more than once by many people), is to have a remarkably complex relationship with the character of Verbal Kint. Trusting in so far as he appears sincere, hurt, broken, yet distrusting inasmuch as we know that he is lying – and in his hands the film is lying to us, as well. To hold those two in sync requires an agreement to *admire his astonishing cleverness*, since it convinces us as well as it convinced poor Dave Kujan. The gap, if ever there was one, between character and performer is here totally elided. We are astonished at the *performance of a total lie*. On these grounds, I think we can see that, whatever the wider arguments about the concept of 'identification', here at least Tellotte has to be mistaken. We have to be simultaneously attracted yet distanced, convinced and therefore made distrustful.

Conclusion

With layer upon layer of hints and deceits, unfolding and withholding, over the course of the film, our watcher gathers first a motley, then a studied array of them, which in review tell something extraordinary: Kint is a liar of a high order and manages to deceive agent Kujan – and us. And the film itself, by the manner of its showing and not showing, speaking and staying silent, systematically supports his deceit. What will the watcher do with all this? All this confusion-turning-to-sense only enters the domain of the useable if, in addition to having this cumulative understanding, s/he also has an appropriate *will* and *motivation*. S/he must feel cheated – and enjoy it. S/he must have liked Kint, felt sorry for him under investigation; must have admired the cleverness of the heist (and the earlier ridiculing of 'New York's

Finest' police conspirators). The more s/he does each of these, in addition to having good memory and sharp senses, the more the film becomes a fully motivated structure. Putting this conceptually, the role of the implied viewer can never be purely cognitive. Our viewer – any viewer who will grasp the story and its point – must have the desire and the commitment to pursue the clues and get a buzz out of realising just how tricky the whole film is. And this can't just be an individuated set of characteristics – the wish and ability to do these things depends on a whole array of historically and culturally specific understandings and involvements which can therefore tell us much about the world into which *The Usual Suspects* was placed.

Of course *real* viewers may not engage entirely in the required ways. They may not be wide awake to clues, deceits, demands. The sound quality might prevent them catching that muttered 'Keyser'. Peer as they might, they could well miss the eyes behind the boxes – I did, first time. Our watcher is not an actual person: it is a *role* waiting to be played, if a viewer is to *become* meaningfully involved. A role, as sociologists will say, contains a number of aspects: roles are culturally acknowledged operations (being Best Man at a wedding; being a 'good listener' to someone in distress; being a Chelsea supporter); roles are complex, and have rules governing the order in which things have to be done, how they begin, proceed and end, and what should happen afterwards; roles therefore have to be learnt – there are more or less tight prescriptions and requirements governing what counts as doing it adequately/properly; and people can perform roles in a hundred ways, badly, or with an ill grace, or ironically, or with delight and enthusiasm. All these apply without remainder to the role of the implied audience.

Every film generates an implied audience position, a role that has to be played if the film is to be made sense of and related to. I am beginning with *The Usual Suspects* because in this case it is just spectacularly evident that this is so. *The Usual Suspects* brings the requirements on the audience sharply and readily into view. We can conveniently summarise what is special here as a function of duplicitous diegesis and, simply because I like the phrase, 'naughty narration'. *The Usual Suspects* is systematically structured to force a watcher who wishes to participate into making false interpretive steps, enjoying the resultant errors, and recognising the cleverness simultaneously of Keyser Soze/Verbal Kint (are they the same? who can be sure?) and of the film – which becomes Kint's tool.

So why would someone want to play the *Usual Suspects* game? Because it offers rewards to a committed viewer – and this is also part of the position of the implied audience. *The Usual Suspects* rewards its viewers with the pleasures of unpacking its cleverness, and at the same time it rewards us by enabling us to demonstrate (to ourselves, to film-going friends) our cleverness in deciphering its deceits. It rewards with frissons of delighted shock the terror of a conspiratorial view of the Underworld: an attractive/dangerous stock of appalling characters. It rewards us if we are willing to play with the notion that authority is a mixture of inept and corrupt – but that corruption may be as nothing in the face of an awesome corruption so demonic that the petty authorities who *think* they run things are just self-deceivers, whereas as we …

4

'An Ant With Ideas ...'

When DreamWorks' *Antz* was released in 1998, it was announced as the next in line of fully computer-generated movies. Following in the tradition begun by *Who Framed Roger Rabbit?* (1988) and *Toy Story* (1995), *Antz* celebrated its own technological achievements, a significant point, as we will see. *Antz* was also important for DreamWorks which, as Hollywood's new studio, had experienced a hesitant start, with half-hearted box office response to their first output (for instance, the George Clooney vehicle *The Peacemaker* (1997)). On a $60 million budget, *Antz* had to succeed. And indeed it did well, launching on a blockbuster-scale 2,400 screens in America, and earning $150 million gross in world-wide box office takings.[1]

Among the more extraneous surrounds of *Antz* was the almost simultaneous release of Disney's *A Bug's Life* – a film inevitably seen as a competitor to *Antz*, because that too was an entirely computer-generated film. But it was also because of the involvement of Jeffrey Katzenberg who left Disney after conflicts with Michael Eisner to join its rival DreamWorks, and then engaged in a long and high-profile legal battle over his contract with his former employer. One aspect of this conflict was Katzenberg's drive not only to outstrip Disney, but to make DreamWorks' animated output into *adult* materials.[2]

But arguably the most important question posed by *Antz* is its position as a special effects movie. Here is a film entirely produced by computer-graphic interface (CGI). Yet, as we shall see, *within* a film whose entire existence is one long special effect, there are moments which have to be seen as special-effects-within-an-effects-film. This raises problems about understanding what a special effect is, which takes us to the heart of a current debate within film studies.

Analytic Description

As the film opens, we hear a voice – Woody Allen's, in a familiar revelatory mode – proclaiming how disturbed he is. 'All my life I've lived and worked in a big city. ... There's got to be something better out there. But maybe I think too much.' He recounts at length his psychological problems as the camera 'tracks' from a city skyline down through grass, into the earth, down tunnels into a chamber where an ant-like figure lies on a couch – at which point it becomes fully clear (where it hadn't before) that this isn't a voice-over. So, right from the outset, we are getting both the Allen persona and a narrative motivation: the search for something better, the will to be an individual in a dehumanising society. His long, very 'adult' speech ends with him declaring that 'this whole super-organism thing leaves me cold. It makes me feel insignificant.' At which the unseen therapist congratulates him on a 'breakthrough' – he *is* insignificant! Despondently, Z returns to work, and we get panoramic shots of the entire colony. Hints of Chaplin's *Modern Times* (1936) are complemented by a mock dystopia with baby ants running along a conveyor belt before being labelled 'Worker' and given a pickaxe, or 'Soldier' and lost under a full-size helmet.

From the start, then, a recurrent discourse among characters about the purposes of life. At the rock face, returning to his work, Z meets old (female) friend Azteka, who rejects his moaning: 'It's not about you, it's about us, the team. It's about this ...' and the camera shows again the entire colony, like a space-hive.

All through the film, the talk is sassy and streetwise, full of colloquial-isms. Azteka, trying to get Z to stop moaning: 'Jeez, will you cut it out already!?' Only Mandible, whom we next see, speaks in a more pompous, self-important style – and is thus untrustworthy. He denounces the 'lazy' workers (though we know already that this isn't so, having seen them hard at work). His speech fills in narrative information: telling us about Colonel Cutter, his enforcer; and about the tunnel, whose building he is pressing ahead with – in four days, it must be ready, then 'we can bid farewell to their kind of incompetence'. Mandible sets out, clearly falsely, to persuade the Queen of the need for a pre-emptive war party against a local colony of termites, and succeeds – we know that those to be sent are all those soldiers loyal to the Queen ... Here enters, from off-screen left, the Princess Bala who is to marry the General. If so, then can't they spend a little time together, like, 'quality time'? The General manages about ten seconds before whisk-ing off with the Colonel. Bala complains to her mother: 'we have nothing in common ... this guy's a stiff'. Mother keeps passing baby ants through her arms, doing her queenly duty. Bala looks down from their high position as music strikes up, to signal off-duty time for the workers.

Cut to the bar, and Z drinking with his friend Weaver, a huge muscly soldier-ant, and still complaining about his lot: isn't there a better life somewhere? From behind him at the bar, an older drunken ant tells of a place he swears he once saw: Insectopia, where you don't have to obey orders and where the streets are paved with food! Z and Weaver scorn him, and eventually he is taken away, for 'his own good'. A dance is announced, and Weaver goes to join in the military-precision setup, filmed for us as a mass event in serried ranks. Enter Bala with two maids, slumming; seeing Z sitting dolefully at the bar, she asks him to dance. He is instantly in love, and joins her on the floor – where he starts doing a sort of jive, declaring the right of the individual to be different. When this leads to him bumping into large guard-ants, Weaver steps in to defend him, and a wholesale brawl breaks out. At this point, Z learns that Bala is a princess, just as she leaves him, dismissively. In love, he seeks a way to see her again, and begs Weaver to let him take his place as a soldier for the forthcoming Royal Review of the troops. Bewitched by promises of attentive female worker-ants, Weaver agrees. At the Review, filmed from high angles like a Nuremberg rally, Z – despite making a fool of himself – fails to catch the Princess's attention; and now finds himself enlisted to fight the termites. He is befriended by an old soldier, Barbados: an ant who will follow orders even when he knows the officers are mad.

War: marching there and singing Marines songs as they go, then finding themselves ambushed by the 'huge' green termites who spit poison (very like the bugs in *Starship Troopers* (1997)). Carnage. Desperate to escape, Z runs, and falls down a hole which is then blocked by a dying termite. (Back at the colony, Weaver sets to with a will, until slowed down by the admiring attentions of Azteka. Their talk leads to their mean foreman withdrawing their privileges, but clearly romance is blossoming.) After the battle: a post-apocalyptic scene, across which wanders a shocked Z. He finds his friend Barbados, dying – just his head, detached from his body, living on for a minute. Before he dies, he says to Z: 'Don't make my mistake, kid. Don't follow orders your whole life. Think for yourself.' Sombre music reinforces that this scene is *really* horrible.

At the colony: the General, commanding yet higher output, hears of the massacre and pretends to mourn – then hears, worriedly, of a survivor, Z, and has to stage-manage his reception so he will be the 'right kind of hero'. Introducing him to the Queen, and trying to silence him, he praises him for being the kind of man to laugh death in the face. Z: 'Actually, I more sort of make belittling comments and snicker behind my hand.' Z again makes a fool of himself when he sees the Princess, and is arrested. Escaping, he seizes Bala, and finds he has accidentally kidnapped her. They tumble down a refuse chute, and out of the colony, she insulting him the whole time. As palace guards close in on them, from above a huge and hypnotic metal object hoves into view; it is (we know, but they don't of course) a magnifying glass, focusing the sun and bringing death to the guards. Z and Bala have to run, and become lost. Climbing a 'tree' like an ant, Z sees in the distance the monolith said to be near Insectopia. Bala, quarrelling, demands he take her home, but he sets out, and she is forced to follow by the sudden emergence of a large biting insect.

Back at the colony, Z's name has become an instant legend. Hero of the war, he has now kidnapped the Princess and gained freedom – might not others do the same? A revolution brews. Intercut Z persuading Bala finally to try consciously for Insectopia; they pilot a leaf across a 'lake'. At the colony, full-scale revolt, with ranks demanding Z, and singing 'All we are saying, is give Z a chance'. Mandible becomes particularly worried when he sees a worker (Azteka) and a soldier (Weaver) joining ranks. Desperate to restore control, he makes a Nuremberg-style speech about duty and Z's failure to perform it, and wins the 'masses' back. Weaver is arrested – we see him, alone, looking distraught as the ants are turned against Z.

Bala and Z awake to discover they are at a place rich in dumped foods (sandwiches etc.) but all made inaccessible by plastic wrappers. Two wasps, who talk and behave like charity-working snobs, offer to help them for the 'goodness of their hearts'; but as they preen themselves, a fly-swat descends and splats the female, and Bala is stuck to a piece of chewing gum on the sole of a human trainer. Z gives chase, and the film slow-mos through a long scene of their chase and eventual survival when a 'coin', with the head of Abraham Lincoln ('Who the hell is that?!' gasps Z as it approaches them), scoops the gum off the shoe and throws it and them into a bin. [See **Zooming In** ... for further detail on this scene.]

At the colony, Weaver is 'tortured' to reveal Z's whereabouts. He names Insectopia only when Azteka is also threatened – and Mandible acknowledges its existence. He sends Cutter to recapture Bala and, breaking a promise to Weaver, to kill Z. As he strides out, he pronounces: 'Gentlemen, you can see how dangerous individualism is. It makes us ... vulnerable.' Bala and Z now find Insectopia. To the non-diegetic music 'I can see clearly now the rain has gone', they find a marvellous trash can, kitted out like a fairground for insects. There is even a hint of psychedelia, in the visual effects that accompany. At the colony, the tunnel opening approaches. Now, with voice-over of Mandible preparing, we see Weaver painfully working at the tunnel face. Cut to Cutter following the scent of Bala and Z, and flying in pursuit. Cut to three brilliantly coloured bugs sitting relaxedly by a camp fire: 'This stuff tastes like crap.' 'Hey, let me taste that. Mmm. It *is* crap' (appreciatively). While Z and Bala discuss their realisation of the differences between palace and workers, the three figures philosophise: 'What if, like, we're just these tiny little things and we're just like part of this whole other huge universe that's, like, so big we don't even know it exists …' 'Hmhm, man, that is soooo deep!' Amid this hippie scene, Cutter arrives and abducts Bala – just as Z has been sent to haul in firewood. The surviving wasp, drunk from a beer bottle, offers to fly Z back in honour of his squished missus.

Bala, looking and sounding just like Princess Leia in *Star Wars*, demands an explanation from Mandible. She is imprisoned. Z, arriving back, makes his way past all the guards to find and rescue her, suffering vertigo on a narrow ledge along the way. They discover the plot to drown all the ants, and rush to prevent the catastrophe. Again, Mandible addresses the crowd, Nuremberg-style, and then instructs Cutter to seal them all in, to be drowned. The water breaks through, with effects that look like they have ceased to be computer-generated. Z calls on all the ants to make themselves into a living ladder to escape, and they break out – just in time – right under Mandible's nose as he makes a triumphal speech to his chosen ones. Here even Cutter turns on him when he claims that 'I am the colony', and he dies, apparently taking Z with him. But Z is (of course) rescued and revived. The film closes with Z's voice-over telling that the colony was rebuilt, better than before, and he has a great new therapist: 'There you have it: "boy meets girl, boy likes girl, boy changes underlying social order" story. … I finally feel like I found my place. And you know what, it's right back where I started. But the difference is, this time I chose it.' As he speaks these lines, the camera pulls back and up to 'reveal' the New York skyline behind the colony.

Preliminary Analysis

The simplicity of the basic story structure, ironically commented on at the end, disguises some tricky issues. There is certainly the classic good/evil confrontation, linked with the achievement of romance. But on this peg are hung a set of other aspects which are challenging to analyse.

- The role of star voices: notably Woody Allen (star persona: angst-ridden, romance-driven, good guy who can't get it together); Sharon Stone (strong sexy woman, won't be messed with and won't just accept a 'woman's role', but in the end interested in a real man); Sylvester Stallone (tough simple guy, on the side of right, will go through hell but will come back in the end); Gene Hackman (bad guy, wise-cracking, devious, threatening). Allen's self-presentation is clearly key to the kind of hero he is (self-effacing, ironising, never quite in control of events); and many of his wisecracks function as bonuses to the basic storyline, not contributing to the onward movement of events. But in other respects his naïve convictions about Insectopia are vital to the film – although at the end of the film it remains distinctly unresolved in what way this ideal dream-place of confectionery, hippies and fairground has affected the future of the colony. Was it just a dream, an illusion – or a necessary dream? The film does not declare a hand on this. But it seems to be a recruited part of Allen's persona, and is vital to the *optimism* of the film.

- The role of special effects *within* a special effects movie: as I noted at the start, *Antz* is *in toto* a special effects movie, and celebrated itself for that. With its range of visual styles – from closely detailed moving insects of many descriptions, to 'water-colour' scapes, through 3-D depth shots, shifts of camera focus, and so on – the film delights in its own visual abilities (by contrast with which the soundscape is relatively simple). But particular scenes achieve something quite remarkable: they are *FX within effects*. This is true in the magnifying glass scene but in particular of the scene where Bala and Z get stuck to the trainer. The film slows, and an extraordinarily detailed set of shots of the laces of the shoes reduces Bala and Z to cartoon appendages. Other shots to a lesser extent achieve the same: the flood of water and the skyline of New York at the end are both arguably instances.

- The political themes at work within the movie: in particular the repeated introduction of 'left'-speak, concerning tyranny, the lack of choice, workers' rights, and the loss of 'individualism'. Most powerfully, there is a recurrent theme about class, and the relations between the powerful and the lower orders. This provides a great deal of the narrative direction and motivation, for example bringing Z and Bala together when she comes slumming to the worker-ants' bar. When she dismisses him as pathetic because he is of the lower orders, he walks off and leaves her, and thus finds Insectopia. And Mandible's final forceful pressure on Captain Cutter to conform to his plans is accompanied by this argument: 'Cutter, you're a fine officer. You have discipline, courage, ability. But you seem to have a certain weakness for the lower orders that I find disturbing.' (This scene, incidentally, reminds me strongly of the presentation of over-acculturated officers within films such as *Patton* (1970) or *A Few Good Men* (1992).)

- The relations between the human and non-human in the film: at times this is even contradictory, for example, when they are near Insectopia,

Z climbs a tall plant without hesitation – very ant-like. Yet when he is returning to rescue Bala at the end, he shows fear of heights and loses the ability to climb. More significantly, at various points their ant-ness is story-relevant, for example, the rescue at the end, the colony-style life, the war with the termites. On the other hand, the ant-ness is so often set aside it makes one wonder why it is there at all. Or, most complicated of all, the acceptance of ant-ness becomes a distinguishing mark among the characters. In the bar scene, Z refuses the aphid beer that Weaver offers him: 'Call me crazy, but I have a thing about drinking from the anus of another creature.'

- From this, a commutation test: take two pieces of dialogue and consider them in a context other than ants. (1) After Z's survival of the war, he becomes a hero and a rallying point for resistance to General Mandible. Thus, when they discover he was 'just a worker':

  > 'A worker? That's impossible. A worker can't do anything except work.' 'Yeah, it's not like we got a choice.' 'We do have a choice. I mean, look at Z – he decided he wanted something and went for it.' (Azteka) 'He's not alone. I used to be a soldier, and I switched places with Z.' (Weaver) 'Wait a second. Are you telling me … I don't have to be here? We got a choice?' 'The authorities don't want you to know about it, but we don't have to work on the tunnel anymore.' 'It's the workers that control the means of production.' 'Hey, Z don't work, I don't work.'

  Imagine this in a political drama – its politics would be so fiercely risky, they could only occur in a straight comedy where the comedic undermined the challenge of the comments, or in a politically-radical film.

  Or (2) consider the death of Barbados, a 'black' soldier ant who befriends Z in the suicide mission and saves his life. As he dies, decapitated, he tells Z: 'Don't make my mistake, kid. Don't follow orders your whole life. Think for yourself.' Imagine this in any kind of war film. It could surely only be something which positioned itself strongly as *anti-war* and *anti-militarist*.

  The translation into this kind of 'animal' movie transforms the dialogue into a different kind of politics. It is rebellion in this filmic world, yet with all the trappings of our world.

- Intertextual references (of which there are many, and probably more than I spotted): for example, in the dance scene (which itself is composed for a few moments like *Grease* (1978)), they mimic the fingers-across-face iconic scene from *Pulp Fiction* (1994). When Bala confronts Mandible and refuses his advances, she speaks words almost identical to Princess Leia's to Darth

Vader from *Star Wars*. The termites in the war scene look and act very like those in *Starship Troopers*, to the extent of spitting poison in the same way. These might be classed as bonuses to experienced viewers, and therefore 'excess' in relation to the narrative. Yet in this context where the story seems to invite shifts of level, as in the role of FX within effects, it seems that the modality of the film is multi-layered. To enjoy *Antz* is to enjoy something which keeps reminding us of its manufacture, of a complicated relation of its story to our world, and of the knowingness and self-knowingness of the audience in their act of enjoyment.[3]

- Finally, that the story is self-reflexive, inviting us to see it as a story with discourses attached: at the end, after the defeat and death of Mandible and the assembled ants rebuild their colony, Z's closing speech is entirely voice-over to us: 'There you have it: "boy meets girl, boy likes girl, boy changes underlying social order" story.' This reflection back over the film, waving its formula in our faces, means that the implied audience of this film is strongly requested to review what the whole has been for. The social order has been changed – yet it hasn't. Insectopia has been dreamed, denied, discovered, experienced – yet it drops out of view at the very moment of its arrival.

- The closure of the film: in a very real sense it is a return to the beginning. While at the start we had an anonymous cityscape, the closing scape is undeniably New York/Manhattan. And Z tells us he has found a new analyst: 'I finally feel like I found my place. And you know what, it's right back where I started. But the difference is, this time I chose it.' But the end isn't the beginning for us, because we have been through all the processes of attending to and responding to the story. We have laughed at, cared about, hoped for Z and the others; we have booed the villains, even perhaps been upset or made sad by the carnage of the war (marked clearly as a waste, and cruel); and we have probably acknowledged (at least some of) the intertextual references to other films and modal references to our world. We have also admired its newness, its effects-ness, its FX within effects (both the modal intrusion of the magnifying glass, and the trainer, and the sudden realism of the flood).

Two questions at least need examining in detail. What exactly is the significance of the creaturing of the film – why use ants, and what do they contribute to its narrative direction and possibilities? Is *Antz* in any significant sense an allegory – that is, a teaching tale which uses its non-human figures as vehicles for moral issues?

The answer to the first question has surely to turn on a difference in scale. Ants offer a world in miniature, and that in some way enables issues to be addressed there that perhaps are less easy to address the closer you return to human scale. *Antz* is not the only recent film to deal with such miniaturisation: think of *Toy Story* (1995), *Small Soldiers* (1998), and *A Bug's Life* (1998). I return to how this functions in *Antz* in the next section.

The answer to the second question has to be cautious: no, but only just. And what is interesting is the several points at which the film brushes against the allegorical. In this respect the scene at Insectopia is interesting. The three bugs (jokingly dubbed 'pests' by Z when they interrupt his very non-antish kiss with Bala – a joke which depends on our identifying their insecthood and at the same time denying it) clearly represent a state of hippiedom. Their laid-back attitude, their cool talk and mock-philosophising hint at marijuana culture. That 'philosophic' exchange is accompanied by a zoom-out which shows them to be just the tiny beings which they wonder for a moment if they are. If bugs *could* philosophise, it is good to think of them wondering like this. But that at least means that, for the implied audience, a recognition of metaphysical insignificance is involved.

Further, the idea of an ant in therapy does require an amount of mental distancing – especially when he is in therapy for failing to feel like a proper anonymous member of his colony! The question is: what kind of mental distancing is expected, and how is it maintained for us? The outline of an answer can be gained by looking at one aspect of *Antz*: celebrated as the first entirely CGI-generated film, therefore in its entirety as a film of effects, *Antz* still contains within it moments of special effects. And they occur precisely at moments when we are reminded of the differences between ants and humans.

Zooming In …

How is it possible to have special effects within a movie which is entirely special effects? The scene to which I am referring comes late in the film, after Z has accidentally kidnapped Bala, survived various dangers, and crossed a 'lake' in search of the fabled Insectopia. At just over five minutes long, the scene is surrounded by (before-hand) the near-insurrection against Mandible, and (afterwards) the torture of Weaver, and the arrival at the real Insectopia, with its Disneyland appearance.

The scene opens with 40 seconds of surprise and delight (with an orchestral summit), then bewilderment as Bala and Z see (what we know to be) an abandoned picnic with all kinds of tempting foods – but which are wrapped in impenetrable cling-film ('What's the problem?' asks Bala. Z, trying repeatedly to sink his teeth in the wrapped burger: 'There's some kind of force-field…'.) Two wasps appear above them, whom they ask for help. The wasps are presented as ultra-class-conscious do-gooders who ooze condescension at the ants, who are 'crawling insects'. 'Good … morning', says the female, Muffy, shouting as if to someone deaf or dim. When Bala introduces herself as a princess made 'all schlumpy' by travel, Chippy, the male, stage-whispers that 'it's worse – they're eurotrash'. Muffy insists on helping them ('Chippy, we have an obligation to the less fortunate. I know you laugh at my hobbies, but this is im*port*ant to me.'). And as they go all lovey-dovey over her 'big heart', the ants slip away, appalled. (3'10')

Now, a sudden change. A whistling sound signals some vast intervention from above. A fly-swat descends, just missing the two ants. As it lifts, we realise that Muffy has been splatted. Now, in slow motion and with music recalling *Independence Day*'s invasion,[4] a giant trainer descends, and Bala gets stuck in a lump of chewing gum on its sole. As Z tries to rescue her, he has to jump on a flying lace and across a series of giant slow-mo strides, and in his turn gets stuck alongside her. The trainer descends like doom. Bala, almost weeping: 'Z … it looks like this is the end … just when I was starting to think I like you …'. Now rearing into the sky again, they see a giant object approaching (a coin) with, on it, the head of Abraham Lincoln: 'Who the hell is that!?' asks Z, as they are hoiked off and flipped among the towering garbage cans. (2'0')

Contributing almost nothing to the narrative's linear sequence (it func-tions simply to move Z and Bala in an unmotivated way to the real utopia), these two minutes are marked as very different from the surrounding film. In dramatic slow motion (the opposite of how ants would experience human movement), the trainer is rendered in highly realistic visual detail, even down to the stitches on the laces.[5] And for the first time in the movie, the ants *lack* knowledge: 'Who the hell is *that*?!' Impossibly, he knows it is a 'person' but his anthood here becomes the barrier. We can know, indeed must know (or at least see the need to know more than Z if the scene is to make much sense. But that then also positions this scene quite differently. Up to this point all jokes have been, as it were, implanted human jokes: psychiatrists in an ant colony; wasps scorning eurotrash ants; and so on. Now the joke is achieved through a recognition of our difference from them. We have to be more than ants, in all senses: larger, more knowledgeable, with our own history. We become, as it were, adults to their children. I venture the suggestion that *these instances of FX within an effects movie mark out moments where* modality shifts *take place*. We are invited at these moments to respond to the film at a new level. What the scene does, therefore, is to drop us for a moment into a different modality of viewing, one which for a few moments reminds us of the differences between ants and humans, of scale, motivation, view of the world, and whole life-chances.

The scenes of FX within effects work precisely to recall the relativity of ants: both their size and their place in relation to us. They are part of a natural order, they meet and eat our detritus (indeed thrive on it). In an interesting way, therefore, ants are shown to *matter*. Yet at the same time, their internal order is not about them, but about us. The battle for 'individuality', fought out in terms of a representation of class, ends in a therapy-centred reconciliation: Z accepts his lot. The implied audience that has recognised, albeit in insect fashion, the wrongness of his former lot, is not asked to view with horror the anonymous communism of ants per se.

Conclusion

Perhaps the most important issue to emerge from this analysis concerns the nature and role of special effects, brought into particular focus here by their paradoxical, doubling presence within an effects movie. Since this issue will return in other analyses (see, for instance, the next chapter on *Titanic*), I shall take a little time here to address this generally.

Generally work on FX has shared a series of curious assumptions, which I would now want to question. First, there has been a search for a general theory of special effects, or in other words, how in principle effects affect films within which they occur – to which, then, special exceptions might be allowed. Second, there is a peculiar commitment to what I would call rational distancing, a belief that it would be better if audiences never forget that what they are watching is a film – as though there is something in principle dangerous about being involved in a film. But then a corresponding belief that although special effects might *seem* to encourage a more distanced response, in fact they are deceitful and trick us into deeper involvement. This second assumption connects with the third, that effects are virtually synonymous with science fiction. In recent years, this has amounted to a claim that science fiction's assimilation of effects is a cutting edge of the tendency for virtual reality to become actual reality – Baudrillard's simulacra writ loud and large.

Most accounts (including my own earlier work on this[6]) have shared Albert LaValley's foundational distinction. In an essay surveying the role of effects within science fiction films, LaValley suggests that effects 'hover between being about the world their special effects imply – i.e. about future technology and its extensions – and about special effects and the wizardry of the movies themselves'.[7] Although I value the insight in this, I now want to qualify my agreement. Indeed, I now see in it the basis for those core assumptions with which I would argue. First, LaValley insists on limiting what will count for him as a special effect to 'the extraordinary use of props and optical devices' – which makes his interest by definition technique-led. This then marries with his claim that special effects must always be about the borders between the possible and the impossible:

> Because of this, we simultaneously revel in the machinery that gives us this deception. Special effects thus dramatize not just the thematic materials of science fiction and fantasy plots, but also illustrate the 'state of the art', what it is capable of doing at this particular moment of time.[8]

This arbitrarily limits special effects to the realm of the celebration of technology – and thus, curiously, almost abolishes the distinction between the two sides he has usefully separated. If special effects celebrate 'new technological wizardry', how is that much different from dramatising where technology might go in the future?

LaValley thus illustrates a tendency we can note more widely, to begin by noting the doubled nature of effects, but then to withdraw the doubling. We can see it again in Steve Neale's short essay on the rise of effects movies in the 1980s.[9] Although special effects may appear to distance the viewer, through the doubled attention they demand, in fact they are a trick, 'reinscribing' us to the 'law of the cinematic institution'. In a different direction, a number of critics have complained that effects undo narrative. By interrupting and drawing attention to themselves as 'special', effects are part of a tendency in contemporary Hollywood to replace narrative with spectacle. So, Robin Baker, in an otherwise useful early essay on the rise of CGI, talks of effects being put in 'for their own sake', to achieve an 'impact aesthetics' – and he goes so far as to direct a moral objection: 'is this desirable?'[10] Or again, Scott Bukatman, while partly celebrating the way he believes special effects have made almost limitless our perceptions of possible space (he uses the opening shot of *Star Wars* to illustrate this), still worries that this ends by being self-denying. Far from making our eyes open wider with a doubled vision, he talks of our new 'immersion' in effects cinema. Narrative, marked by 'history, depth, purpose', is replaced by pure play, a 'fetal cyberspace' that worries him by its lack of effort and loss of rationalism.[11] Again and again, we see this emphasis on the negative and risky, in special effects. The worst for this is Michael Rogin whose diatribe against *Independence Day* dislikes not only its politics but in particular its special effects. He writes of their 'convincingly counterfeiting reality' creating a 'visually coercive bodily stimulation', which undid normal psychic inhibitions and put audiences at risk. I would want to claim the exact opposite. I believe many audiences were able to gain conscious pleasure from the effects *against the grain* of the film's overt celebration of America. When the White House is blown up, I remember the explosions of laughter and applause among audiences, which sounded very much like an enjoyment of what could be taken as an anti-American spectacle. That is impossible on Rogin's account.[12]

The account of special effects that in many ways constitutes the endstop, the limit-position, for others to measure themselves against is Brooks Landon.[13] Landon's book is a strange marriage, between a scarily encyclopaedic knowledge of science fiction in literary and filmic forms – and in many of its crossovers with other media (comics, music videos, and the like) – and a global theorisation that places science fiction, and its (for him) essential incubus, special effects, right at the heart of a new cultural formation. Special effects are not only a typical mark of science fiction but are virtually definable by their relation to this genre. Science fiction, on his approach, is the genre that celebrates *cinema itself*. It constantly provides both an account and an image of the new, and – by its inclusion of special effects – constantly presents the technologically new. This is especially true for Landon with recent science fiction, which now also both plays with time, narratively, and thus simultaneously evokes cinema's own fundamental play with time. It takes part in an endlessly mobile boundary between science and fantasy ('both joined by the technology of the cinematic apparatus' (p.92)) – all of which demonstrate cinema's, and especially science fiction films', central role in the 'new postmodern culture'. Special effects are just naturally and inevitably part of this panoramic array. Indeed, he goes further. Citing Bruce Franklin, he suggests that science fiction, in all its manifestations (not just cinema, therefore) now *constitutes* 'reality'. We *live* it.[14]

This is a whopping great theory, which works only if we agree with certain moves Landon makes. First, we have to see special effects as essentially declarative – they *want* to be noticed, and thus prove their, and provoke our, allegiance to technological novelty. His second move is to associate with Vivian Sobchack's pessimistic account of the very time-travel films that, to both of them, mark the apex of this kind of film-making. Perhaps, he says with her, the very emergence of films self-consciously playing with time, and using effects that demonstrate time-shifting to us, is a mark of the end of the genre: 'not only does the future appear used up in SF film, but also to a great extent we've come to suspect that *the future of SF film has itself been used up*' (p.112). This is because, at the very moment of SF's pinnacle in the box office, it has become wholly predictable. Substituting repetition for origination, the 'future as already over' for the meta-narrative of progress, science fiction films do not now even 'pretend to be interested in the ethos of speculation about intersections between science and humanity' (p.112). So, having evoked a model in which special effects virtually equals science fiction, with the corollary that their very existence requires them to shout their name as technology, Landon has almost to give up on the very project he has embraced. The genre is self-destructing. There is no 'future' in it.

The problems are in his assumptions. As my study of *Antz* suggests – and my discussion of *Titanic* will take a stage further – the kind of special effects film that Landon is fascinated by was much more historically specific than he allows. And its meaning was, arguably, very different. As I argued with Kate Brooks, special effects in movies such as the two *Terminators*, *Robocop*, *Total Recall* and the like, were for their key audiences not symphonies to technology, but visions of possible political futures that could be simultaneously enjoyed in the spectacle of the effects, and glimpsed as threatening in what the effects indicated. Landon's model of audience immersion does not allow this kind of playing opposite a film. That film-makers such as Spielberg and Cameron are now largely deserting the science fiction arena, and using their effects-machines for other narrative purposes, I would argue, is best explained, not by the increased possibilities of CGI or by the death of a genre, but by a new politics of Hollywood.

Other critics' accounts of special effects are more complex, and I do not have the space to deal fairly with them here.[15] Instead, I put my position and leave it open to readers to compare arguments and conclusions. My argument is that special effects have to be *signalled* as special, in whatever film they are used. In an important sense, as many film theorists have pointed out, the whole of cinema is a special effect. From the moment a camera points at a scene, and a microphone records sounds, everything is non-natural. Quality of film, distance, focal character, movement, point of view, etc.; illusions of voice-proximity or distance, balance of sounds, layering of dialogue, sound-effects and music, and more; editing and sequencing – all these and an indefinite number more make any film a special composite. And as films have developed both technologically and narratively, what counts as the 'ordinary' has necessarily evolved. So to become 'special' in any film, some moments have to be signalled apart. Therefore, necessarily, effects are essentially singular. Only at the most abstract level can an overall definition be given. To find out the role of special effects in any film, therefore, we need to address certain questions to them:

- How are the effects marked as different from the 'ordinary' of the film in which they occur?
- At what point(s) in the narrative sequence do the effects occur? What consequences do they have for the continuance of the narrative?
- What therefore do they make 'special' about the scene(s) they mark?

We will see, when we look at *Titanic,* how this enables us to unpick its proposals in a striking way.

5
Titanic: A Knight to Remember

There is no questioning the cultural importance of James Cameron's *Titanic* (1997). Actually, there is no questioning the cultural importance of the *Titanic* disaster. Almost from the moment of its sinking, on 15 April 1912, the ship passed into mythology. Richard Howells has recently documented the extraordinary rush to turn the sinking of the *Titanic* from a tragic, perhaps even a criminal, event into something of deeper significance. He recounts the way the ship was retroactively named 'The Unsinkable' – a naming that has stuck so firmly that Cameron's film actually opens with a character saying: 'So this is the ship they name "The Unsinkable".'[1] So strong was the pull to a particular kind of mythology that an obsessive desire to probe the 'truth behind the *Titanic*' has subsisted ever since. To this day, there is a club of interested people with its own publication, the *Titanic Communicator*, which of course added to the awards given to Cameron. To the delight of these myth-makers, there even exists a story, written and published fourteen years before the disaster which, if you are in the right frame of mind, can be seen as predicting it.[2] At the time of writing, the Internet Movie Database was (incompletely) listing 52 'Titanic' books currently in print.

Howells shows the way the sinking of the *Titanic* provided a metaphor and a mythic narrative to sum up the significance of 'modernity'. The *Titanic*'s sinking was quickly embedded within discourses of human hubris and 'Nature's' response. Real human mistakes, failures and responsibilities were mythified and provided a long-lasting story of overweening human ambition, bathed also in stories of passing class arrangements and the cultures that accompanied them.

This was by no means the first film version of the sinking and its consequences. Within three months of the event, a silent movie version starring one of the survivors (*Saved from the Titanic*, 1912) had been rushed out.

Seven other film and TV movies appeared before the most recent. Even so, it is arguable that the mythic power of the *Titanic* was fading by the time Cameron took it up. *Titanic* was Cameron's eighth film as director. Almost all the others had been in the overlapping genres of futuristic thriller, action and science fiction. He had made his name in particular with his two *Terminator* films (1984, 1991), his contribution to the *Alien* franchise (*Aliens*, 1986) and *True Lies* (1994).[3] All had used spectacular special effects which were woven powerfully into the fabric of the films' narratives. This in turn became one of the features most publicised in advance of the release of Cameron's film. The other feature was the cost.

Titanic cost in the end more than $300 million, far more than any film before. Its outrunning of its budget was notorious, and predictions were circulating far and wide that this movie could sink its studio backers. A bloated leviathan, it might live up to the name and fate of its subject. In the event, and partly because – despite scathing press commentary – the scuttlebutt about the film proved enormously positive, the film broke all records. Box office takings world-wide amounted to more than $1 billion, with special video releases (at inflated prices) no doubt raising this by a factor of 50 per cent. Among a host of other awards, it won eleven Oscars, including Best Film and Best Director, giving Cameron the opportunity to mimic Leo diCaprio's triumphal 'I'm the King of the World!' as he received his own award.[4]

But important as all these are, perhaps just as important is what *Titanic* did for audiences. Its mixture of disaster, special effects and romance was a potent universaliser, attracting both men and women, couples and families, young and old. It did exceptionally well in both home and foreign markets. It also reinvented the phenomenon of repeat-viewing. Groups of young women, in particular, went to see the film many times over. This phenomenon, famous with movies such as *Gone with the Wind* (1939) and *The Sound of Music* (1964) and a very few others, has not been extensively seen for quite some time, except with the rather different phenomenon of *Star Wars* where re-seeing the trilogy has been at least in part about becoming an expert, extending the narrative, and participating in a self-conscious fan club. What can we learn about this multifaceted phenomenon from its character purely as film?

Analytic Description

A woman's voice sings quietly and hauntingly over a sepia sequence of a ship at dock, with ghostly slow motion images of people waving, long shadows cast, dissolving into the sea at night and the single word title

TITANIC. As that dissolves away, the shot enters the sea and shows – still just with the voice – the lights of two submersibles moving away down from us, and disappearing to leave … black. End of singing voice.

Sharp cut to engine noises, shot in parallel with the submersible, as they search for something, using a sophisticated sonar (shown on/as screen). Lights move across the sea bottom. Glimpses (no more than that) of an old encrusted wreck: like seeing through a porthole. Cut in shots revealing that we're seeing a video screen. Now we see a man (Lovett) in the submersible filming, who starts a voice-over to what he's filming, then turns the camera on himself, as he describes the slow death of the *Titanic* in sombre tones. Laughter from nowhere: 'You're so full of shit, boss.' Camera reveals bearded cynic (Bodine).

After more of this 'fun', they prepare to send in a robot sub, and we inspect the *Titanic*'s interior through its inboard camera. As it moves past objects (a chandelier, a child's doll, held in close-up longer than would be naturalistically the case), we half-hear ghostly voices, then slow atmospheric music. On the submersible, they see what they want, and manoeuvre the robot in to reveal – a safe. Triumphantly: 'It's pay day, boys.'

On the surface, the safe is lifted aboard and cut open. Amid the mud, and rotted goods, no sign of what they were seeking. A disappointed call to shore tells their backer only some old papers have been found. One is being washed clean, revealing a charcoal drawing of a nude young woman, wearing a large pendant. Suddenly excitement rises again – that was what they were after. Cut to another location, an old woman at a potter's wheel with, in the background, a TV news item about the salvage and the ethics of its search. The woman is drawn to the set, calls her daughter, and exclaims as they show the drawing: 'Well I'll be goddamned.' Cut to ship, Lovett urged to take telephone call. It is the old lady, who asks him have they found the 'Heart of the Ocean' yet? He is taken aback for no one should know of this but them. Who is the woman in picture? 'It's me', she says. Cut to shots of a helicopter approaching search ship, intercut with the men on board debating: is she a fraud? She is installed in a cabin, then brought to their search centre. Lovett coolly tells her the story of her fabulous diamond while she gazes at the drawing, and has a fleeting recall of the scene when it was drawn. She can answer all Lovett's questions, so he is forced to believe her claims. We see her handling with memories items they've retrieved. They show her a dramatic computer simulation of how the *Titanic* sank: 'Pretty cool, huh?' 'Thank you for that fine, forensic analysis of it, Mr Bodine. But of course the experience of it was rather different.' So, will she now tell her story? She examines the monitor screens and has another flashback, tears springing to her eyes. She will tell it … her way.

'It's been 84 years, and I can still smell the fresh paint.' Behind her, the *Titanic* appears like a dark blue ghost from the video monitor filling the screen to dissolve in a matched shot to a full-coloured quayside scene of the ship, and thousands of people watching or readying to board. Orchestral music celebrates the ship's scale. A car pulls up and a young woman – Rose, hat concealing her face – alights. She lifts her head to look – and it is the woman in the drawing – Rose. Unimpressed by the ship, she is corrected by a smooth aristocratic man, Cal Hockley, who instructs her on the ship's size. 'So this is the ship they call the "Unsinkable",' says Rose's mother, also alighting. Sharp class contrasts are set up for us: a porter being tipped and moved out of the way; the rich entering the ship untroubled, other passengers being checked for body-lice. Voice-over: 'It was the ship of dreams … to everyone else. To me, it was a slave ship. … Outwardly I was everything a well-brought-up girl is supposed to be. Inwardly I was screaming.' Cut via the ship's hooter blasting to a quayside bar, and a group of gamblers. Two friends, Jack and Fabrizio, risk everything on a game. Winning, and celebrating wildly, they gain two tickets to sail on the *Titanic*, and race up the gang-plank just in time, the camera tracking their race. 'We're the luckiest sons of bitches in the world, ya know that?' Departure. The ship's huge screws turn, music surges, the *Titanic* dwarfs the tug that pulls it out.

Settling in: huge contrasts of life-style. Four to a cabin for Jack and Fabrizio, who are nonetheless content. Suites of luxurious rooms for Rose. She has her chosen paintings put on the walls, puzzling over one by a 'something Picasso'. 'Like being inside a dream, or something – there's truth but no logic', she muses. 'Picasso', sneers Cal, 'he won't amount to a thing, trust me'.

Voice-over introduces us to another character, 'the Unsinkable Molly' Brown who is 'New Money' (seen also as lip-sync with her mother making the comment). Dissolve to shots of open sea, with swelling music as they set out for America. Captain to Officer Murdoch: 'Let's stretch her legs.' A montage of shots in the engine room enacts the ship building up steam, then the screws revving, the bow cutting the waves, Jack and friend running whooping to watch their progress. All shots run left to right, as they head out. Everything collaborates to create a sense of triumphal power and harmony. The weather (sunny, late afternoon with shadows). Porpoises running ahead of the ship. Willing stokers labouring to build up steam. The captain smiling contentedly, receiving a cup of tea. Music, rising orchestrally splendid. Jack, standing right at the bow: 'I'm the King of the World!' Finally the ship passes under the camera to steam ahead as the music fades down.

On the last vestiges of this, we hear: 'She is the largest moving object in all history.' At table in the first-class dining room, the men discuss the ship while Rose and her mother sit, silent. Rose lights a cigarette, but is 'prevented' by her fiancé from smoking, who orders her food without asking her. Molly, a 'new woman', comments acidly, and the conversation remains brittle with tensions. To their discussion on the size of the ship, Rose asks if they have ever thought about Freud's ideas on male preoccupations with 'size'. She departs, to her mother's apology, and Cal's dismissive 'I'll have to watch what she reads …'. 'Freud – is he a passenger?', asks Ismay, the *Titanic*'s owner.

Third class deck: Jack sketching, skilfully. Stewards walk the first-class passengers' dogs, reminding those in third class of their place in the scheme of things ('among the shite'). Jack sees, and is instantly smitten with, Rose, sees also her pushing Cal aside. Slow dissolve to a scene of first-class passengers, with Rose's voice-over overlaid on this: 'I saw my whole life as if I'd already lived it, an endless parade of parties and cotillions … always the same narrow people, the same mindless chatter.' Rose sits, head down and in despair. We see her snap and run, weeping, to the stern of the ship and climbs over the rails to throw herself off. Jack, who has been lying looking at the stars, sees her. Teasingly, he tries to talk her out of it. In a long scene, which introduces them to each other, he describes scenes from his life where he fell into bitterly cold water, and what it was like. When she decides to come back, she slips and screams and he has to grab her to save her. They tumble to the deck, as others arrive. Accused by Cal of assaulting her, he is seized and handcuffed, until Rose says, covering herself, that she nearly fell and he saved her. Ungraciously Cal agrees to invite him to have dinner with them – thinking that he can thus humiliate this nothing.

In her cabin, shot all in warm reds and browns after the dark blues of the previous scene, Cal now brings forward giving Rose the Heart of the Ocean, trying to buy her affections, perhaps her body. Dissolve from her speechless response to her apologising to Jack on deck, and telling how desperate she feels about the forthcoming wedding. But when Jack asks if she loves him, she refuses to answer: it's inappropriate for him to talk to her like that. She tries to deflect her embarrassment by examining his drawings, and discovers how good they are. Through them she begins to learn about Jack's life in Paris, drawing prostitutes, and sympathising with the poor. This long scene is left hanging, as Jack says he 'sees her', that she wouldn't have jumped. There follow a series of vignettes, of the upper-class women suddenly taking a stroll on deck to try to avoid Molly, linked by a camera track to Ismay urging the captain to 'go out with a bang' by running at top speed to New York, then back to Jack telling Rose about his life. 'Why can't I be like you, Jack, and just ride off into the sunset?' As they share a dream of going horse-riding and on a rollercoaster, they are bathed in a warm brownish sunset lighting. She's taken aback when he proposes that she first learns to hawk and 'spit like a man', is dragged, mock-resisting, into the game – and is caught in the act by her mother and her strolling companions. Elderly Rose's voice-over forewarns of her mother's crushing suspicions of Jack.

Dinner is announced, Rose and mother go to dress, and Molly gamely takes Jack aside to see what she can do for him, dress-wise. Going to dinner, a scene full of intensifiers: as Jack hesitantly enters the first-class dining area, to the faint sounds of the orchestra playing light classical, the camera shifts between point-of-view shots (as if 'we' were being bowed in, then gaze round at the marvels), and high and low angled shots emphasising his awkwardness. Cal's voice enters behind with an echoey quality, as he sweeps round in proper conversation with a countess. Unrecognised in his finery by Cal, Jack is caught by Rose and camera rehearsing shaking hands as she stands atop the grand staircase. In virtual slow motion, they greet with close-up exchange of looks, then Jack kisses her hand – instantly dissipating the mood by saying 'I always wanted to do that since I saw it in a nickelodeon'. Cal, introduced to him, responds: 'Amazing – he could almost pass for a gentleman' and turns dismissively away.

The long dinner scene is an exercise in class relations. Molly advises Jack as they enter to act wealthy and they won't know the difference – and they don't. Elderly Rose's voice-over punctuates it: 'he must have been nervous, but he never faltered.' Cal and mother attempt to put his wrongness on display, but are neatly riposted. Jack even makes an impromptu philosophical speech about taking each day as it comes, and 'making it count' – which Rose turns into a toast, and all are forced to drink to this. As Jack leaves at the end, to go back to 'row with the other slaves', he slips Rose a note which says 'Make it count – meet me at the clock', and he takes her to a real party in third class. Abruptly it's drinking beer, loud music and uninhibited Irish gigs. Rose has to dance, and is soon caught up, the camera whirling in participation. Sudden drop out on mid-note to Cal talking business with the other rich men, then back to the dance. Her growing involvement in the fun is being watched by Cal's manservant, Lovejoy. Slow dissolve to next morning, Cal and Rose having a refined breakfast. He knows that she went dancing, and in a cold fury he requires obedience of her, throwing the table over and threatening her. A deeply shaken Rose is helped to her feet by a sympathetic serving girl. Back at her cabin, her mother, sharply tightening Rose's corsets, fiercely warns her against Jack, and a stern reminder of their precarious financial situation. They are dependent on Rose's marriage to Cal, or – emotionally blackmailing her – mother might end as a seamstress. This important scene ends with this exchange. Rose, trapped by the situation says: 'It's so unfair.' Her mother responds: 'Of course it's unfair. We're women. Our choices are limited.'

Church service, in first class. Unseen by Rose, Jack tries to get in to speak to her, but is firmly rebuffed and removed at the command of Lovejoy. Rose, then, walking the deck afterwards with her mother overhears the captain receiving an ice warning, but he reassures that this is 'quite normal' – in fact he is increasing speed. Jack sneaks into the first-class area, catches Rose just after she has had her vague worries about the lifeboats set aside. He insists on talking to her; he tells her he can see inside her to the real, trapped Rose who will burn out if she marries Cal. This scene works largely in over-the-shoulder close-ups with a high emotional charge via their faces. She walks away with a struggle. Next scene sees her sitting at table with her mother and two other women, seeing and hearing the emptiness of their lives epitomised in a small girl learning napkin etiquette. Cut from her blanked face to the ship's bow and the sunset, Jack leaning silently. Out of focus behind him enters Rose. Rose's theme enters behind as he leads her to the rail, makes her climb up eyes closed. He 'flies' her and great sweeping camera motions circle them. Their hands clasp, they look, and kiss, alone on the prow in the deep red of the sunset, to a musical crescendo. [See below **Zooming In …** for a closer look at this scene.]

As the camera circles them one last time, the music fades as the shot dissolves into a matched shot of the sunk wreck, now seen to be on the video, with Rose watching it who turns and says: 'That was the last time *Titanic* ever saw daylight.' As the others discuss the captain's mistake in raising speed and ignoring the ice warnings, the camera drops them out of focus turning on Rose's face. She is looking at the screen again, a cold blue shot of her sunken room which matches back to its live state in rich red-browns. In the mirror we see Jack and Rose enter – he is to draw her. Seeing a Monet painting, another scorned by Cal, he strokes it with hands and words. Rose gets out the Heart of the Ocean, and says she wants to be drawn like his French girls, in the diamond and nothing else. When she stands in front of him naked, the scene switches to a series of extreme close-ups as they feel the erotic possibilities of this, then the artist in Jack takes over and we see his hands charcoaling in, and asking her to be still. The camera moves in on her still perfect face, right into one almost unfocused eye, and that dissolves in perfect match into the wrinkled eye of old Rose. The others are listening in stunned silence. After a brief exchange we are back on the *Titanic*, Rose putting away the drawing, Jack returning the diamond to the safe.

Two brief interlude scenes have Cal angrily commanding Lovejoy to find Rose, then after a full shot of ship and flat calm sea, the captain and first officer discussing the difficulties of seeing bergs in these conditions.

Back at Rose's cabin, Lovejoy comes looking, giving chase when they exit hastily via the second room. They dodge him in a lift, then run in slow motion through a red-lit engine area into the storage area. In an old car, after playing at driver and lady, they come together and make love. Cut to outside high then close-up shots of the ship at night, and the deadly cold. Inside, in a car steamed with their breath, they hold each other. Now stewards come searching, and Cal finds the drawing in his safe. The lovers just evade capture and run onto the deck, where Rose pledges herself to Jack. At that moment, as lookouts turn back from smiling at their kiss, they sight an iceberg. Chaotic action, fast cutting and running camerawork: end of extradiegetic music. Through the reactions of the first officer we see the desperate attempts – and failure – to avoid the berg. Underwater shots show it hitting, then the first burst of water. Jack and Rose pull apart, shocked as the iceberg slides past them. A desperate rush by the engineers to get out, as huge automatic doors descend.

A series of scenes as the captain begins to assess damage, as the third-class passengers find water swilling in, while stewards advise those in first class that there is nothing to worry about. Long slow shots of the ship lying still. Cal demands action for a theft. Passengers play with the ice. The lovers arrive back at the cabin, to find officers waiting to arrest Jack for theft of the diamond, which Cal slips into Jack's jacket. As he is led away, Rose no longer sure what to believe, cut to the captain learning from Andrews, the ship's builder, that with five areas flooding, the *Titanic* will sink – in little more than an hour. Held shots on stunned faces show the impact of the realisation.

All scenes for a while are short, and intercut to emphasise rising activity in response to the coming disaster, but also confusion, uncertainty, turning to shock as people realise. Cut back to Cal confronting – indeed hitting – Rose, until they are interrupted by a steward determinedly requesting them to dress warmly, put on life-belts and go on deck. Then to confusion in third class as they get the news as well. The captain instructs the radio operator to send the distress call. Outside, readying the lifeboats. Fast swivel-shots enact the urgency. Inside, the band plays, ignoring the confusion. Rose hears from Andrews the true gravity of their situation. Jack is padlocked to a stanchion, and left under the eyes of Lovejoy. News arrives that only the *Carpathia* has responded to their distress call; a held shot on the captain's whispered 'My god ...'. The camera cants and swings over the activity on deck to show the captain finally being aroused from shocked stupor by an officer wanting the command to load the women and children into the boats. The officer begins the assembly of first-class passengers, with a mix of deference and urgency. The band sets up and strikes up, 'as the captain ordered', to alleviate panic. Down in the cramped third class a conflict: while one steward rushes along urging people into the lifejackets, the camera pans up desperately crowded stairs to reveal another steward stopping people going on deck with a locked grill. Outside a first boat is lowered. A distress rocket goes up and bursts, bringing reactions of adult fear, but a delighted expression on a young girl's face. As the embers fall, the camera has pulled back to show the ship's head going down in the still, dark water. The camera tracks in to a porthole just submerging. Inside is Jack, looking helpless. Cut inside: Lovejoy, leaving, pockets the key to his padlock and delivers a parting punch to Jack's stomach, 'compliments of Mr Hockley'.

On deck Molly is organising women onto the boats. Cal asks if there is yet space for him, but is moved back. Rose's mother primly hopes that the boats will be class-separated, or at least not too crowded. Rose turns on her, and tells her the truth – that half the people will die, because of the shortage of lifeboats. Behind them, Cal quietly puts in: 'Not the better half, I hope.' From this comes the final confrontation as Rose sees all that Cal is, and refuses to get on the boat with her mother. When Cal grabs her and denounces her as 'whore to a gutter rat', she hawks and spits in his face, and runs.

Inside the boat, first seen through porthole, Jack is calling for help. Water begins to run down his corridor. Rose, searching, encounters Andrews and he tells her where Jack will be held. Water rises. Rose forcibly overrules a lift steward and they descend – to find water rushing in. She wades alone through the darkening corridors, and eventually hears and finds Jack, but no key. Outside: shots of the ship tilting. Rose goes hunting for help, water up to her waist. All is empty and echoing. She stops in despair. The lights go out for a few moments, then cut in again. When a solitary steward tries to drag her up to deck, she has to punch him to stop him. Finally she sees an axe, and grabs it. Descending, the water is shoulder high and freezing. She works her way back to Jack, and taking the risk of chopping his hand off, frees him. Together, they struggle desperately upwards.

Outside, a boat pulls away from the *Titanic* which now has its bow under water. Silence reigns. A distress flare is fired. A high and distant shot shows the *Titanic* as a tiny isolated spot in a still ocean. The camera then closes in again on the ship, to show a series of vignettes of women being parted unwillingly from loved ones, Cal striding angrily around but readying to look after his own life, then a moment of light relief: Rose and Jack burst through a locked door, only to be confronted by a steward who says they will have to pay for damaging White Star property … Andrews protests to a feebly resisting officer that some of the boats are being launched less than half full. Down below, third class are still locked in, and now threatened

film ever made. Its title, with its bare simplicity, invokes something of not only scale but also stupendousness. The word itself, 'titanic', carries such qualities.[5] The film is punctuated by shots which demonstrate the scale of the ship, and – what is more – the proportionate size of humans to it. When the *Titanic* first sails, we visit its screws, then the engine room. It is like a scene from a Bosch painting – vast machinery, hellish fires throwing light onto sweating near-naked figures – except that the crew all appear as willing participants in the activation of this giant.

- The *relations of the two stories*: the *Titanic* will sink. Known extra-textually by surely every person in the world-audience, it is 'told' right from the start as we watch the salvage attempts and see the life on board as tragic precursors to this. But apart from those shots that we need to show us the massiveness of the ship, all else is organised in and through the story of Rose. These are interwoven in a very significant set of ways. First, the ship is shown as the embodiment of perfection (luxury on a scale never before experienced) and for that exactly becomes the embodiment of her enslavement. Second, the film has it collaborate in her transition. This is shown in a dozen ways. When they run through the ship, on their way to their lovemaking, no one blocks their way. When they need the prow of the ship to themselves – on a perfect evening, with a stunning sunset – incredibly, no one else is near them to interrupt their idyll. And of course Rose knows exactly where Jack will be, although nothing has been said to tell her: go to the prow. When the first ice warnings come in, Rose is on hand to hear them. When the ship hits the berg, Rose and Jack have timed their arrival on deck to see it, and Rose then meets the only person, Andrews, who can tell her how serious this is – and he does, volunteering information to this lone young woman which, in most hands, would be a cause of panic.

- Their *names*: Rose de Witt Bukater names a class to perfection. This is old American wealth and pomp, even if it has fallen on hard times. Jack Dawson bespeaks absolute ordinariness – it could be the alter ego of a superhero. But 'Rose' and 'Jack' are something beyond this, and – although the retelling could not without being dull show this – it is just astonishing how often they speak each other's names. They *invoke* their names to each other.

- Jack and Rose as *representations*: Jack epitomises perfect ordinary humanity. He has not one prejudice or weakness, only strengths and warmths. As an artist, he has and embodies sympathy with the downcast, the poor, the helpless. As a man, he is full of hope, integrity. As an individual, he handles every situation without embarrassment, with directness. Jack is virtually the 'spirit of American democracy', with his Irish, Italian,

Russian friends, his ordinary, popular culture, yet his total unfazability. Rose, meanwhile, is a modern woman waiting to get out. The contrast with Cal is telling. Cal epitomises all things arrogant, selfish, class-driven – and therefore narrow. Where he is crude and dismissive, she smells the future. The Picasso scene is important in this respect: as audiences, most of us will have heard of Picasso, therefore our judgement on this stands ahead of them, and awaits their judgement on him. Cal dismisses Picasso as of no possible interest, but Rose senses – though as yet lacking the words for it – a new body of meanings: 'Like being inside a dream, or something – there's truth but no logic.' (Jack is interesting in this – like someone who manages magic, he has to *touch* the Monet, to feel its power.) She also has read Freud, and knows his significance, where Ismay displays his limits to us (with our modern knowledge) by asking if Freud is a passenger. She too has been untainted by her class, or if touched at all, so superficially that her cleansing is only a matter of moments. Introduced to spitting, it only needs her to say 'No, Jack. Jack, no' (note the invocatory use of his name) twice, and she is persuaded. Introduced to sex – from a class that in reality was deformed by terrible Victorian fears of this – she surrenders to her body almost immediately, welcomes it, and has an (implied) orgasm at first go. But what is equally important is what she becomes through her encounter with Jack. She turns, by the film's indication, into a perfect modern woman – one entirely of Jack's making. When we see, at the end and as she is about to die (that she dies is an implication, not a demonstrated event), we see her photographs. Although she went on to have children, and jobs enough to have become self-sufficient, we see no sign in her memories of the father, or of where they lived. She carries with her the icons of Jack's transformation of her. Is this not a modern version of the 'woman saved through love'?

- *Past and present*: the overall narrative of *Titanic* is constructed through a set of relations of the historic ship, and the attempt to salvage its relics – and through a relation between them constructed cinematically. Each has its own sharp contrasts. If the past was a contrast of extravagant wealth and struggling poverty (which is not indexed in the present at all), the present has a *moral* danger – greed overwhelming proper respect. As an illustration, Bodine – who mixes in his character cynicism (this woman must be a fake), hippie traits (bearded etc.), nerdishness (his ease and delight in computers) and simple crassness (his 'Pretty cool, huh?' as he gets excited about the computer simulation of the *Titanic*'s break-up has to be just about the neatest encapsulation of this last!) – has the virtue of common kindness, but has to learn to respect the past. The *Titanic* is not mere salvage, it is stored-up lessons: of courage, tragedy, virtues that the present-day needs if it is not to become purely money-driven. In short, one of the key organising discourses is the *lessons of history* for the present.

- *Cinematic intensifiers*: there are so many of these, any selection is arbitrary. The use of slow matching dissolves to mark transitions and continuities, simultaneously. The use of musical crescendos to bridge scene-changes. Many scenes are colour-marked, with deep tonal contrasts (warm browns to cold blues, for instance). Observing versus participatory camerawork (e.g. the third-class dance scene versus cool, distanced examination of men talking). But at crucial moments, these drop out. Generally, the present-day is a realm of factuality except where the past is being visited. The *Titanic*, at the opening, is a place of ghostly sounds and sympathetic music. But once turned to the 'present-ness' of the characters, and such mood-indicators depart. Only at the end, as Rose prepares to die, do the past's intensifiers enter the present. And in the past, intensifiers drop out for those scenes which need us to experience tragedy. Once the iceberg hits, all extradiegetic sound stops. It returns, first, via the unique 'commentary' provided by the orchestra whose playing transcends its diegetic origins to become the unspoken mood of those waiting to die: Andrews, standing alone in the state room; the captain, alone on the bridge; the woman, soothing and tucking up her children below. Only as the *ship* itself becomes a personality again – seen in long-shot, then from a high distance position emphasising its isolation – and begins to sink, do intensifiers re-emerge. Once gone, silence returns until Rose begins to revive.

- The *voice-over*, and its relation to what we see: elderly Rose is our guide at crucial moments, remarking and marking the stages of unfolding of the story, and their wider significance. But she does not control what is seen. She is like an entrance to events, a door to the past. But we see and know things she could not have seen or known: the engine room, for instance; the captain on the bridge at the start and close; Jack's attempt to see her at the morning service – where we see her not seeing him; Cal's decision to plant the diamond on Jack – so that we know she should not have hesitated over his guilt, and his later cynical ploy with the abandoned child. All these are examples demonstrate an *ideal omniscient narrator* who nonetheless always *speaks as if she* is *Rose*.

- *Transformations*: the only character who changes significantly in the course of the film is Rose. Others are revealed – Cal, in particular, is proven a fake, his manservant a brutal sidekick; mother is shown as a sad, puffed up figure. Jack achieves something, through his love for Rose. But he does not change. Rose emerges in the course of the film like a butterfly from a chrysalis. In every way that it can, the film collaborates in the emotional charge accompanying that emergence.

Zooming In …

I will illustrate the workings of these patterning principles in one crucial episode, occurring one and a quarter hours into the film and lasting just 3'30'. Choices are coming to a head for Rose. Her mother has warned her of their precarious situation, she has had her violent confrontation with Cal, and Jack has been prevented from seeing her. Now he has just caught her promenading after the church service. But Rose has, just, resisted his appeal: 'It's not up to you to save me, Jack.' 'You're right', he replies, and with an emotional effort she breaks free from a near-kiss saying: 'I'm going back. Leave me alone.' Jack is left alone, hurting. The scenes that follow embody almost all the processes I have identified.

A light musical bridge (the muted sound of the ship's orchestra) carries us to the first-class dining room. The camera descends from a shot of the majestic ceiling lights to compose on Rose's mother and friends sitting perfectly attired at table, drinking tea. They are discussing the problems in dealing with the bridesmaids' dresses for Rose's wedding. The camera moves between the talking women to focus on Rose, who is sitting silent and disturbed, but unnoticed. The sound drops back as the camera lingers on Rose's pained face, as if she is hardly hearing any longer. She looks left and the camera repositions in close-up on her. We see what she is seeing: at a neighbouring table a woman corrects her young daughter's posture. Rose watches; the small girl does as she is told, primly adjusting her napkin on her lap with white gloved hands. Behind Rose, we hear the women indulge in polite artificial laughter.

Sharp cut, visual and sound, to the high angle shot of the prow of the ship cutting the waves, an intense roar of water. The prow moves across the camera's field, to reveal Jack, standing disconsolate. Move to close-up on his still face, lit by evening sun. The camera turns across him to reveal Rose walking into the rear, out of focus. The film's main theme begins lightly before she speaks: 'Hello, Jack.' He spins round. 'I changed my mind.' Shot and reverse of them exchanging happy looks. A side shot, against an intensifying sunset backdrop, has them moving together into centre frame. The musical theme is now fully established. Rose begins to speak: 'They said you might be up here …' but is shushed to silence by Jack who takes her hand and in a series of shifting midshots and close-ups leads her to the tip of the ship. She half-smiles, hesitant but expectant, as he gets her to close her eyes and climb up onto the railings. He holds her lightly. Shot from above and below we see them against ship, sea and sky. 'Do you trust me?' 'I trust you', she answers.[6] Slowly he adjusts her arms until she is standing like a ship's figure-head, then – seen in a tight two-shot – tells her to open her eyes.

Alone with him on the prow against a deepening sunset, she looks out and gasps with delight. 'I'm flying, Jack!' The camera begins a series of three sweeping shots around them, as if it too is flying and they are surging past it. Couple, surging ship, sunset sky, musical theme and camera behave in perfect, held harmony. Close-up again: he sings softly in her ear: 'Come, Josephine, in my flying machine', and she laughs softly back. He folds her arms around her and holds her and she tilts her head towards him. They kiss tentatively, then fully and the camera sweeps round them above them one more time as the music climaxes, Rose's long white scarf blowing free in the breeze. But in mid-movement a shift occurs. The music dies back to a lamenting flute, and a long slow dissolve (8 seconds) merges past and present in a perfect matched shot. In the last seconds of the dissolve, the white scarf lingers like a ghost on the drowned wreck, even while we begin to hear underwater sounds of straining and creaking metal. This single shot then continues into a pull-back to show us the wreck as on a video monitor and, panning right, introduces elderly Rose's face looking almost at us. In a clear voice she tells: 'That was the last time *Titanic* ever saw daylight.' Reverse shot to the salvage team listening. Lovett: 'So, we're up to the night of the sinking.'

What does this sequence reveal, and perhaps confirm? First, in plot terms, it marks two transitions: Rose's commitment to Jack; and the beginning of the disaster. Rose's decision to go to Jack becomes a journey into something new – she 'flies' (an epithet which returns at the end, when we see the photograph of her in a flying suit). She becomes a symbol at the prow of the ship. This act is surrounded with emotional intensifiers: their total alone-ness (on a ship filled with more than 2,000 passengers, on a glorious evening …), the ship surging powerfully, a pluperfect sunset, breeze lifting her scarf to wave free, camerawork forging an alliance between them, all to a soaring orchestral accompaniment. When she opens her eyes, she 'sees' differently. Rose becomes for the first time a free individual and climaxes it with a freely-given passionate kiss. But as perfection is achieved, it is withdrawn. The final camera swoop segues to the drowned ship. Their doom is marked even as they achieve happiness. The very perfection of this transition – the longest dissolve in the entire film, with a perfectly matched shot and the ghosting scarf – raises the status of both their love and its coming tragedy. All are combined into the one shot, which continues to reintroduce our narrator who stresses the symbolic nature of the moment ('That was the last time *Titanic* ever saw daylight') – yet, except for the faintest of pauses, registering her listeners' response to all this, the normality of the plot resumes without hesitation ('So, we're up to the night of the sinking').

This all suggests that here the ordinary becomes special, the special ordinary. The entire scene depends on a series of computer-generated effects (sunset, ship cutting the water, combining with shots of Jack and Rose; computer-matching shots) along with more ordinary filmic effects (timing in the music, laying in the sounds from the wrecked ship, and so on). But they do not declare themselves *as* effects.[7] They declare themselves as emotional intensifications of the narrative meaning of the scenes as transitions. The *Titanic* itself gives her a taste of symbolic flight, but is doomed to take it away at the very moment of its achievement. Dialogue is minimal, and indeed consciously restricted (Jack's 'Shh …' to Rose). Rose *becomes* through the way she appears and is shown experiencing. But who is seeing this? We are but also, by impossible implication, the salvage team are. We are receiving the enacted version of what they are being told. Our privilege as watchers is to experience Rose's transformation, and her giving herself to it and to Jack. We were inducted into her inwardness in the preceding scene, when she heard and felt her oppression in the dining scene, and the slightly dropped sound led us to 'hear' it as if with her.

Why does this matter? Because it reveals two processes at work in the film. First, as well as witnessing not only Rose's transformation, there is an invitation to impute the salvage crew's transformation. At the start of the film, they are cynical money-grabbers, playing at understanding the scale of the tragedy but really in it for the potential wealth. But now they are faced with a truth larger than they had realised. Here was human hope and tragedy on a grand scale. Nothing directly signals such a change, but because of what we as audience have been shown – and see them as having seen – the film surely asks us to ask such a change of them. And it is precisely the special effects, acting as narrative intensifiers, which generate this requirement of us.[8] This proposition could in fact be tested by careful audience research, which would examine how engaged viewers impute responses to the salvage crew at this point. If correct, it would suggest that the significance of the film lies in the way in which it invites audiences to think about historical responsibilities. The *Titanic* may be of the past, but it has lessons for us to think about. To judge the crew at this point is to join in a moral consideration of the proper ways to think about our past.

Conclusion

What may we derive from this? Special effects function in *Titanic* to achieve several specific goals, and at different points they are in harmony or conflict. First, they enact for us scale: they are the means by which we experience the ship as epic. Second, they give us experiences of innerness. Third, they provide a range of emotional intensifiers. And fourth, they bridge past and present. It is also important to note one thing that is *not* achieved by way of FX: this is the ship's luxury. That is displayed pro-scenically, but is not accentuated by any heightening cinematic devices. The only point where it might be argued that this is not true is at odd moments of elderly Rose's rememberings, and at the very end where, in dream as she dies, she experiences going back. In this sense, the effects of *Titanic* belong to the combination of tragedy (epic scale humbled by nature) and emergence (the birth of a modern woman).

But with this, Rose's story is magnified through its association with the ship. She becomes superordinary, without ceasing to be ordinary. She becomes a mythic individual, while remaining individuated. She is perfect, yet her perfection is in becoming less opulent, more 'democratic'.[9] *Titanic's* invitation, then, is to play the role of *inheritor*. This is 'our' past, and we are as we are because of it. Its enlarged people, its glories and tragedies on a scale we can hardly repeat, are here ours to experience by proxy. It is the very act of participating that is the lesson of the film.

6
In the Jungle, the Mighty Jungle

The Lion King (1994) marked Disney's ascent to the position of top studio in Hollywood after lean years in the 1980s. Costing $48 million to make, and earning $313 million at the North American box office, *The Lion King* eventually earned Disney over $1 billion in profits, after taking account of its overseas earnings (more than $400 million), its runaway success on video, and the full range of licensed merchandise and promotional tie-ins.[1] This does not take into account the earnings from the released-to-video sequel *Lion King II: Simba's Pride*, nor the incalculable but unarguably valuable gains all these brought to Disney's spreading chain of specialist city centre stores with their melange of tapes, toys, clothes and memorabilia. *The Lion King* was big, period. The fact that it went on to become a major stage play, designed by avant-garde producer Julie Taymor, on Broadway and abroad says something about Disney's own conception of the scope and expansiveness of this story-world. The rise is spectacular by any standards: in 1984 Disney's profits had been only $224 million, by 1994 they had risen to $4.8 billion. In the eyes of many, it confirmed the position of Michael Eisner, under whose tutelage all this had been achieved, as the most powerful man in Hollywood.

This was Disney's first full-length animated feature to be based on a story entirely developed in-house. And its use of some highly recognisable star voices – notably James Earl Jones as the wise paternal lion Muphasa, and Whoopie Goldberg as the leader of the hyenas – continued the evolution of star presences as 'contracted semioticians' (lending their meanings, but having no rights) with contracts to match.[2]

The scale of success of *The Lion King* is a thing in itself, and must raise questions about just what in the film resonated with its family audiences.[3] But that success also engendered a range of combative responses. Success indicates dangers, perhaps harm already done, to many commentators.

Critics read the film for messages of many kinds. And these join force with longer-established critiques of the Disney ideology, from Jack Zipes' arguments about the seizure and transmogrification of folk-tales,[4] to Janet Wasko's fears of the merchandising machine that a company like this has become.[5] And the film did have effects, even sadly being associated with the suicide of a young boy who left a note saying he wanted to be with the Lion King. To understand *how* this film spoke with its audiences, then, matters.

But this is about more than the film. Disney itself, man and corporation, has long been a name and a metaphor for ideas bigger than any individual film it releases. Disneyland and Disneyworld, with their theme parks and 'Imagineers', are the epitome of well-managed and guaranteed pleasures and fantasies – whether people view that as good or ill. Peter Kramer points up the way this has become in the public eye an integrated 'Magic Kingdom', a world of safe satisfactions.[6] This is now being taken a step further by some, making Disney a metaphor for wider social processes. Paralleling the debates about 'McDonaldization', the sociologist Alan Bryman has proposed 'Disneyisation' as a model for understanding the processes refashioning work as well as consumption and leisure time.[7] In the teeth of arguments like this, understanding a keynote film like *The Lion King* becomes ever more important.

Analytic Description

With just a dedication, and 'Walt Disney Presents', the film begins. A chanting 'tribal voice' signals in a sequence of animals which turn to greet the dawn with awe in their intelligent eyes. We are on the savannah and, species by species, animals and birds nod to one another in recognition of … a summons. Like a moving watercolour painting, birds cross a waterfall, elephants move past a snow-topped mountain, a whole flight of birds cross a delta, in layers, and antelopes leap like ballet dancers out of the mist. Now a woman's singing voice times in with the continuing chant, to sing low and serious: 'From the day we arrive on the planet, and blinking, step into the sun …' – and the camera offers its first close-up, of a giraffe mother and her offspring cresting a hill into the rising light. The panorama of images continues as visuals and song comment on each other, with everyone – ants and elephants equally – carrying on their lives. On the crescendo of the song – 'It's the circle of life. And it rules us all' – a sudden fast tracking shot homes in on a pinnacle of rock, where a majestic lion raises his head to the sky, while the other animals bend their heads. First, a parakeet, then an aged baboon greet him as monarch, to his delight. As the song dies away, we see that the lioness holds a cub, whom the old baboon (Rafiki) has come to bless, shaman-like and then to hold aloft to the vast circle of other species. As he does so, the song restarts at the crescendo, antelopes rear up, elephants trumpet, monkeys gibber and zebras paw the ground in acknowledgement. Even the sky blesses the cub (Simba), a vent in the clouds allowing a shaft of sun to strike him, as in an allegory. Cut out of the song, on a drumbeat, to silence and the title: *The Lion King*.

In a cave, an arrogant lion, Scar, plays with a mouse he has caught. The parakeet, Zazu, interrupts to warn that the king Muphasa (Scar's 'big brother') is coming, demanding to know why Scar failed to attend the ceremony. The hostility between the smarmy, deceitful Scar and the strong, noble king is stark, taking both human (the insulting words they trade) and animal (the king's roar of threat) form – but it doesn't quite come to a head, this time. Scar declines a challenge, and stalks off, sneering. Idyllic nature shots and sounds now dissolve us to the next scene of Rafiki making primitive magic-paintings of Simba, whose glowing image dissolves into the cub, bouncing around, demanding his dad allow him to go and play. Simba is given a lesson in the philosophy of kingship by his father. Simba will one day be king, but 'there is more to being a king than getting your own way'. As the lesson proceeds, the film tours the grasslands of their domain, catching antelopes springing. But there is a place, he learns, where he is forbidden to go, 'beyond the borders of our kingdom'. There is a gap between Muphasa's solemnity, and Simba's childish 'Wow!' to everything new. His father instructs him. There is a balance in the world, everything is connected, 'from the crawling ant to the leaping antelope'. Faced with the question, 'But don't we eat the antelopes?', his father explains: 'When we die, our bodies become the grass and the antelopes eat the grass. And so we are joined in the great circle of life.' And a focus-pull is staged to take us past them to the savannah kingdom.

A humorous intermission has the lions practise pouncing on a protesting Zazu. Then news arrives: the hyenas are encroaching on the kingdom. The king goes to deal with them, sending Simba home. There, the malcontented Scar incites Simba – who is showing off about being the future king – to break his father's interdiction about the forbidden place – and soon he and Nala, his friend, sneak off to visit it, shaking off Zazu who is sent by their mothers to accompany them. Song two ('I Just Can't Wait to Be King!') manages this trick/transition. It is presented like a Busby Berkeley-staged dance routine with added elements of farce, with all species co-operating in the spectacle. The final moment – of a hippo settling his vast behind onto Zazu – segues back into the narrative, and the cubs nip off while Zazu protests. They tumble unexpectedly into the elephant's graveyard. At first excited, they become terrified when the hyenas appear. Cackling and threatening, the hyenas joke about eating the lions. After a fearful chase through the graveyard, Muphasa appears just in time, summoned by Zazu, and tames the hyenas – who are now shown up as stupid cowards.

Shamed, the cubs return home with the king. Simba, summoned to take his punishment, suddenly sees the comparative size of his paw with his father's print – and knows how small he really is. The telling-off turns into a bonding session as father and son romp together in the starlight. But when Simba says they will always be 'pals', his father philosophises again, saying he won't always be there, but that old kings go up into the stars and watch over them from there – so Simba can never really be alone. At the close of this thought, dissolve to the hyenas moaning and scrapping at the licking they got. They are parodies of mocking underlings, sneering at those above and hating everyone more competent than they are. Enter Scar. Scar curses their incompetence; he had wanted them to kill Simba, and Muphasa. He sings a song (borrowing the structure and tune of 'The Circle of Life' to make a parody of that) which insults them yet draws them into his plans. The scene gradually uses more and more fascist iconography, even marching lines of goose-stepping hyenas (of which there now seem to be thousands), ending in a garish display all over a huge crag.

Dissolve out to a canyon, and Scar is arranging a surprise for Simba. As he leaves to do whatever it is, Simba calls after him: 'Hey Uncle Scar, will I like this surprise?' Scar – almost looking at the camera – says: 'Simba, it's to die for …' Now we see that the hyenas are awaiting a signal from him. Getting it, they stampede the wildebeest herds, straight at Simba's position. Scar summons Muphasa to save the stranded Simba. In a desperate fight against the tide of stampeding bodies, Muphasa rescues Simba but, battered by his efforts, he can only half-scramble up the rocks to beg for help from Scar. With a sneering 'Long live the king …', Scar tosses him back to his death. Simba sees him fall, but doesn't see Scar's part in his death.

The stampede departs. Going to the lifeless body, Simba tries to rouse his father, not understanding death, then huddles under his paw, hiding (sombre music highlighting his helplessness) – until Scar comes and tells him he will have to go away, forever. Slinking away, thinking himself responsible, he is chased by the hyenas until he crawls away under thorn bushes and they give up. They jeer his departure, promising to kill him if he ever returns. [See below **Zooming In** … for a close examination of this scene.]

Cut to Scar back at Pride Rock pretending to mourn Muphasa's death, and taking up the position of king, with the shadows of the hyenas rising behind him. Rafiki watches, mournfully, then smears a despairing hand over his image of the lost Simba. Dissolve to a high shot of Simba collapsed on baked earth, and the shadows of vultures descending over him. As they close round his body, enter a crazy jokey pair – Pumbaa a smelly warthog, and Timon the meerkat. They decide to adopt 'the little guy', and carry him to cover. But Simba only wants to die. In a spirit of mad optimism they teach him their happy-go-lucky philosophy: 'Hakuna Matata' – 'No Worries' – which becomes the third song. They draw him, via the song, into their crazy world of carefree playfulness and bad jokes, including one where Pumbaa nearly makes a smelly rhyme with 'down-hearted', until Timon stops him: 'Not in front of the kids!' Soon, all three are singing in chorus, and rollicking. Hungry, they eat grubs from under a tree – overcoming his distaste and eating a wriggling larva, Simba looks out directly and parrots Pumbaa's 'Hmm … slimy, yet satisfying!' Now in their wilderness paradise, we watch a series of transitions: of landscapes, and of Simba, from cub, through juvenile to young adult lion – all to the rhythms of 'Hakuna Matata'.

Dissolve to Pride Rock, against a now desolate landscape, with Zazu imprisoned, and the hyenas nearing revolt because there is no food, and the lionesses – whose job it is, insists Scar – refusing to hunt. Back to our trio, relaxing at night. They share their theories of the stars – Timon's confident statement that they are fireflies that got stuck, Pumbaa's hesitant thought that they are balls of gas, billions of miles away … and then Simba, reminded of his father's words about the old kings – and become sad.

Day, and the scent of Simba carries back to Rafiki who realises he's alive! Then, in the middle of a rendition by Timon of 'In the Jungle, the Lion Sleeps Tonight' Nala appears, hunting Pumbaa. Simba fights her, then suddenly recognises her. A romantic feeling ensues between the two young adults. We hear a recall of the opening chant, and they sing their thoughts about each other. Simba learns the situation at home, but refuses to go and help – his guilt won't let him go back. Nala leaves, angry that he won't take his responsibilities. Torn inside, Simba calls on his father, but gets no reply. Then he sees, but doesn't recognise, Rafiki who taunts him until he follows to 'see' his father. In a pool he sees a reflection that speaks to him: 'You are more than you have become. You must go back and take your place in the circle of life.' Resisting at first, Simba finally accepts his destiny and returns to Pride Rock, crossing deserts and finding the desert that his home has become. Outwitting the hyenas with the help of Timon (who has to play a drag queen to distract them), he finally overcomes his fears to confront Scar. Scar nearly turns the lionesses against Simba by telling his role in Muphasa's death. But at his moment of triumph he betrays himself, the tide turns, and a great – but at times hilarious – battle breaks out, with Rafiki using kung fu to whop some hyenas, and an offended Pumbaa ('They called me "pig"!') charging others. Scar remains treacherous to the end, but finally falls among the hyenas, having just blamed them for everything. They turn on him, just out of 'camera'. As refreshing rain returns to the parched Pride Rock, Simba and Nala greet, and Simba climbs the rock to assume his place, to triumphal music.

Dissolve slowly to a now renewed landscape, verdant and alive, and a circle of honouring animals. A new cub is being presented to them by Rafiki as the final return of 'The Circle of Life' bursts in then slams to a close on the title: *The Lion King*.

Preliminary Analysis

What can be learnt from this analytic description? What preliminary generalisations and hypotheses will it support? Each of the following may seem at first sight obvious, but let's explore them individually, for the ways they are combined, and for what questions they raise:

- There is a current of didacticism in the film, centred around the idea of the 'circle of life'. The song recurs several times, and at crucial moments, carrying a sense of climax. It is also referenced twice in Muphasa's teaching speeches to Simba. The circle of life is both natural and moral. It is how things are but therefore tells the characters what they have to do. Simba won't become what he is, the king, if he doesn't choose to take responsibility. The film, then, operates with a principle of 'natural morality'. This 'circle of life' clearly feeds off ideas current within popular ecology. The earth is our home, we are all on this planet together, everything is interconnected. But it works those ideas into a particular framework, and conducts us through them alongside a distinctive narrative. What is distinctive, then, about the way these ideas work in *The Lion King*? The remarkable thing is that the circle is *not* complete. Though the film closes with a repetition of the opening, although Muphasa teaches Simba that everything is part of the circle – from the crawling ants, to the leaping antelopes, and to the lions themselves which turn back into the grass that the antelopes eat – one species is excluded: the hyenas. They are *not* part of the circle, as far as the film is concerned. What are they, why are they excluded, and what can that tell us about this film?
- This is a musical, in part. There are five songs, of which four are performed by the characters; and the occurrence of a song leads to a shift in the manner of the filming. In the opening song, the words '… come blinking into the light …' coincide with a baby giraffe doing just that. At its climax, as the voice climbs, so does the camera, to the king's rock.

Editing adopts the rhythm of the music, the normal laws of physics and behaviour are set aside so that the songs become show-stoppers. In the second and third songs, weather, colour, movement, all collaborate with the mood of the song – while they last. The moment they end, normality returns. Zazu being sat on has a circus significance when it first occurs as part of the song, but changes meaning the moment the song ends. Songs, then, are like time-out from the narrative, yet they also enable crucial narrative transitions. Simba and Nala escape Zazu via the tricks of the song, Scar organises his hyena militia through his song, Simba is able to grow up outside narrative time in 'Hakuna Matata'. So, what are the songs adding to the film, and what's their relation to its didacticism?

- The film offers a series of knowing moments to the audience. Sometimes these are, as it were, full-frontals: a character will address the camera and us, directly. When Timon stops Pumbaa from rhyming 'down-hearted' with 'farted', for the sake of the children, this is for *our* benefit. When Simba sucks on a grub, swallowing hard to down his nausea but saying 'Slimy – yet satisfying', this is for our mock-discomfort. When Muphasa is killed, we know that Simba does not see Scar's treachery. And when Simba cries helplessly, he turns his face as if to us. In a multitude of ways, the film *addresses* us and weakens the boundaries between filmic world and audiences.

- A conflation of animal and human qualities infuses the film. Clearly the animals are there for their ability to signify appropriately: centrally, the lions for their 'nobility' and the hyenas for 'scavenging cruelty'. Animal ethnology would virtually reverse this, of course. Male lions spend much of their time living outside prides, and are known to kill cubs which are not theirs – hardly familial characteristics! On the other hand, hyenas are strongly social animals. But this is not the point, except inasmuch as it emphasises that these are allegorical lions and hyenas. *The Lion King* is premised on the *idea* of animals and their behaviour. Yet even here, there are oddly blurred lines. As in reality, it is emphasised that it is the lionesses' job to hunt; however, if becoming king can bring responsibilities, why might that not include hunting? The question isn't apt because of the particular way the film organises the animal/human interface, and doesn't invite questions beyond its own terms. Consider one or two examples. Much of the time, for example, Simba and Nala behave like televisual children. Things are 'weird' and 'cool'. As teenagers learning their responsibilities, Nala and Simba converse like high school dream kids:

> Nala: Wait up! What made you come back?
> Simba: I finally got some sense knocked into me – and I've got the
> bump to prove it!

Their talk suggests exemplary ordinariness. Yet at the same time there are moments when they are purely lion – when they rub heads, for instance, or when anger turns into a roar. The wildebeest are there at Simba's coronation and show appropriate awareness. Yet they are stampeded as purely animal, and their respect means nothing when they trample Muphasa. They are human, or animal, at need. And at times the relationship between the two is highly self-aware, as when – near the beginning – Scar declines Muphasa's challenge. When Zazu, disappointed, asks why, Scar replies: 'Well, as far as brains go, I got the lion's share, but when it comes to brute strength [looking at Muphasa], I'm afraid I'm at the shallow end of the gene pool' (all said, in a mock-supercilious English accent). What rules govern this connection between nature and morality?

- The film shifts, again rather knowingly, between the literal and the allegoric. Nowhere is this better displayed than in the scene where meerkat, warthog and lion discuss the meaning of stars. To the meerkat, stars are fireflies that got stuck to that 'blue thingy' up there; the warthog had always thought they were balls of burning gas billions of miles away (but this correct account is scoffed at by Timon); but Simba recalls his father's mythic account, that the kings of the past are up there, watching over us. Their co-presence doesn't deny the allegoric meaning, it reminds us that this is precisely what it is.

- Importantly, the film closes as it opened, with the slamming sound introducing the title at the end as at the beginning. The circle is closed – and we who have watched know that it is closed. The end is another beginning – and we know it. Therefore though the filmic *world* may be identical at start and close, *we* are not. And within this are a number of moments of repetition, some obviously ritual, others to do with learning. Rafiki the baboon makes his 'portrait' of Simba, that portrait recurs as a device to signal narrative events (is he dead? is he alive after all?). Muphasa's advice to Simba keeps being recalled and re-enacted. Simba's childish 'Danger? I laugh in the face of danger' which, first time, led to their near-death in the jaws of the hyenas, is brought back to him by Nala when it is time for him to face his responsibilities. And so on. These moments of repetition function simultaneously to communicate the progression of the narrative, and to add knowledge to character motivations. But they do not quite work like repetitions in, for example, folk tales where the Rule of Three operates: say or do something three times, and it takes on magical significance. Instead, if anything, they are more didactic – the first time innocent, the second time demanding or showing learning. So, if the film is about a circle of life, what relation does the circular nature of the film hold to that?

How might we add together these components to try to define the film, and its role for us? I want to approach this via a disagreement. The film critic Robin Wood has argued that in the 1980s a new trend of cinema emerged in which the Law of the Father was reinscribed, and in the process audiences were in effect reduced to childishness.[8] Wood had in his sights films such as *ET* (1982) but the claims he makes, if true, would apply almost without remainder to *The Lion King*. Arguably, as Kramer notes, it embodies perfectly an Oedipal narrative: the child must grow up in the shadow of the father, and then carry the guilt for the father's death. By taking on the responsibilities of adulthood, he overcomes guilt and ascends to the position of the father and wins the female.

Neat and attractive as this account is, it is fundamentally false as a vehicle for analysing the film. And most importantly, it cannot be used as a basis for making any argument about the construction of an audience as infantilised males (as Wood attempted, for which Peter Kramer criticises him). Strictly, we need only point out that while *Simba* may feel guilt over the death of his father, *we* know very well that he is not guilty. We have been given privileged access to Scar's guilt, by being shown several scenes withheld from Simba, and by being able to interpret as 'evil' (where Simba as child is deceived) various pieces of unctuous behaviour – none more so than his response to Simba's question, before the stampede, whether he will like the surprise: 'Simba, it's to die for …'.

But to put it thus negatively would be to miss an opportunity, for this would simply propose a Bordwellian alternative, that we are more knowing than a psychoanalytic account can allow for. I want to extend the argument: that a psychoanalytic approach such as Wood's is the *least* able to account for the structuration of emotions by the narrative process. Let us therefore consider: what kinds of *caring* are required for an audience to participate effectively in *The Lion King*?

Zooming In …

Take the death of Muphasa. Imagine three kinds of engagement with this scene, three ideal-types of emotional involvement: we might *care for* Simba, we might *care with* Simba, or we might *care as if we were* Simba. What would be the consequences of each? Here follows a close examination of

$4\frac{1}{2}$ minutes between the end of the stampede, and the moment the vultures descend on Simba's body.

Misty greys blur and almost conceal things as Simba rushes forward on the tail of the departing stampede, calling desperately and pathetically: 'Dad …!' Echoes, then silence. He moves towards the camera, with a bewildered expression. A last wildebeest clatters into frame, leaps the camera, is shown departing. Cut to Simba's face seeing something fearful as the dust clears. Low choral voices enter as the camera tracks him circling his father's body, confused and fearful: 'Dad? Dad. Come on.' He tries repeatedly to rouse him, but fails. Simba runs back from the body, calling 'Help … help … anybody …' in a cracking voice. Echoes again. Close-up of his face, tears forming. He moves to the body and climbs under one paw, sheltering desolately against it for comfort. (2'0')

Over Muphasa's shoulder, out of mist, emerges Scar, shot from a low angle, like Simba's. With quiet accusation he murmurs: 'Simba – what have you done?' Simba backs away, pleading he didn't know, it was an accident. Yes, of course, 'but the king *is* dead'. Shock registers on Simba's face. 'What shall I do?' Scar: 'Run. Run away. Run away, and never return.' Simba bolts, away from the camera, running awkwardly like a frightened child. Scar smirks. Behind him, out of the mist, emerge three skulking hyenas. Without turning, Scar pronounces harshly: 'Kill him.' They charge. Simba, ahead, finds his way blocked by a huge cliff, then turns to see the hyenas closing in. He scrabbles up the cliff face just ahead of raking claws, then has to launch himself down a precipitous slope, tumbling head over heels until he lands in the safety of a thorn scrub (the camera accompanies his headlong fall). Behind, the hyenas screech to a halt, the hindmost bumping the first into the bushes. As he emerges, covered in spines, the others shriek with mirth. Brief interlude as they sneer and argue among themselves. Then, a high shot shows a desolate evening landscape, cast in reds, as they jeer and threaten the distant, departing Simba if he ever returns. ($3\frac{1}{2}$'0')

Cut to Pride Rock, shot in cold evening blues, looking bare and dead with no sign of vegetation. Scar is announcing the death of Muphasa and Simba with pseudo-grief, then his own ascent to the throne. 'Yet out of this tragedy we shall rise to greet the dawning of a new era, in which lion and hyena come together in a great and glorious future.' His words, already unbelievable from what we know he is and from the way he says them, are contradicted further by the shot of huge skulking hyena shadows cast on the rock behind him. Camera pulls back and pans right, to show Rafiki watching from a distant rock, in disbelief. He shakes his head. The scene behind him dissolves, to show his ritual painting of Simba. A tear rolling down his face, he turns to the painting. Shown in close-up centre-frame,

Rafiki smears his hand across it, acknowledging the loss of the future king. Dissolve from this held image to an almost matching high vertical shot of Simba lying motionless on parched, cracked earth. The shadows of vultures cross his body.

Narratively, this is a key scene. It is the moment of Scar's, and evil's, triumph. It is the moment of Simba's loss. An audience must both understand the events and their significance, and also care about them. Consider, then, those three conceivable ways of caring, and how they might affect how we could comprehend what is happening.

Caring for: to care for Simba would mean to recognise that he is not guilty but to see that he is hurt, confused, childlike, and in difficulties – and wish he weren't. This is a position of cognitive superiority, a position in which emotion towards a character is mediated through knowing filmic traditions and conventions, and through an emerging grasp of the narrative pattern of *The Lion King* – that a villain is at work who will surely in the end get his comeuppance; that Simba who is a helpless child now will not always be so; that life is hard, but justice will in the end be done; that happiness will return. Such a viewer, therefore, will expect Simba to escape the hyenas sent to kill him, even while urging him to run. And s/he will know, when we see Simba on the parched desert floor, surrounded by vultures, that he cannot be dead.

Caring with: to care with Simba is to be caught in the slipstream of the film, experiencing the events and the associated senses of right and wrong, hurt and helplessness, as they happen. It is to feel how awful it would be if you were Simba – but aware that you are not, and responding via the difference. But such a viewer, if s/he is to parallel Simba's feelings, could not yet know the conventions of Disney films, that all suffering must be manageable and that all will turn out right in the end. Scar is known to be villainous, for we have seen that, unambiguously, as he signals to the hyenas to start the stampede. Therefore, when Scar confronts Simba over Muphasa's body and demands of him 'What have you done?', a degree of confusion would have to follow. For Simba does not understand death yet – he seems to think his father just won't wake up – and reacts with shock when told that Muphasa is indeed dead. To feel with Simba at this point, therefore, will be to experience bewilderment. When such a viewer saw Simba lying on the parched earth, after the dissolve from the despair of Rafiki the baboon – who *does* at this point believe Simba to be dead – again, there would have to be uncertainty, doubt, confusion. *Is* he dead? Will he be eaten? Such a viewer is, if you like, 'learning the ropes' of cinematic response. If s/he were in Simba's position, how awful it would be! And you can imagine them turning to their parents and asking: 'Is he alright? Will he be OK?' to which no doubt the parent would say some variant of 'I'm sure he will be – wait and see.'

Caring as if...: this is the position implied by the concept of 'identification', if that has any meaning. Whatever s/he may know, the operations of desire (and its opposites) are autonomous. So, to care for Simba is to become as if you were him, for now. It is to enter in/be entered into by the character – a completion within you of that which was incomplete, an ever-recurring lack. What follows, logically, from this account? When such a person experiences, as if Simba, the death of his father and the denunciation by Scar, he (and a female watching must 'play the male' here) should *share Simba's sense of shame*. Whatever the conscious mind might say about Scar's treachery, this other part is crying 'Guilt!' Given that Simba now only wants to die of shame, why run from the hyenas?

It's even harder to know exactly what an 'identifying' viewer could be feeling when Simba is lying apparently dead on the desert floor.[9] The camera indicates death – only Pumbaa's surprise discovery a little later controverts that. 'Caring for' has little problem, since s/he knows enough of the conventions of Disney movies to know that Simba can't be dead, really. 'Caring with' can be very worried, and hoping that he may be OK. 'Caring as if' is in an impossible situation.

The Lion King assumes not only the ability to know ahead, but also to watch symbolically. In the long scene which follows, the viewer watches Simba recover with the attention of his friends, learn to eat grubs and squirmy things, perceive a kind of paradise playground – and then watch Simba, in the course of one silhouetted walk across a fallen tree, transform from cub to juvenile to young adult. Such things are nigh on impossible unless there is a maintained distance between the identity of a viewer and that of the lion. 'Identification' with Simba would be a painful, confusing and impossible process. If this were the only way in which emotional responses could be conceived, films like this would inevitably fail. But in fact we can see, from an analysis of a film such as *The Lion King*, something of how human emotions must work within film-watching. A mixture of cognition and caring, attribution and affect mutually modifying has to be at work. What is interesting with *The Lion King* is to see that an *ideal* viewer has to play a double-game. S/he needs to be cognitively alert to such things as Scar's deceit – able to recognise the marks of villainy and therefore awake to the clues as to his deceits. At the same time, knowing too well in advance would produce a cynical 'What's the point? I can see where all this is going' response. To know like an adult while caring like a child ... this combination is crucial, but there is more to be said about it. So, what exactly do they know and care about?

A Bad Case of the Hyenas

The representations in the film, as we have seen, play between the animal and the allegoric.[10] While all the animals are capable of recognising a summons to celebrate the birth of the young and future king, they can drop back into animalhood at narrative need. Hence the stampede: the wildebeest there follow their purely animal fear of predators. But in the end all are contained within the mythic circle of life – except the hyenas. Let us therefore use them as a test-case. What are they?

They are narratively crucial. In a world where, without them, evil would be embodied only in the ambitious but fundamentally weak Scar – who even has a touch of the intellectual about him, at various points – the hyenas act as his shock-troops, bringing disorder. With their arrival at Pride Rock, blight also comes: barrenness, the departure of other species. In character, they despoil for the sake of it, vandals of the savannah. They are greedy, sneaky cowards. They sneer and jeer at everyone, including each other. They have no proper respect, except when visited by fear. Socially, they are outsiders in all senses. They live at the geographic margins of the film. They are not admitted to the circle of life – but why not? True, they produce nothing – but then nor do any other characters or species. Yet it is obvious from the outset that they have no place in their world. It may not ever be possible to be rid of them, but they are absolutely refused admission to the moral order. They are the threat that Simba exists to counter. They are the justification for kingship. Lions may eat antelopes but they have three things on their side: they look noble, they rot down into grass, and they keep the hyenas at bay. The hyenas are, to all intents and purposes, the allegoric underclass. Most disturbingly, and the point where allegory swims closest to the surface of direct comment, they speak with 'black' voices. They are recognisable as simply bad because of the near jive-speak they affect: mocking, negative, threatening.[11] If you doubt this, compare their speech as they capture the young Simba and Nala with the speech in *Falling Down* (1993) when Michael Douglas' character finds himself surrounded by street punks.[12] The key difference is the resonances and tonalities of black talk, as rendered often on screen.

Why isn't this evident? What allows *The Lion King* to seem to be an innocent film, for the delight of the young and the adult-young? What protects it is its combination of two things: its allegoric distance, and its discouragement of unpacking of its meanings. On the one hand, *The Lion King* clearly presents itself as teacherly: Simba has to learn, and the lessons he has to learn are lessons that apply to us as well. But the lessons it teaches are not to be taken as such: they are emotional truths. It just seems right that Simba should ascend to the throne – once, of course, he has learned his lesson that he has responsibilities, which are … to acknowledge the circle of life (and even he walks the edge of being outside the circle) and to keep down its outsiders. Even the death of Scar is not to be laid at the door of Simba, because, as he says, 'I am not like you'. The rabble-rouser must die at the hands of the rabble.

This leaves, still, the generous components of musical show in at least two of the songs: Simba's childish 'I Just Can't Wait to Be King', Timon and Pumbaa's 'Hakuna Matata' in particular, and some aspects of Scar's fascist anthem, 'Be Prepared'. In each of these, any trace of literalness is abandoned for spectacle, and circus-like performativeness. Choreographed animals perform dramatic and architectural feats in time and mood with the songs. Light and scenery collaborate, to lift these elements out of the narrative flow. And it is in this, surely, that their significance lies. Very like the set-piece musical numbers in classical Hollywood musicals, which Richard Dyer and others have understood as moments of spectacle in which the glamour of stardom is presented to-camera,[13] what seems to be celebrated here is the sheer presentational excessiveness made possible by the new digital animation techniques.

The Implied Audience

This film walks a riskily fine line between fiction and didacticism. Working allegorically, it only keeps its narrative integrity as long as you don't ask difficult questions of it. A viewer mustn't (a) get irritated with this rather rude child Simba, with all-American language, (b) doubt the rightness of monarchs, (c) wonder about the way the hyenas talk, (d) think it's strange that the weather changes the moment old Muphasa dies, and so on. Equally s/he mustn't be so knowing about a Disney film as not to care a bit when Simba suffers. All this adds up to a combination of adult knowingness and childish sentiment. But as I have argued in detail, this isn't comprehensible via some notion of unconscious lack completed at symbolic levels – it requires a form of conscious participation, to take the allegory into some working relation with the lived world where its reactionary moral stances might be activated.

How can this happen? I pose the idea that to activate the allegoric force of *The Lion King* requires the conscious participation of audiences, in the following kinds of ways. Imagine a child, leaving the cinema, saying to a parent: 'Why did Simba have to go back?' The parent, accepting that the giving of an answer has to be a narrative explication, might say something like: 'Well, he had to go back because we all have to accept responsibilities, don't we?' Imagine a child asking: 'Didn't you think the hyenas were really scary?' To which a parent might reply: 'Yes they were, weren't they, all greedy and no good to anyone – let's hope we don't meet anyone like that.' And so on. Each time an adult explicates to a child the internal logic of *The Lion King*, s/he *activates its ideological presence*. In living out the fusion of the adult knowledge (how such films go, the narrative motivation of characters, the inner moral logics of the film) with a childish emotional participation, the dialectic of such conversations will bring into the lived domain the working ideology of the film.

7
'Like Food Processors, But Nasty'[1]

The making of *Starship Troopers* (1997) was permeated by a debate which has worried Hollywood more widely for a while: the issue of 'fascism' in films. *Starship Troopers* was directed by Paul Verhoeven, whose films have not been afraid of controversy – think of *Basic Instinct* (1992), and *Showgirls* (1995). But Verhoeven himself, having grown up in Holland during the German occupation, had personal connections with questions of fascism. In another direction, he was also director of two of the top-rated 'action' thrillers of the 1980s: *Robocop* (1987) and *Total Recall* (1990).[2]

Costing $95 million (the largest proportion of which went on the special effects, in creating the Bugs and their world, the actors being almost all unknowns and therefore relatively cheap), *Starship Troopers* grossed around $120 million at the box office, takings sufficiently modest to scupper immediate talk of the sequel at which the film hints at its close. Still, it did well enough to spawn a 40-part digitally generated TV series, being made at the time of writing.[3]

In the early 1990s, for reasons that are not yet entirely clear, there grew up among film-makers around Hollywood a nervousness about dealing with what were termed 'fascist' themes. 'Fascism' is not a simple, descriptive term, but an idea around which a bundle of issues and fears seems to accrete. In the period immediately after World War II the term came into active use, and hung like a cloud over certain kinds of cultural development, including film-making. In 1949 two American sociologists wrote a book in which they virtually prophesied that 'leaderless youth' could become the foot-soldiers of a nascent US fascism. That book became a source for a 1955 film which many saw as potentially exciting the very dangers the book had foreseen: *Rebel Without a Cause*. It was in this context of a wide political debate about the dangers of a new youth culture that in 1959 Robert Heinlein wrote the original book, *Starship Troopers*.[4] Heinlein, an arch-conservative of a very particular American kind (deeply reactionary politics sometimes expressed in utopian forms[5]), offered a solution to the dangers of disaffection among young people which, to many, again looked like the very thing it was claimed to guard against.

Heinlein's book was always more than just a story. Taking early retirement from the military in 1934, because of tuberculosis, Heinlein took up writing after World War II. His first stories were pure adventure. But in the late 1950s, as he was beginning work on his utopian novel *Stranger in a Strange Land*, he was roused to fury by seeing an advertisement by a group of people calling for an end to nuclear testing – among them, some of his own acquaintances. Failing to get a response from President Eisenhower, Heinlein took up his pen to produce *Starship Troopers* as his panegyric to the state and the military, and rewrote *Stranger in a Strange Land* so that it celebrates a principle of leadership. *Starship Troopers* aroused a lasting controversy over those charges that it was 'fascist'.

The decision to make *Starship Troopers* into a film took place in a context where, a year earlier, the screen adaptation of the British comic character 'Judge Dredd' had also been beset with fears of producing a 'fascist' film.[6] The parallel debate about *Starship Troopers* is well told in its *Making of* book.[7] Verhoeven would truck no compromises. If they were going to adapt this book at all, it had to deal with the 'fascism' of the original. Here is how scriptwriter Ed Neumeier dealt with the issue in one interview:

'I think Heinlein was essentially writing a social critique questioning whether democracy was a valid way to do business', says Neumeier. 'A lot of people were horrified when the book came out and called it fascistic. I think what's interesting about what he did is, he created a civic lesson for us. At the end of the book, when I was 12, I was actually thinking, "Hmm, what kind of government do I want?"'[8]

The decision was exactly the opposite of that taken with *Judge Dredd* (1996). There, the producers backed off from possible controversy, and used the persona of Sylvester Stallone to provide a moral lynch-pin to the story. Here, the decision was to run with the original story, problematic politics and all. Producer Jon Davison, who in 1987 had worked with Verhoeven on another film whose politics had an in-built ambiguity, *Robocop*, stated the grounds:

'One of our first concerns was the tone of Heinlein's book', admits Davison. 'In fact, I used to be secretary of the Philadelphia Science Fiction Society in my early school days, and also used to subscribe to lots of fanzines.

And I can still remember, even years after its initial publication, the storm of controversy surrounding quote, "Robert Heinlein's fascist novel", unquote. So that was definitely our primary concern – how were we going to deal with this? Our answer was, by being faithful to our source. Ed and I agreed early on that there was no point in doing Robert Heinlein's *Starship Troopers* and then changing his viewpoint.'[9]

How should we understand the film that was the outcome of all these debates, and this history? It's worth noting that as a film it tended to produce extreme reactions: of love and loathing. In Britain there were complaints at the '15' rating it was granted – and if the basis of such classifications is body-counts, one can see why. But there is a curious quality about the film, a not-quite parodic quality, that will need careful examination.

Analytic Description

The film opens with a military tattoo beating under the titles, opening into a militaristic insignia, and a filmed recruitment advert for people to 'Join Up Now', showing various people who are 'doing their part' – the last, to the amusement of those around him, being a small boy who grins at the camera. Recruits earn citizenship. (First playing of repeated motif: 'Would You Like To Know More?', shown as a moving caption across the bottom of the screen, and simultaneously spoken to 'us'.) The advert becomes a news broadcast, telling of the threat of Bug Meteorites, and then a live report from the invasion force as it attacks the Bugs' home planet of Klendathu. The Bugs, when they appear, are huge articulated killing machines. As we watch, we see things go horribly wrong, as the force is overwhelmed by the huge (in numbers and size) and ferocious Bugs. The report breaks down with the horrible death of the reporter at the scene ...

One year earlier: a classroom, American-style high school. A group of late teenagers being lectured on the duties of citizenship by a passionate teacher who, we suddenly see, is missing one arm. Johnny Rico, handsome, clean-cut, is not paying attention. On his lap-top (they all have these) he is preparing to send a kiss-message to the nearby beautiful Carmen Ibanez. The teacher, Mr Rasczak, highlights that they don't yet understand the meaning of citizenship, even if they know the words. Class ends. Johnny meets with Carmen, but she is more interested in her math result – will it be high enough to get her into space-pilot training? Yes! 92 per cent. Johnny's score is put up – 35 per cent, his friends josh him. Meantime another young woman, Dizzy, looks on at Johnny's obsession with Carmen with helpless desire, and a love triangle is set up. The scene bridges to the next, with

Carmen predicting the need to be tough to survive Space Academy. Cut to biology class: a fierce, caustic teacher stalks the laboratory telling the class (of our characters) about the Bugs and their adaptive strengths. As Johnny dissects a small Bug and pulls out its sticky innards, Carmen heaves, and vomits. Not so tough, after all …

Cut to new scene: at his home, a schoolmate Carl is conducting a telepathy experiment on Johnny, who is failing miserably. Carl 'messages' his pet skunk to go and plague his mother – it does, to their teenage amusement. Cut straight from here to a school football game, with Carmen cheering on Johnny who performs athletic miracles (back-flips and flying somersaults like something out of a Hong Kong martial arts movies) to score. Johnny sees, and is jealous of, Carmen's interest in the captain of the opposing team (Zander), and almost loses the game for his side through being distracted – to the chagrin of Dizzy, who has been captaining the team with tough efficiency. Eventually they win, with a touch-down one tenth of a second from the end of play … (In all these scenes, characters interact, fooling around and joking, like half-grownup teenagers only able to take one thing seriously: sex.)

Cut to Johnny's home, impeccably wealthy and upper class, and a row erupting with his father over Johnny's wish to enrol in Federal Service. Father has other plans, for him to go to Harvard and not 'waste his life'. Johnny cries his right to choose, in stereotypical fashion: 'I just want to get out on my own. See the galaxy for a couple of years.' Mother tries to mediate, with a (com)promise of a paid-for trip to 'the Outer Rings', where Johnny has always wanted to go.

At the graduation dance: rich and beautiful couples dance, with frequent reminders of the unresolved romantic triangles. Johnny seeks out Rasczak for advice about volunteering for Federal Service. The advice is hard: 'Figuring things out for yourself is the only freedom anyone really has. Use that freedom. Make up your own mind, Rico.' As we see the incipient conflicts between Carmen's growing interest in Zander, Johnny's passion for Carmen, Dizzy's undeclared passion for Johnny, and Carl's more distant wish for Dizzy, the scene ends with Carmen whispering to Johnny that 'My father's not home tonight …', and the camera pulls out to a wide shot of embracing dancers.

Slow dissolve to the insignia, zoom out to reveal it is on a giant banner at a swearing-in parade. Our central three are all there to volunteer, Carl getting military intelligence, and Carmen pilot training. Johnny will join the infantry: 'Good for you. The Mobile Infantry made me what I am today', says the recruiting officer – as he spins round in his wheelchair revealing lack of both legs. The three pledge eternal friendship. Back home, Dad refuses to accept Johnny's decision; Johnny walks out on his family. At a futuristic spaceport, he waits to say goodbye to Carmen, but she can barely respond to his request that she say she loves him, before she is whisked away in a high-speed shuttle.

Cut to another Federal advert: children being allowed to play with giant guns, by smiling military men. ('Would You Like To Know More?' – henceforth asked by an insinuating voice.) Then, an advert for an execution of a murderer, to be shown live. ('Would You Like To Know More?') An invitation to be tested for telepathic skills. ('Would You Like To Know More?') News of a Mormon space colony which ignored advice about the dangers of Bugs ... we see the bodies lying, ripped apart. ('Would You Like To Know More?') Cut to a scene at boot camp: a brutal training sergeant is haranguing the new recruits, including Johnny, saying none of them is worthy of him. Would anyone like to try? One (hillbilly) tries, gets his arm broken. ('Medic!') Anyone else? At that moment, Dizzy arrives, accepts the challenge. She loses, but wins approval for having pushed the sergeant hard. At their meal, pecking order conflicts arise with Ace, who taunts Johnny as a 'rich kid'. Johnny rejects a friendly approach from Dizzy – hints that she's pursuing him, which angers her. Out on the training ground, Johnny and Ace compete, but Dizzy outdoes them both, and pushes them into the mud.

In the (unisex) shower, afterwards: one recruit draws everyone into saying why they joined up. Only Johnny, sullenly, refuses. Dizzy, entering the shower and stripping, says he's joined up for a girl. Is it her, she's asked? She smiles ... Cut to: Johnny talking to someone about the camp, and a shot of their locker room. We realise after a few moments that he is recording a message to Carmen on a futuristic device. His friends, including Dizzy, horseplay in the background. Camera pulls out to reveal that the message is in fact being watched by Carmen. She then turns away to race with a friend to her task: to pilot a shuttle out to their huge training ship. She flies it, and we see it, like one of the fighter ships attacking the Death Star in *Star Wars* (with similar music). As she takes her pilot's seat in the main ship, there, in the other seat, is her instructor, Zander: looks pass between them. To the almost-concern of Zander and the senior instructor, she undocks the main ship with style and an edge, then takes it to warp speed, the FX of which dissolve into Johnny, in the middle of a mock battle to capture an 'enemy's' flag. Dizzy, alongside him, proposes a ploy using their football skills, and together they triumph. Johnny is made squad leader, and gratefully proposes 'friendship' to Dizzy. Now he gets a reply message from Carmen, telling him that she's going career, so it's goodbye but let's be 'friends for ever'. Behind him, Johnny's horse-playing friends back away as they see he's hurting.

Now a live-ammo exercise, with Johnny in charge. In the midst of it, one of his squad is killed because of a stupid instruction Johnny gave him. At his trial, we learn that, shocked by the death, two others are leaving down Washout Lane to go home. He is sentenced to Administrative Punishment: a brutal public flogging, shown in detail, with his body stretched taut above the military insignia. As the images fade, the sound of the lashes overlays a scene in deep space, of Carmen and Zander at the helm of a huge space vehicle. She has replotted his course, correctly, he has to admit. As they're about to seal their mutual admiration with a kiss, a giant asteroid looms into view. They have to manoeuvre extravagantly to avoid it (and are mightily praised for their skill) but lose their communication pod in the process. Therefore they are unable to signal back that it is, as they have guessed, an arachnid missile.

Back at boot camp, Johnny is packing to leave – he's washed out. He calls home on a VidPhone to speak to his parents. But as they joyfully tell him he's welcome home, they hear something strange ... and their message breaks up. As he turns away, Dizzy tries one more time to dissuade him, but he is just bitter. He begins the walk down Washout Lane just as a newsflash comes in over a huge public screen in the exercise yard. War! The meteorite hit and obliterated Buenos Aires, their home! Johnny rushes to withdraw his resignation. Cut to news programme, footage from Buenos Aires, which segues via a recruiting advert into a live report from the battle fleet as it prepares the ground assault. [See below, **Zooming In ...**, for a closer examination of this scene.] Johnny meets Carmen, who's piloting the *Ticonderoga*. It's tense, and made worse when Zander enters, mocking the infantry. They brawl, and are hauled away by their respective sides, Johnny and Co. to get tattoos saying 'Death!'

The mission: classic scenes of soldiers readying for battle in the shuttle. In the *Ticonderoga*, they see plasma bolts shooting up from the ground, and gradually realise that there has been 'one goddam big mistake' – this is no defenceless planet. Ships are hit and burn. Below, the shuttles land, and troops disgorge into a blue-black battle scene. The first thing they see is giant Bugs squirting the plasma out of their bodies into the sky; they nuke these. Then the battle Bugs arrive – thousands of them. Unbelievable mayhem and carnage. Suddenly we are back with the scene with which the film began. The battle scene fades to black on the death of the reporter, many of Johnny's platoon, and apparently Johnny himself, wiped out.

'Federal News Flash: 100,000 Killed In One Hour.' The military commander resigns, a new leader pledges new tactics: 'To fight the Bugs we must understand the Bugs.' A TV mock-debate follows on whether there can be intelligent Bugs.

As the surviving ships and troops limp away, Carmen learns Johnny is believed dead, and weeps. But we see him in a tissue regeneration tank, being repaired as his colleagues smile in at him. Three days to go! Cut to scene with Johnny back in action, meeting his new platoon, with a new no-nonsense lieutenant – it's Rasczak, with an artificial arm: 'This is for you new people. I only have one rule. Everyone fights, no one quits. If you don't do your job, I'll shoot you.' As the mission proceeds, we hear that a new tactic is being deployed: bomb heavily first (we see the massed Bugs on the ground, then the bombers come …), then Mobile Infantry clean up. On the ground, they kill surviving Bugs – then a giant acid-spewing Bug, the size of a house, surges out of the ground. Johnny leaps on its back, and blows it apart with a nuclear grenade. Made up to corporal (the other having been killed), he makes Dizzy his squad leader. That night, they rest and relax. But when Dizzy invites him to dance with her, he turns her down – until Rasczak gives him advice, for once: Don't turn down a good thing. Johnny now goes to her. They dance, smooch, and at last go off and make love.

Recalled to duty, they patrol through a mountain pass, stones tumbling ominously from above. A signals man sent to try to get a message out is seized by a winged Bug, and is mercy-killed by the lieutenant ('I would expect any man here to do exactly the same for me'). Arriving at a metal defence fort, complete with look-out tower, they find bodies everywhere, and a man with his brains apparently sucked out of his head. In a cupboard, a cowardly general is hiding, begging not to be killed. Then, as they struggle to re-establish a communications link, Bugs! Uncountable hordes pour towards the fort, like 'Indians' swarming towards a Western fort. All defenders open fire, and a desperate battle ensues – which the Bugs are clearly winning. The defenders retreat into the inner area, to await the rescue pod which they have finally managed to summon down. As it lands, one of the acid-spewing Bugs erupts from the ground inside the fort – and Lieutenant Rasczak falls into its pits, losing his legs. He commands Johnny to shoot him, as he had shot the man earlier. Dizzy blows up the huge Bug but, as she turns to celebrate, she is attacked from behind and fatally wounded, and dies in the shuttle in Johnny's arms, saying that it's OK as she had Johnny before she died. Here, Johnny meets Carmen again who all this time has thought him dead. He wants the planet nuked, but from the mother ship comes a refusal – they have other plans.

Dizzy is buried in space. Johnny makes a powerful speech about how he now understands the meanings of citizenship. Carl appears, to explain the plans for the planet – there is a Brain Bug down there, and they want Johnny's platoon to go back and help capture it. As they land and prepare for battle, Johnny looks over his new recruits, and wonders at how young they are. He recites Rasczak's words precisely: 'This is for you new people. I only have one rule. Everyone fights, no one quits. If you don't do your job, I'll shoot you.' Then: 'Saddle up!'

Above, plasma bolts are striking the mother ships, Carmen and Zander's among them. These two just escape before their ship explodes. Their shuttle plummets to landfall, careening into the ground and penetrating a tunnel full of Bugs, where they are captured rather than killed. Johnny has caught their distress message, and goes in search but his military rationale overrides his urge to hunt for her. But as they enter the tunnel to hunt an utterly loathsome Brain Bug, he senses her, and leads two others in a rescue bid. Almost too late – Zander, encountering the Brain Bug, defies it but it punctures his head and sucks out his brains. Carmen, about to meet the same fate, injures it with Zander's knife – and in the moments this gains, Johnny arrives with a hand-held nuke. The Bug recognises its danger and backs away. As they retreat up a tunnel, one of the soldiers is wounded and stays to fire the nuke and save the others. They just escape the blast – and re-emerge to find the Brain Bug captured. Carl steps up to it, and 'listens' to its thoughts: 'It's afraid!' To wild cheering, the troops recognise that this is a turning point. And Johnny guesses that he sensed Carmen through the agency of Carl.

Amid scenes of celebration, there is a cut to Federal News: the captured Brain Bug is being 'tortured', with a 'Censored' blank on the screen to protect us from the sight … ('Join Up Now') There follows recruitment footage of (now captain) Carmen with a baby-faced crew, and (now lieutenant) Johnny Rico with a platoon going into battle; 'They'll Keep Fighting – And They'll Win.'

Preliminary Analysis

This is a packed story. Apart from the scenes of all-out war, almost every other scene performs at least a double function: usually, evolution of the romance triangles and advance of military training or skills testing. Within an overall driving narrative, which has very few moments of respite, the film nonetheless incorporates elements of complexity and disruption which viewers have to navigate if they are to manage the film. Key among these are:

- *Repetitions:* throughout the film, key slogans and lines of dialogue get repeated and in the process accrete meanings. In every one of the Federal broadcasts, we meet: 'Would You Like To Know More?' … these including news items, information on how to volunteer, and gory items such as the execution. On four occasions, a serious injury to a soldier is met with the singular cry of 'Medic!', before the action resumes. The teacher/ lieutenant's speeches are very consciously replayed: first, his rule about mercy-shooting, then his speech to new recruits. These signal, therefore, the increasingly successful *militarisation* of the central characters as they are shown understanding and accepting the realities of military life and with that citizenship. A prime example of this is the slogan yelled as the troops are led into bloody battle, first by the lieutenant, then by Johnny once he has adopted the military mantle: 'Come on, you apes, do you wanna live forever?!' These repetitions accumulate a grim humour round them. What, then, is the part in the film overall and its proposal to audiences?

- *Representations:* the film's central characters embody a strange and at times inconsistent mix of 1950s high-school teenagers (clean-cut and straightforward, having conflicts with parents, and romance among themselves) even down to the cheer-leading at the football game and the macho competitiveness that this embodies. Yet at the same time there is no clear gender separation, as we discover Dizzy leading the team with physical force – and then proving herself a more than competent soldier. With these come the easy attitudes towards sex, including the shower scene which refuses to make an issue out of nudity.

Class as wealth is a narratively relevant factor. Johnny is marked as foolish for his failure to study at school, and the benefits of hard study are evident for Carmen and Carl. Yet there is a problematic association of class with future success – Johnny Rico's father may think he can buy his son's success, but the real happiness lies in the commitment to service of Carmen, Zander and – eventually – Johnny. Ace celebrates, early on, his ordinary background against 'you rich kids', but by the end of the film has accepted a foot-soldier position.

There is a curious way in which the central characters are simultaneously stereotypically American, yet not so. There is a loose ethnic mix among both central and marginal groups of characters (strong hints of hispanic and black, as well as white, and smaller hints of oriental). Yet the only place actually mentioned is Buenos Aires – as if by the time of the film the 'American way' has spread everywhere. What world is being presented as the future, then, and who are its inhabitants?

The other side of representation, of course, is the Bugs. Awesomely effective, multiform, innumerable, they seem to have no purpose other than to kill humans. In fact, it is hard to think of them having lives other than as killing machines. They exist to rend, eat, drain, destroy. It seems nonsensical to ask any questions about them: why do they so single-mindedly kill? How did they evolve such multifarious forms?

Don't think about the improbable capacity to spew flame-thrower acid from the mouths of one variety, or the impossible physics of firing plasma-bolts from their bottoms hundreds of miles into space. Certainly don't ask how such a capacity might have evolved. Just don't ask. Don't ask about Bugs that can spread across planetary systems, yet don't seem to have a single mechanical device to their name.

But that is the point. Because we cannot ask about the Bugs while maintaining any normal participation in the film, they can only function as fantastical tests of us, our strengths and weaknesses, our politics and forms of government. So, when ground forces are sent into action against myriads of Bugs who are known to be almost unstoppable, armed with little more than machine guns, an audience has a choice: either suspend all normal considerations and stay for the mayhem; or wonder why – in which case the government seems *stupid*.

- *Genre mixes:* the film makes repeated references to many genres, as we will see in our close examination of one scene: the battle at the fort. Among the genres/texts referenced pretty directly are: SF/*Star Wars*; westerns/ John Wayne; horror/the *Alien* series; war/military rites of passage; teenage sex romance/*Beverley Hills 90210*; parody. Some are very directly referenced, provided one has the necessary knowledge ('Saddle up!' and the filming of the entire fort sequence). Others are more like available points of comparison (the virtual inhuman indestructibility of the Bugs, inviting comparison with the creatures in the *Alien* series).

- *Level shifts:* repeatedly in the film, we encounter sudden shifts of presentational level, such that we have to re-adjust as to whether we are seeing live action, or news action, or recorded message, or advertisement, and the film segues between them, without warning and without discontinuity. We don't know until after a shift has taken place, e.g., Johnny recording his message to Carmen, twice we are 'tricked' about the status of the images we are seeing.

This is the other side of relatively invisible camerawork and soundscape. Only at particular moments does the camera function as independent witness or self-consciously comment on a scene. Its 'invisibility' is well-illustrated in the shower scene, where nudity virtually becomes nakedness (in John Berger's terms[10]), neither withholding breasts and buttocks nor accentuating their visibility. They are simply there, because people do strip to shower.

In the same way, the soundscape is rarely used as explicit commentary. Unusually, the flogging scene uses a sound-bridge to the following scene, emphasising the harshness of what we have seen by continuing to hear each blow to Johnny's bare back. The only times the organisation of sound becomes more than what is narratively necessary is in the level shifts: between actuality and news coverage, or recorded message, or recruitment message. At such points there is ambiguity as to whether the voice is simply occurring within a scene, is being heard by characters within their narrative position, or is addressed to a virtual 'us'.

In fact, almost more remarkable is the virtual absence of establishing shots. Some scenes have them: the graduation dance opens and closes with high angle overview shots; certain war scenes show the general terrain before action begins. But as often we are pitched into scenes and have to work out, once there, where we are, why we are there, and at what level (contemporary filmic action, news report, filmed letter, or whatever) the scene is operating. How do these jumps between levels of narration work on the film as a whole, and its creation of an audience role?

Zooming In …

The scene I've chosen comes just under an hour into the film, immediately after the news of the devastation of Buenos Aires and Johnny's plea to be allowed to stay in the military. The scene is a cut-in Federal broadcast, lasting in film-time for just over two minutes.

The Federal logo (futuristic 3D metallic) shimmers with flames, then a zoom out shows the slogan **WAR** made out of flames. Sombre music, with military drums under which take over, then fade out under voice-over: 'Out of the ashes of Buenos Aires come, first, sorrow.' (Cut in news shots of urban devastation, rescuers lifting bodies out of rubble. Close-up of photograph in damaged frame, cut to close-up of dead dog.) 'Then, anger …'. Survivor (to camera): 'The only good Bug is a dead Bug!' Superimpose caption (futuristic font) across bottom of screen: WOULD YOU LIKE TO KNOW **MORE**? (Last word flashes.)

A high angle shot of conference chamber – VO: 'In Geneva, the Federal Council convenes …' From a low angle, first mid-shot, then close-up on Sky Marshal Dienes (declaiming): 'We must meet the threat with our valor, our blood, indeed with our very lives to ensure that human civilization, not insect, dominates this galaxy now and always.' Sound of mass applause, and high angle shot of crowds standing applauding. Repeat caption: WOULD YOU LIKE TO KNOW **MORE**?

Cut to shot of grey laboratory with large machines, one section floor-to-ceiling bars. (Styled caption over: KNOW YOUR FOE.) Carl turns and walks towards camera. VO: 'Every day Federal scientists are looking for new ways to kill Bugs.' Close-up on Carl: 'Your basic arachnid warrior is not too smart, but you can blow off a limb … (long shot of Bug having limb shot away) … and it's still 86 per cent combat-effective. Here's a tip … (Close-up on Carl) … aim for the nerve stem and put it down for good.' Shot from behind: Carl massacres the Bug. VO: 'WOULD YOU LIKE TO KNOW **MORE**?'

Cut to playground with children. ('Everyone's doing their part. Are you? The war effort needs *your* effort – at work, at home, in your community.') Styled caption over: DO YOUR PART! Teacher standing behind, excitedly cheering on their stamping on Bugs, in close-up. Mid-shot of the teacher clapping and giggling. Fractal dissolve to shots of ships in deep space. (Styled caption over: COUNTDOWN TO VICTORY.) A panning shot of a shuttle landing on mother ship. VO: 'We now break to take you live to Fleet Battle Station *Ticonderoga* deep inside the arachnid quarantine zone where the men and women of the Federal Armed Services prepare to attack.' Background sound, as heard through a headphone: 'BSQ uplink, on two … one … you're on …' On the fourth word a reporter appears, walking towards retreating camera, in a bustling corridor. Reporter: 'No one here on the *Ticonderoga* knows exactly when the invasion of Klendathu will occur. But everyone's talking about it, and the talking says: tomorrow. Here's a bunch of MI kids that look like they could eat Bugs for lunch.' Reframe to include Dizzy: 'Hmm, yum, yum, yum …' Reporter: 'So, trooper, you're not worried about fighting arachnids?' Ace enters camera space, speaks to reporter/camera: 'Hey, shoot a nuke down a Bug hole, you gotta lotta dead Bugs.' An unknown soldier pushes into camera, speaks to 'us': 'I just hope it's not over before we get some.' Reporter: 'Some say the Bugs were provoked by the intrusion of humans into their cultural habitat, that a live and let live policy is preferable to war with the Bugs …' Reframe to include Johnny in background, he turns and speaks to camera: 'Johnny (interrupting): Let me tell you something. I'm from Buenos Aires, and I say: Kill 'em all.' On his last words, he pushes his face into extreme close-up, then turns and walks away, arms around friends' shoulders. The reporter gives a look to camera. Cut to a new angle on the scene, the trio talking among themselves in excited anticipation, followed by a tracking shot alongside trio walking together down the corridor.

This scene is complex in its simplicity. In tone, first, it opens with the horror of the destruction of Buenos Aires, yet shows this to us in a stagey way ('The only good Bug is a dead Bug!' pronounces a man who might be reading an autocue.) The Federal Council scene is filmed like a political speech with camera angles emphasising strength. But the words over-reach and can easily sound faintly ridiculous. The scene with Carl has a clinical nastiness as he casually disposes of the caged Bug. And the schoolyard scene is emphatically bizarre.

There are numerous shifts in level. From news footage, via repeating caption ('Would You Like To Know More?'), we are in an educational pro-gramme, then a military advert. There follows a cut to live action, however improbable that might be (instantaneous perfectly composed shots from deep space, half-way across the galaxy), cued in by an overheard studio director's instructions. The camera then joins the scene in the corridor just too late, giving us the reporter's voice as voice-over for a moment. And at the end of the scene, without any visual indication we leave the Federal broadcast altogether and re-enter narrative space.

The doubling of these with the bounding narrative requires high-energy participation where, even though we may know in general how things will progress, there is an overall 'without warning' driving feel to the whole. One moment soppy romance, the next gung-ho training, then speedy manoeuvres jumping to fascistic TV adverts segueing into body horror. The role of the implied audience has to be found within this very pacing and the transitions it hurls.

The Implied Audience

For *Starship Troopers*, it is necessary to distinguish at least two layers of requirement of an implied audience. The first, a strictly narrative layer, must be capable of managing the time-shifts within the film in order to follow its story-construction: that we begin near the end, and cycle back round through the disastrous opening battle – begun in hope, ended in carnage, but then, through the events seen after this, returned to a new hope based on a more intelligent plan.

But in the course of managing these time-shifts, the film makes a series of starkly opposite demands of us. Opening with a quick gear shift from patri-otic optimism to bloody battlefields, it then dives back and lets us bathe for almost an hour in, first, the stunning good looks and easy lives of Beverly Hills look-alikes – who turn out to come from Buenos Aires. Their romance- and prom-centred lives shift without seeming to change into the brutal regimes of boot camp, where a lesson in discipline is a broken arm, a knife through the hand, or a public flogging of unrelenting brutality. Elements of sardonic or bizarre humour sit within seconds of rank body horror: affirm-ing pictures of young children being encouraged to play with machine guns, and of a teacher jumping with childish delight as her charges squash wood-lice in the playground are followed by disembowelling and beheading by insects as gruesome as any you have met on screen. It is this very shifting, dislodging any steady position the moment you might achieve it, that suf-fuses *Starship Troopers*. There are no warnings, no spaces for standing away.

Romantic lead gets laid, after long periods of frustration. Romantic lead wins gung-ho fight with SuperBug, exploding it with perfectly aimed grenade. Romantic lead is torn apart by next Bug, and dies in her new lover's arms.[11]

In fact the difficulty in coping with the position of the implied audience of *Starship Troopers* is the number of radically different generic positions it asks you to occupy, and then to drop at a cut's notice. The genre mix I noted earlier is absolutely *not* a blend – the essence of the film is that the genres sit pointedly alongside, or even on top of, each other. The scene with the Brain Bug captures this perfectly. Carmen and her chosen love (whom quite likely we think she wrongly chose, since the central character has the real hots for her, and she has said no) are still smoulderingly in love, looking beautiful, and caring for each other like something out of a high-school drama right up to the moment when the Brain Bug drives its horn into Zander's skull and drains his grey matter, and we see his cheeks sucked in by its force. This is asking a very particular kind of skill of its audience: to be involved, yet detached; to join in with the game of genres and enjoy each for its own, yet ride the swift changes. One enthusiastic review caught this ambivalence perfectly:

> It's as if Verhoeven wants it both ways. He clearly wants us to see how ridiculous all this is even as he *revels* in the ridiculousness itself. Yeah, our society could descend into a fascist state if we don't question authority – now let's go kill those Bugs! The federation rules! The weird fusion of barbed commentary and visceral actions works – depending on your own toleration for each. Myself, I was laughing at both – with the occasional queasy realization that I was cheering on a fascist state.[12]

It is the willingness to ride, and at that enjoy riding, that queasiness which must characterise the position of the implied audience.

So what does *Starship Troopers* tell us about fascism? If we consider the film as an *attempted commentary*, we may discern something of the perceived meanings of 'fascism' and the film's response to them. So, in what does *Starship Troopers* seem to see a 'fascist' potential? Curiously, the answer seems to centre around the media: in the use of symbols; in the use of the media to popularise and distribute those symbols; in the use of the media to conflate and confuse news, advertisements and propaganda. The points at which the film passes beyond an SF/horror/western/action high-octane romp are those where the film 'speaks out to us' simultaneously showing and ironising its own capacity to seduce us into the virtues of devotional citizenship. Is this the limit, maybe, of a contemporary Hollywood film's ability to think about totalitarianism?

8
Dear Meg, Dearest Tom

Sleepless in Seattle was a major hit of 1993. On a budget of $21 million, it grossed $227 million at the box office, and confirmed Hollywood's opinion that there's money in them thar women audiences.[1] It also confirmed the place of its stars Tom Hanks and Meg Ryan on the A-List of Hollywood earners. A romantic comedy, it followed fairly directly from Meg Ryan's success in *When Harry Met Sally* (1989). It was Hanks' first directly romantic role.

Sleepless in Seattle's combination of romance and humour is very ordinary, but interesting from an academic point of view since these two areas have been the subject of much work recently. Romance became a hot topic of cultural theory in the late 1970s when various feminist investigators saw in it a means of investigating the ways in which women live their subordination. For one group, romance was in fact an important mechanism of mental oppression. Romance was to women what pornography was to men.[2] But in an opposite direction, a number argued that this was to join in the devaluation of those things which women choose and enjoy.[3] The relative stand-off between these two positions eventually led to some different work which emphasised the role of romances in the production of female subjectivities: that is, the ways in which romantic narratives might play a role, and perhaps a historically shifting role, in giving women the materials necessary if they are to manage the demands made on them by social oppressions. Whatever the approach, it is clear that many feminists saw in romance something through which they could articulate important elements of a separate feminist politics, centred around representation, and the differences between men and women *per se*.

A similar process has attended the ways in which film humour has been considered. An area largely avoided until recently by cultural theorists,[4] such work as there is tends to reflect with a special awkwardness the efforts of film analysis generally. A divide opened up between those who looked on humour as a form of deceit, making palatable ideas and narratives that were essentially alienating, and those who saw in humour signs of disruption.[5]

It is interesting, though, that there has been relatively little attention to the overall genre of romantic comedies, less than their importance to Hollywood's history would seem to require.[6] Studies of romance have looked mainly elsewhere (novels, serial fiction, magazines and comic books being the main forms analysed); and studies of humour have either worked at high levels of theory and generality (often with strong psychoanalytic leanings)[7] or have looked at forms such as sitcoms, stand-up comedy and particular comics. Such work as there is reveals very starkly the difficulties in making sense of humour while still allowing that it *is* funny. Take for instance Neale and Krutnik's much-cited study of popular film and television comedy.[8] This has an acute chapter dealing with the 'comedy of the sexes'. This distinguishes romantic melodramas (typified by the *noir* tradition) and comedies (where their prime interest is in 1930s screwball comedies and, less, the 1950s comedies). With the melodramas, they arrive with relative ease at what we might call their 'principles of meaning'; they offer, say Neale and Krutnik, a 'narcissistic eroticism' (p.135). But romantic comedy poses more problems, because of their 'play with relative levels of knowledge' (p.142). In many situations, we know things that a woman character won't admit about herself – we know she is still pursuing the wrong man, but will find out her mistake. This, they argue, puts a distance between us and the woman's desires, since we know how she *must* end up. In 1930s films, this imbalance was accentuated by what they call an 'expository imbalance' (p.144); what the hero tells the heroine is more likely to be true than what she says back.

This account comes close to dealing in the kinds of terms I am advocating in this book. Here is a recognition that the meaning of a film cannot be determined without considering the position required of a participatory audience. But their account stops short, and in effect undoes that step down this road. First, they try to see this as a special condition of comedy – and in laying this out, reintroduce a series of claims about cinema-going generally that I would simply reject:

> The difference is, indeed, most clear in the cinema situation: one watches a drama largely in silence, in rapt attention, whereas with comedy laughter 'disrupts' the 'passively consumed dramatic illusionism' and one is pulled away from the world represented on screen. And as comedy frequently calls attention to its status as fiction the spectator is more aware that

he/she is watching a *film* rather than looking in to a 'realistically' constructed world.[9]

There are too many arguable claims for me to respond to adequately here.
First, there is not one piece of evidence that people ever stop being aware
that they are watching a film – of whatever kind it is. Indeed, if they did,
they would become completely confused, since they wouldn't know how to
cope with all the processes which only make sense if we know we are reacting to films (switches of camera position, editing, temporal discontinuities,
etc.). Second, they have obviously never watched audiences watching exciting films, where gasps, exclamations, people clutching each other and so on
are very much part of the process. Third, that word 'realistically' conceals
cans of wrigglies. Beyond certain documentaries, I defy Neale and Krutnik
to find one film for which it would be possible to delete those scare-quotes,
such that viewers *could* participate without having developed an interpretative schema advising them as to the kinds of behaviour and event that
can happen.

But actually, this isn't an empirical claim. The notion of 'ordinary' cinematic behaviour is their sheet-anchor, against which comedy is straining,
and to which in due course it is brought back. Comedy only temporarily
licenses audience activity and freedom. In the end, they believe, we are as
much contained as we are by, for example, melodrama. We can see the
problems in their account through a telling example they use, from the
1959 film *It Started with a Kiss*. This film, they nicely show, embodies a gag
which is directed at the audience. Joe, an ordinary soldier, is pursuing
Maggie, who thinks she wants to marry a rich man. But when they kiss, she
melts – and kisses him back, again and again, clearly intoxicated. The scene
then dissolves to a bedroom strewn with discarded clothes, and reveals a
woman's hand enclosed in a man's on the sheets of the bed. As they say, the
association of scenes does seem to imply that kissing has led to sex – without marriage. However, the man's hand unwraps, to reveal … a wedding
ring:

> The joke is that the elision of the wedding scene has provoked for the
> spectator a 'false' expectation of transgression. The climax of the gag –
> the exposure of the ring – is that moment when this expectation is con-
> founded, and the spectator reviews and corrects it. The pleasure of such
> gags is intrinsically linked to the resetting of boundaries: sex outside
> marriage is quickly converted into sex within marriage. The transgres-
> sion is 'refamiliarized'.[10]

Neale and Krutnik are reading the outcome of the joke as a reaffirmation of marriage for and by the audience. This is surely wrong. This makes it seem that in 'reviewing and correcting', the audience shed their sense that the sex might have been premarital, and see it as all one terrible mistake. But in that case, I would argue, it wouldn't be funny at all! Let us ask instead: what are the necessary conditions for an audience to identify this as a gag? To be funny, the audience has to identify that they have been *played with*. That is, the film was tricksy – it made them think they had had sex outside marriage, but then made them go 'Doh – they had got married in the slow dissolve!' That is funny if the idea of sex outside marriage was (a) conceivable, and (b) not automatically immoral. An audience who find premarital sex offensive, would find the scene shocking, since the idea of making a joke out of it is itself offensive. An audience who find it funny, who see it as a gag, rather than as a rather tasteless ploy, must find the *possibility* of premarital intercourse in a film quite attractive. Neale and Krutnik only posit audience activity in order to deny it any real space.

It will hardly be surprising that I see far more mileage in Kristine Karnick's broadly Bordwellian approach which analyses *The Awful Truth* (1937) to ask how we are cued to recognise comedy and to fold it into our developing understanding of the film.[11] She first examines the way comedy modifies what is otherwise potentially a deeply melodramatic plot, but then proceeds to ask not only what contribution the comedy makes to the narrative, but also how it can be that certain scenes remain funny upon repeat viewings – a point which really would cause difficulties for Neale and Krutnik's notion of 'refamiliarization'.

With this background of debates, it is interesting to see what can be learnt from close attention to a major earner such as *Sleepless in Seattle*, and to ask in what ways a Hollywood film – with its star combination, its tight narrative and its high cinematic values – develops the idea of 'romance' and 'comedy'.

Analytic Description

The film opens with soulful piano music, introducing a long shot up the slope of a cemetery to a man standing by a young boy, both looking at a grave. The man's voice, as if in close-up, says: 'Mommy got sick. It happened just like that. There was nothing anybody could do. There's no reason. If you start asking why, you go crazy.' The camera pulls away from them and sweeps slowly up to show the context: behind them, the skyscrapers of a large city mistily fill the background. Cut to a city street, then into a design office: the man, as yet unnamed, stares abstractedly out of the window, only just managing to respond to a colleague, then, when another (his boss) offers him the address of his shrink, the music ends and with a touch of bitterness he pulls out a wad of cards and starts to read out their offerings: ' "Loss of Spouse Support Group". "Chicago Broken Family Network". "Parents Without Partners", "Partners Without Parents". "Hug Yourself ... Hug a Friend ... Hug a Shrink". "Work Hard" ... Work is the only thing that will see you through this [For the first time, we see the man (Sam/Tom Hanks) in close-up – long pause] ... Never mind him, he's just a guy that's lost his wife.' He's thinking about making a real change, moving to a new city, 'anywhere where each time I go round a corner, I won't think of Maggie'. An unsignalled flashback/recall: he's with Maggie and his son Jonah, going to a ball-game ... Back in the office he declares his decision: he'll move to Seattle. The airport, and saying goodbye: a woman from the office telling him it *will* get better in a few months. Still hurting, Sam pushes aside her advice, saying, 'I know, I'll just grow a new heart ... Look, it doesn't happen twice'.

Cut out to continuation of titles, with Jimmy Durante singing 'As Time Goes By', the song providing an emotional continuation of the opening themes (e.g., 'Woman needs man, and man must have a mate – that no one can deny'). Slowly behind the titles we see an image of the world, with a map of the USA emerging from the darkness. The song ends as one shooting star leaps from behind the earth. Title: 'Baltimore: one year later.' City waterfront street: a young and handsome couple (Annie/Meg Ryan and Walter/Bill Pullman) entering separate cars on their way to a family event, with the man trying to remember all the complex relationships he is about to meet. The woman is coolly – yet perhaps distantly – confident in him. Cut to their arriving in their separate cars at a large suburban house, he still rehearsing the list. 'Am I what they had in mind?' 'Oh Walter, they're going to love you!' she says, and kisses him on the cheek. Inside, a family celebration, and Annie is called upon to announce her engagement to Walter. This has a slightly awkward 'Gee I am *sure* I am delighted to be doing this' feel to it as they all congratulate the couple. Walter is taken with a fit of allergic sneezing, and a strange, good-natured competition follows to prove which of the men has the worst allergies. Their good-naturedness takes on a kooky quality, as if they aren't really running their own lives – they are run by their allergies, their social graces, their relations (father answers the question to Annie about when and where they will get married). Everything is not quite authentic.

Cut to Annie with her mum trying on a beautiful inherited wedding dress, and Annie telling mum how she met the 'wonderful Walter'. Again, that edge of the expressed feelings being a touch inflated as though she has to work at them. They discuss whether it was 'destiny' that they met by having their almost identical sandwiches switched at the deli. Annie insists she doesn't believe in destiny, 'it wasn't a sign, it was just a coincidence'. Mum goes all nostalgic telling her story of having a 'coincidence' with Annie's dad, as the camera moves into a still, tight two-shot on their faces. Their exchanges achieve, by a mixture of words and looks, a 'meeting' of old and new. Mum 'knew' she would be with Dad for ever – 'it was magic'. Annie conveys doubt at this old idea. Mum 'knew' they would be good in the ('How do you call it today?') 'sack'. She quickly shushes her daughter's response that she and Walter have already … still, they share that that part of it is working 'like … clockwork'. They discuss Walter – what a 'formal' name, murmurs mum. When they look at Annie in the mirror, and go to hug their mutual congratulations, the beautiful dress rips. 'Oooh, it's a sign', exclaims Annie. 'You don't believe in signs', responds mum. Cut to couple leaving, Annie picking up on the formality of 'Walter' and asking him did he ever have another name? Annie urges him to go on, while she pops back in for something.

The car journey, to the jolly music of 'Sleigh bells ringing', revealed to be on Annie's car radio. She sings along, then switches station and picks Dr Marsha Fieldstone talking about 'wishes and dreams', to avoid 'Jingle Bells' sung backwards. Dr Fieldstone is hosting a phone in and Annie hears eight-year old Jonah phoning in with a wish for a new wife for his dad (Sam) who is so sad. The sound quality is not like that of a phone-in via car radio: it is close, almost intimate. We watch Annie running the gamut of a series of emotions; amusement at exchanges over Jonah's age and his still being up, sympathy over his dad, mock-horror at Dr Fieldstone asking for Jonah to get dad to the phone. Cut to Sam's apartment: a long slow scene has Sam mock-summoning his son ('I'm not going to handle this alone!') with shots of son absent behind stair well. Sam and Jonah gradually move together as father and son as, despite himself, he is drawn into talking about his feelings – which he doesn't find easy. Annie listens (the quality of the sound on her radio identical with that of the live action) and her face is seen in glowing close-up as she becomes affected, and begins to answer for Sam. At one point she almost jumps when she finds she and Sam have said the same words in response to a question. The scene ends as Annie jars back into the ordinary world, as she/we hear a lorry zoom past her, and Sam tells Jonah that this was 'fun … and helpful', with a sideways look.

Annie, stopping off for a drink, hears the two women at the counter discussing the radio phone-in. The sound of the renewed interview bridges us back into Annie in the car, with tears rolling down her face as she hears, and we also see, Sam telling what he hopes to do with his life: 'Well, I'm going to … get out of bed every morning, breathe in and out, and after a while I won't need to remind myself to get out of bed every morning. And then after a while I won't have to think about how I had it great and perfect for a while.' This very long scene ends with the completion of the emotions as Ray Charles ends a version of 'Somewhere Over the Rainbow' to shots of Annie arriving in her car, Sam sitting with Jonah asleep against him, and a night scene of boats floating in the harbour.

At Annie's magazine office, the phone jam that followed Sam's call is being talked about and the women get talking in silly fashion about how they get all weepy over anything affectionate, while the men look on, shaking their heads. 'You know what it is? There are a lot of desperate women out there looking for love. ... You know it's easier to get killed by terrorists than it is to get married over the age of forty.' Though they dispute the truth of this, the women agree that it *feels* true. Later, over lunch, Annie tries to pass off her interest in 'Sleepless in Seattle', but when she tries to recall Walter it goes hazy. New Year, and we see Walter and Annie celebrating midnight with plans to go to New York (Walter's allergy fears looking like a generalised caution about everything), while Sam is alone at home with a sleepy Jonah. As he lifts the child into bed and kisses him goodnight, a song enters over his 'aloneness': 'Lonely Nights' provides a commentary on his pacing the house and outside, looking at the fireworks going up – which are also on his television (he is surrounded by good feelings he can't take part in). Maggie enters, and he addresses her as someone in the present/ not present: 'I miss you so much it hurts...'. No reply from her still face – and she is gone when next the camera looks.

Next day: everyone else wants to talk to Sam about the phone-in. Woman client: 'It's so nice when a man can express his feelings.' This is a topic of mild mockery. Sam wants out of their talk around him. Cut to back home, and thousands of letters are arriving for 'Sleepless in Seattle'. Jonah starts reading the letters out, and assessing the women for Sam. Sam is having none of it – this isn't how you find potential partners. Everything has to be done by careful steps, starting with you seeing them, liking them, asking them out for just a drink, so you can back out if you don't like it. 'I wonder if it still works this way ...' 'It doesn't – they ask you', replies an all-knowing Jonah. Jonah talks knowingly about sex – don't they scratch your back like he's seen in the films on cable TV? As if in response, over the end of their teeth-cleaning session comes 'Making Whoopee'. Cut between Sam mock-wrestling Jonah and Annie and Walter going to bed, carefully cleaning themselves. Walter snores quietly, a figure of fun. New song, as Annie gets up: 'In the Wee Small Hours'. She turns on Dr Marsha Fieldstone (perfect sound again) replaying Sam's words. Focus in close and closer on Annie's face, reacting. The song ends on his words 'it was like ... magic'.

Cut between incidental scenes: Annie visiting her shrink who babbles jargon at her while she spirals round her fantasies about Sam, and takes comfort from his own admissions of pre-marital nerves; to Sam having a drink with a worldly male friend who instructs him in how the rules of romance have changed since Sam was last 'out there'. Arriving home, Sam finds Jonah with a girlfriend, Jessica, another knowing, confident child who puts him out of joint. [See below **Zooming In (1)** … for a close examination of this scene.] As he faces their self-confident togetherness, a song starts up: 'I'm Back in the Saddle Again', as he winds himself up to ring a possible date, Victoria, awkwardly – only to find that she is managing him totally from the other end of the phone (we hear only his end). The song wraps round his clumsiness, and bridges to the next scene – Cary Grant on a TV set (in *An Affair to Remember*), being watched by Annie and her editor/friend Becky. 'Those were the days when people *knew* how to be in love.' 'That's your problem – you don't want to be in love, you wanna be in love in a movie.' Annie is struggling to compose a letter to 'Sleepless in Seattle'. Her friend criticises her efforts, coolly reminding her of Walter. 'What if this man is my destiny?' Abandoning the letter, Annie joins Becky in watching the film, mouthing Grant's words in unison. 'Men never get this movie', says Becky. Cut to Sam's place, Jonah having a nightmare and calling for his mum. Sam, tender dad, asks what mum would have done to soothe him; she'd have sung 'Bye Bye Blackbird'. They discuss her tenderly, Jonah upset because he is 'starting to forget her'. Sam brings her back for Jonah with a story – she could peel a whole apple in one go, in one piece. As they hug, in the background, a blues rendition of 'Blackbird' works its way in, and segues to the next scene, 'matched' shots of Annie walking night streets alone sitting on a bench, and Sam doing the same on his deck.

Sound-bridge to the next scene, of Annie using journalistic ploys to worm for information on Sam and where he lives. Orchestral music accompanies, comments on each bit of her search, to the point where she recruits a detective agency to get photos. Cut to Sam nervously preparing to go out on his date, with cool Jonah and babysitter humouring him. Still working through Sam's mail, Jonah finds the letter from Annie (Becky posted it without saying), and senses that this letter is different. Sam will have none of it. It is not a sign that the woman agrees on who was the greatest baseball player – the real sign is where the letter comes from: the other side of America.

The date: Victoria is keen, she had thought he would never call. Disrupting this promising start, a call comes in – from Jonah, wanting them to go to New York to meet Annie. Sam is furious, but Jonah just ignores his complaints. But as Sam returns to the table, and makes a joke about Jonah, Victoria lets out a shrieking cackle of laughter – and we know she is inappropriate, impossible. From above, high angle shot of photos being taken of Sam. Next scenes, as Victoria comes to their place to cook them a meal, the camera focuses on Jonah's reaction as she laughs repeatedly: she is *wrong*. She fails all Jonah's tests, and he walks the edge of rude. He watches them, sees his dad being tempted despite her wrongness, and calls the radio programme. Annie gets called in bed by Becky, telling her to go listen to it. Annie hides in the cupboard to listen, as the camera cuts, in a farce-like scene between Jonah denouncing Victoria over the air, Annie hiding in a cupboard to listen, and the radio providing voice-over. 'Now he's kissing her on the lips – what am I going to do?' Jonah 'interrupts' this by screaming and claiming 'a black widow spider …' Farce-style matching shots of his/Annie's screams (as Walter opens the cupboard door on her),[12] then of both climbing stairs, then of Jonah/Annie lying sleepless in bed. Then of Jessica/Jonah plotting his going to New York, and Becky/Annie plotting her going to Seattle. She goes.

At the airport, Sam is saying goodbye to Victoria, then explaining his philosophy to a dismissive, bar-swinging Jonah that all he is doing is dating her. He is trying to understand what a 'woman' is, why they do things the way they do. He's 'trying her on for size', to see how she fits because nobody's perf … and through the Arrivals door walks Annie. Sam stops, silenced, and tries to follow, sensing that she is somehow special. Light piano theme adds its hint. Sam loses her. As they walk out, Jonah offers his philosophy in return, which he learnt from Jessica – basically, that they are fated to meet Annie. Long series of scenes, held together by a complete song ('We Go Together') in which Annie seeks out Sam's place, misses and follows him by car, watches him romping with Jonah. The song closes with her phoning Becky to tell her what happened. Next day at the beach, again trying to see him. As she is about to, an unknown woman arrives and Annie, standing stunned, is almost run over. She and Sam see each other, each stumble out a 'hello'. Cut back to Baltimore, and Becky slams on their favourite video: it's a sign, that's how it happened there. Now Annie finds a letter from 'Sleepless' which *we* recognise was written by Jonah, not Sam. We next see Sam with the woman from the beach – it's his sister, now with her husband. Sister also recognises the likeness to *Affair to Remember* – instantly crying over her own retelling of it (Jonah looks on, puzzled). The movie references intensify as Sam and friend recall crying over *The Dirty Dozen* – now it is Annie's turn to look bemused. Cut to the Empire State Building scene, being watched by Jessica who is also crying over it. She uses her mum's travel business to fix Jonah a flight to New York.

Long scenes of Annie and Walter meeting up in New York, Annie trying her hardest to be 'happy' with him. He is kind, loving – and yet … When he gives her his mother's diamond ring, it is exactly what she would have chosen for herself: 'You see what I mean? There are people who would like a relationship to be full of surprises, but I am not one of those people. No, siree.' Cut to Sam and Jonah having a set-to over Sam going off for a 'getting laid' night with Victoria. Jonah wants him to go to New York, to meet Annie. No way – didn't Jonah see *Fatal Attraction*? 'You wouldn't let me.' 'Well I saw it and it scared the shit out of me, it scared the shit out of every man in America.' When he goes to say goodbye to Jonah, he has vanished. Cut to Jessica having the information squeezed out of her: New York. Map motif – he's there, to lively jazz music, getting a taxi to Empire State, 'going to meet my new mother'. Jonah goes up to various women on the tower. Annie's not there. In a restaurant facing it, Annie keeps staring out the window, eventually owning up to Walter about her fantasies about 'Sleepless'. In between, Sam sitting anxiously on a plane, map motif, then running from the airport to grab a taxi to Empire State. As night comes on, Empire State turns on its lights – and Annie has to go. [See below **Zooming In (2)** … for a close examination of this scene.] The bouncy, lively music orchestrates all this, slowing to 'commentate' Jonah giving up (with a slow 'Blackbird'), dropping his bag and sitting down in the gathering dark. Long shot of Empire State takes us back to Annie, giving back the ring and – seeing the lights on the building – having to leave, to see if 'Sleepless' has come. Sam finds Jonah, they hug, reconcile. The building is emptying round them. Comedy of near-misses as they leave as Annie arrives. She has to persuade the guard to let her look: 'Cary Grant, right? … One of my wife's favourite movies.' Annie finds Jonah's bag left behind – and as they return to look for it, their eyes meet … and they can't take their eyes off each other as they say 'hello' shyly, take each others' hand, and the final song ('Make Someone Happy – and you will be happy too') commentates closing shots that move out from Empire State to resolve into a lit-up map of the USA from which rockets of celebration rise.

Preliminary Analysis

What patterns and processes are made visible by this? Some are obvious – although their obviousness, I will want to argue, is just what is interesting here. It is 'obvious' that this film deals in several bodies of ideas: the changed conditions of romance and love in the 1990s; of knowing what is allowed, or even is good practice if you want to date someone – especially if you are older; the tricky mixing of romance and sex today; 'fate' and 'destiny' and whether there is an ideal partner out there for each of us; films themselves – old and new – as sources of our ideas about love and sex, and how to deal with them. The film flag-waves each of these through characters' talk. To call these obvious, in fact, is to say something about this kind of movie: it not only wears its heart on its sleeve, but also its themes in its dialogue. Romantic comedies work by *being* 'obvious'. But that does not mean there are not non-obvious things to say as well – provided they don't claim to undo, or subvert, that obviousness. I would want to argue that such films are funny to the extent that they provide an immediately recognisable feel of belonging to a group-shared set of problems-that-ought-not-to-be-problems-but-surely-are. They couldn't be funny if they weren't recognised – the extra comes in considering what is tied up in that process of recognition. Let us then consider some of the processes at work in enabling these recognitions.

- *Narrative direction:* although it may seem too obvious to be worth saying, it can't be ignored that the narrative premise of the entire film is that a man doesn't know how to find a new love, whereas a woman does. Sam fumbles and stumbles his way back into the public arena, in search of what he lately acknowledges is a hole in his life. Annie, moved by something she doesn't understand, does the pursuing. Not only is this the premise behind the action in the film, it also provides the basis for a lot of the incidental dialogue. 'Things have changed out there.' Men and women, boys and girls do things differently now.

- *Role of the music:* two kinds of music occur. One kind is truly incidental, coming in to accentuate particular scenes, and given emotional pace and colouring. For instance, the scene where Jonah flies to New York begins with a lively jazz accompaniment, but as he loses hope, that disappears and is replaced by a high, 'lonely' orchestral theme which peters out. But the songs do more than this: they accompany scenes where virtually nothing else is happening. They become in a significant sense the 'action' of those scenes. What kind of action? Consider the scene where Sam's loneliness overwhelms him – or does it? All we *see* is him walking, and sitting, in his apartment. Though his face certainly does not look happy, neither is it overwhelmingly sad, withdrawn perhaps. But the accompanying song – plus our prior knowledge of his situation – in effect becomes a commentary on his inner life. It is not his thoughts, but it is a guide to them. This may stay at the level of, simply, generalised feelings of loss and loneliness. But in as much as the situation may prompt more specific feelings and thoughts of regret, despair, expectation or whatever, the film does not provide them. What it does is to cue viewers to provide them from their own repertoire of likely responses to a situation like that. Also important is that the songs are always completed, whereas the accompanying musical themes can be fragments, hints, gestures.

- *Cinematic qualities:* only in a very few ways, and at occasional moments, does this film use techniques of presentation which encourage a conscious noticing of them. A rare high-angled shot, ending a sequence of two-shots and shot/reverses; a fast tracking shot; the use of the repeated 'relief' map of America to symbolise journeys between west and east. The rarity of these suggests a movie in which *participation in the flow of events* is the prime quality. This is confirmed by the way the film gives us flashbacks into Sam's relations with Maggie, his dead wife. The first is entirely unsignalled, as if he had suddenly revisited a memory – and we have to go with him. The second is signalled, in that Sam's words to Maggie speak to her both as present and as dead. Her presence within the pro-filmic scene, though, is wholly unmarked. We experience her as Sam experiences her: present, yet gone.

- *Sound* is, of course, a cinematic quality, but in *Sleepless in Seattle* it is sufficiently important to be worth a separate discussion – in particular the role of the radio phone-in. This has a most important narrative function. It puts Jonah centre-stage in precipitating Sam's return to romancing; it causes Sam to unlock his emotions; it makes Annie begin her search; and it occasions the nationwide passion for speculating about 'Sleepless in Seattle'. Its narrative motivation is sustained and strengthened by its quality. Unlike any radio I've ever heard, it is wholly undistorted, equal and even at whatever place it is heard, without a trace of tinniness. It is in short an ideal radio sound, with even a trace of added intimacy. This is, I would suggest, *utopian* sound, giving us not just clarity, but hearing-as-insight. Though we move from Sam's phone, to Annie's car radio, to a radio in a diner, to a portable radio/ghetto blaster held close to the ear in Annie's cupboard, the sound quality never loses the close, confidential tone – it is perfect eavesdropping.

- *Stars:* Sam and Annie are of course played by two A-List Hollywood stars Tom Hanks and Meg Ryan, and Bill Pullman (Walter) is not far behind. But it isn't easy to see how the narrative utilises or is in any sense adjusted to their star personae. In a general way, it is true that Tom Hanks has gained the persona of the honest plain-speaker who finds the words don't come easy, and with depths of humanity – his performance in *Forrest Gump* (1994) epitomises this. Meg Ryan, already associated strongly with romantic comedy as a genre, combines quirk and feist via her highly mobile face. Yet there are a number of things about this film which indicate a going-beyond, a way in which star personae have become an inadequate explanation. Work on stars was particularly strong in the 1980s, and achieved much by, first, some excellent historical research on the role of stars within the studio system.[13] In addition, there was significant contemporary work on the rise of the hard-bodied males of the 1970–80s, whose cinematic presence was very directly a function of their look.[14] But as Barry King has shown, we cannot ignore the changes first introduced by the post-1949 restructuring of the political economy of Hollywood. Under this, no longer directly contracted to a single studio, most stars had to take more responsibility for the maintenance and updating of their personae. King shows how this affected the boundary between star-performance and acting.[15]

Investigations of stardom have declined recently, and therefore have not looked closely at new circumstances emerging in the 1990s. Given this book is not an investigation of stars *per se*, I can only point to the signs I see emergent in a film such as *Sleepless in Seattle*. Oversimplifying, I would suggest that for one tier of stars at the moment there is a signal difference from the classical period. Whereas in the 1930–40s stars had to be, as it were, 'naturally transcendent', today such stars have to achieve ordinary naturalness in order to demonstrate the stardom. We know of course that this is who is playing the two parts, but that is not allowed to shape directly what they have to do. What Tom/Sam and Meg/Annie manage in *Sleepless in Seattle* is an *arrival at inevitable ordinariness*. They appear to transcend stardom to become wholly natural – and in that very achievement they regain their very star quality. And this is self-consciously marked, in the internal discussions about 'what films used to be like'. Despite his friend's advice, Sam/Tom can't be like Cary Grant – he was a 'star'…

Yet for all this, they remain stars. An ingredient is added to the narrative by their associative meanings, which somehow deepens both the feelings and the comedy.

- *Juxtapositions:* the narrative bounces us, as audience, between the two worlds of Sam and Annie, as Sam struggles to re-enter the arena of public romancing, and as Annie starts her combined self-inquisition and search for 'Sleepless'. With the associated discourses about 'destiny', plus the generic components identifying this as a romantic comedy, there cannot be any doubt but that we are prepared, from the earliest moments of the film, for a narrative direction which will finally bring them together. This is made unarguable at the points where Annie finds herself saying things in sync with Sam's phone-in talk, and headily predictive when, first, Sam spots Annie unrequitedly at the airport, when Annie watches Sam and Jonah from afar, and when their eyes meet across the bonnet of a truck. What this means, of course, is that in important ways we, as audience, know things about the future of these characters which they as yet don't know about themselves. We see their destiny coming, and are watching to see how it will come.

- *Representations:* Sam and Annie belong to almost-perfect, white middle-class worlds: Sam, an architect, living in a delightful waterside apartment; Annie, a magazine journalist, inhabiting a world of plentiful dinner parties and beautiful clothes. Outside their romantic concerns, neither seems to have a care in the world. Their positions in society, in other words, provide merely a backdrop to their lovelorn lives, plus a set of constrained opportunities for romance. Both are very much placed in a present, aware of itself as a changed world in which the rules which used to govern romance have become problematic. How and why, are not their concerns. It is given that men now have to relearn how to relate to women – in ways that will allow the outcomes to be as 'natural' as, in theory, they used to be. And it is hardest for those at full maturity, because the rules have been changed from under them – note the repeated-though-disputed 'It's easier to get shot by a terrorist than for someone over 40 to get married'. This amusing statistical self-awareness clarifies the film as concerning the problems of a generation. Jonah, therefore, is different. Jonah takes his first steps towards a romance with Jessica with ease. They know – they've seen it all on cable TV. Jonah is a curious child/adult mixture: on the one hand with his teddy bear and nightmares over his lost mother, on the other hand discussing women scratching men's backs during sex.

  In one important respect, though, Jonah's position can't be understood without connecting him to the previous issue, about foreknowledge. Jonah is rude. Taken abstractly, his behaviour is appalling – he dismisses Victoria without thanking her for cooking his supper, he turns away from her and sticks his tongue out at the airport, he interferes mightily in his father's love life. Yet these things become much less rude, more the necessary reactions of someone who 'knows better', if we and he *know together* that Victoria just isn't the one. It's not just her hyena laugh – that is the clue. Jonah *knows*, irrespective of all knowledge gained through cable TV, that Annie is the one. He has an irrefutable child-wisdom.

A general issue is visible inside these points, which concerns our knowledge compared to that of the characters. I've argued already that we need to see several important ways in which our relation to the film has to be built on knowing things that the characters in the film can't. We know that Sam and Annie have to meet, they don't. We know that Victoria is wrong (as does Jonah, which partly excuses his otherwise rudeness), Sam doesn't. But our knowingness takes many forms beyond this.

Take the repeated debates about characteristic maleness and femaleness. In a series of conversations, characters discuss what makes men and women 'tick'. Under what conditions are they *funny*? A person who agreed wholly with, for example, the statement that all women want is a cute butt might nod in recognition, but would be unlikely to laugh – unless at Sam's not knowing this. A person who saw a woman crying simply at the act of recalling/retelling the story of *An Affair to Remember* as simply natural would probably not laugh – unless women crying *per se* is funny to them. But if, in each case, audiences respond via recognition of the kind of talk being referred to, but with a sense that this is an exaggerated, even parodic version of what they recognise, then they gain in absurdity and humour. So, men crying over the final scene in *The Dirty Dozen* looks like a counterpoint to women crying over 'chick movies'. But the characters don't behave as if they were doing this in order to get a laugh. That is how they are; they behave as if these things are real to them. The position from which these can be found funny is therefore again one of audience difference. But it isn't as simple as superiority. To find the 'cute butts' joke funny, it has to be recognised as something conceivable in our social environment. We are therefore not only laughing at the characters but at something in or around ourselves. With these kinds of issue in mind, let's closely examine two parts of the film.

Zooming In (1) …

The first covers two narratively important scenes in that they signal Sam's screwing up his courage to get 'out there' and look for a new romance. They immediately follow Annie going to her shrink and getting an odd kind of reassurance that perhaps she is just nervous of commitment to Walter. Our scenes are introduced by a false continuity shot, as Annie leaves through a door, and Sam plus builder-friend emerge through a different door.

They are discussing how men can know 'what women are looking for'. As the camera tracks them walking away down a street, friend tells Sam they want 'pecs and a cute butt'. Sam, bemused, asks: 'So how's my butt?', and bends down and lifts his jacket up so his friend can take a look. 'OK.' 'But is it "cute"?' 'I don't know', replies his friend. In a busy bar, over a beer and burger, the conversation carries on, shown in a series of two-shots and shot-and-reverses, and carries on as 'normal' conversation with hesitations and stumbles, interruptions, incomplete sentences and so on. How long is it since Sam was 'out there'. 'Jimmy Carter … 1978.' 'Things are a *little* different now', says his friend. He elaborates: 'First you have to be friends, you have to like each other, then you neck. This could go on for years. Then you have tests, and then you get to do it with a condom. The good news is, you split the cheque.' When Sam protests he couldn't do that, friend says he will be made Seattle Man of the Year when 'they' find out.

Sam's friend throws him a poser: 'Tiramisu'. 'What's Tiramisu?' 'You'll find out.' 'Great, some woman is going to want me to do it to her, and I'm not going to know what it is.' 'You'll love it.' 'This is going to be hard, much harder than I thought.' His friend suggests he try to date Victoria, the decorator on his current job, Sam protests, awkwardly: 'How would I do that?' He should ring her up and ask her over in 'his own suave way', telling him to 'think Cary Grant' when he asks her to come and discuss colour schemes or fabrics. What, says Sam, you think Grant asked a woman something like that in, say, *Gunga Din*? No, says friend, 'I don't think *Gunga Din* is a swatch kind of a movie.' Their conversation deteriorates as Sam goes into role, acting out Grant asking a women in his distinctive style to 'come over and look at my swatches'. As they debate these final points, the camera cuts to a high-angled shot down across the whole bar.

Cut to Sam arriving home in pouring rain, entering his house and going looking for Jonah who doesn't answer his greetings (the camera tracking him through his actions). Entering Jonah's room, he sees nothing and turns to go when he hears something. The camera reveals the back of a large pedestal chair, which swings round, being paddled by two pairs of feet. In the chair, huddled *very* close together are Jonah and a girl, clutching a portable record player. The camera cross-cuts the kids' cool control, and Sam's uncertainty and confusion. 'Dad, meet Jessica.' 'Hi', says Jessica, coolly. Sam: 'Well, hello, it's nice to meet you', with an element of forced formality. Jonah: 'Dad, did you know that if you play this backwards, it says "Paul is dead"?' Sam: 'Yeah, I knew that …' Jonah: 'How did you know that …?' Sam looks as though he doesn't know how he got to be talking about this, then Jonah: 'Dad. Could you shut the door?' Caught off guard, Sam says: 'Sure' and turns to do so. 'H and G', says Jessica. Sam: 'What?!' 'Hi and goodbye', she explains, and four junior feet paddle the chair back round again. Sam shuts the door – then quietly reopens it with that parental look which says, 'I want to know what you might be getting up to'. This ends the scene. It is followed by Sam going downstairs and plucking up the courage to ring Victoria for a drink.

These two scenes are short (under 4 minutes, the pair) but very dense. What is funny here? What *kind* of funny is it? And what does an audience have to agree to, to find it funny? On close examination, a lot of curious things start showing.

In the first scene:
- *the case of the cute butt*: Sam's friend tells him about 'cute butts', but this is a mystery peculiar to women. Asked to say if Sam's butt is cute, therefore, he simply can't answer – it is a logical impossibility for a man to

understand what women will find attractive. This is hidden in the 'depths' of women. But that is only funny if an audience at least recognises the idea of a completely separate but incommunicable language of desire in women;

- *the general manner of their talk*: its almost parodic version of ordinary talk – awkward, stumbling, at times almost incoherent – becomes itself a part of the very thing that they are talking about. Sam can hardly get his thoughts into speech, so his friend's more learned exposition counterpoints him. To find this funny, an audience must register the difference but also be aware that Sam's stumblingness is an index of his inner uncertainty;

- *surreal moments*: the vision of asking someone to 'come over and see my swatches' is funny if an audience has access to the repertoire of mock-invitations like 'come up and see my etchings', with which it half-rhymes;

- *strategic dating*: the way Sam's friend lays out romance like a battle-plan is funny on condition that an audience senses the tension between the supposed naturalness of attraction, romance and so on, and the military two-step with which it is depicted;

- *'Tiramisu'*: this exchange posits something which in all likelihood someone in Sam's position (middle-class job, with cultural associations) would surely have heard of, but hasn't. His ignorance, yet wish to know, makes his misunderstanding of it (as a possible sexual position?) gain in humour, the more of the following an audience is able to do: know more than Sam what 'Tiramisu' denotes … be willing to see this pudding as a sign of dating; be willing to play with its associations, and allow the possibility of some bizarre sexual practice called by this name … and recognise the dilemma that Sam's friend's game sets up for him – already nervous, he now sees a world of problems he hadn't even dreamed of until now…

In the second scene:
- *knowing what comes 'naturally' versus 'naturally' knowing*: Jonah and Jessica are just getting on with things, mixing a bit of cuddling up with truly amazing things like learning about obscure bits of pop-lore, whereas as we've just seen, Sam … Of course Sam knows about 'Paul is dead' and it is just a pointless fact to him, whereas to Jonah …;

- *reversal of roles*: Sam is not in control as he feels he ought to be. The 'child is father to the man'. He is more uneasy at his son's presumed romance than his son has been with the father's;

- *insiders and outsiders*: in his son's bedroom Sam is caught out using inappropriately formal language, and then caught out not even recognising a bit of kids' jive-talk ('H and G') – which marks him as not belonging to their world. They politely exclude him, with a swing of the chair.

There is a series of strands of humour-generation here, which only work if an audience registers knowledge gaps and conflicts. Sam needs knowledge that isn't really communicable *as* knowledge, but he will continue to behave inappropriately until he gets it. This suggests that the kinds of humour operating in *Sleepless in Seattle* have everything to do with shared knowledges and, peculiarly, shared ignorances. We might call these the 'conditions of humour'.

Zooming In (2) …

But *Sleepless in Seattle* is more than a comedy, it also has its moving moments, and its goal of rectifying Sam's grief, and lack – as we know, from very early on – must be fulfilled as we see the film establishing those narrative parallels, filmic juxtapositions, and the formless frustrations and desires in Annie. My second close-up, therefore, looks at one important moment of this kind: when Annie finally ends her relationship with Walter. The setting is New York: Jonah has arrived at the Empire State Building, but has failed to find Annie. Sam is on his way. The preceding shot showed Jonah slumping down unnoticed, in failure, on the observation platform, with a sad orchestral theme commenting.

This dies away to a single held high note as the camera shifts to a long shot of the building lit up at night. Cut to Walter, in mid-shot over Annie's shoulder, looking at her and saying: 'So … he could be on top of the Empire State Building right now.' Virtually all subsequent shots follow an over-the-shoulder shot-and-reverse pattern to whoever is speaking with, as the scene progresses, an increasing number of close-ups. Faint, almost inaudible, ambient murmuring comes from around them. Eye contact between them is maintained almost without a break. Annie: 'No … I guess he could be … no. [Cut in Walter looking back.] It's not him, Walter, it's me … I just can't do this.' Walter (slowly, direct to her eyes): 'Look … Annie. I love you. But let's leave that out of this. I don't want to be someone that you're settling for. I don't want to be someone that *anyone* settles for. [Cut in Annie looking back.] Marriage is hard enough without bringing such low expectations into it … isn't it?' Annie, still and direct: 'Walter, I don't deserve you.' Walter (dropping out of eye contact): 'Nah, I wouldn't say that … [gives slight, almost boyish laugh] … but okay!' (He re-establishes eye contact.) They laugh, quietly, together. Annie, in shot, gives him back his ring. Walter takes it, looks at it, puts it away. Annie: '… You OK?' Walter: '… Yeah.' Annie has a long intake of breath, and is now able to move a little and begin to look around. Her glance goes out of the window: 'Oh …' Walter: 'What?' Camera shoots Annie from the window, so she is virtually looking straight at it: 'Look …' Annie is held for one second, then reverse shot to show the Empire State Building, and a pink heart of lights coming on upon its side. On piano, a light romance theme enters: 'It's a sign.' Walter (back to over Annie's shoulder): 'Who needed a sign?' Annie: 'Walter – I have to go', her voice cracking with feeling on the last word. The next shot has her exiting the building to grab a taxi.

This scene, just on $1\frac{1}{2}$ minutes, has difficult things to achieve. Given there are no bad characters, only ones who are not quite 'right', Annie's break-up with him has to clear the way for her coming perfect romance with Sam. That's hard. Walter has to free her unequivocally, or she will be scarred with having hurt him. But he has also to do it in a way that doesn't accrue too much emotional credit to him, or *we* may see her as marked with some cruelty. Walter, therefore, cannot show hurt, he can only break eye contact at the vital moment, and return with self-deprecating and slightly bantering humour – and thus liberates her back into the sparky but mildly inauthentic humour that has marked their relationship. It is also important that she cares enough to ask, 'Are you OK?', and impossible that Walter should say anything other than 'Yeah' with a smiling sigh. He thus is confirmed as the ultimate good guy who is therefore also not the right guy.

Here, more than anywhere else in the film, we do *not* know better than the characters. We are absolute onlookers to their momentary vulnerable humanity. The scene has to have total emotional honesty, very largely achieved by that eye contact, but without exaggeration – and the absence of any extradiegetic music marks this as a plain scene between two others. Camerawork is consistent and held to dialogue until the completion of the break – whereupon a reversed point-of-view shot can take us back into the necessities of Annie's romance. The film returns to its 'knowing' relationship the moment Annie gasps: 'It's a sign', and immediately transcends it with Walter's, 'Who needed a sign?' Inner inevitability has wholly taken over.

The Implied Audience

What conclusions can we legitimately draw from all the above?

Imaginative universe: the most important thing about this is that in this film's universe, all normal laws and rules may continue provided they submit to the priority of the 'rule of romance'. So, it is inconceivable that any of the following should happen: that Annie should miss crucial bits of the radio broadcast by going through a tunnel or other signal dead-spot; that Victoria should not have some invalidating trait such as her laugh; that Annie's boss should not allow her to go to Seattle; that Jonah should be challenged when he flies to New York; that the guards at the Empire State Building should refuse Annie's entrance, even though it is after closing time. And so on. The world of romance is tidy precisely in order to allow focus on the tension of a possible relationship. The key element is that everyone who can, should acknowledge the centrality of the need for, but the problems of getting, 'love'. This is how and why the middle-class jobs, housing and social position of Sam and Annie function: they remove potential obstacles and complications. A world where you can afford to fly out at a moment's notice is a world better enabling romance. In such a world coincidence always equals a sign from heaven – we know this, it is the problem for the characters that they don't. In that sense therefore we have to be more committed to the 'utopia of love' than they do. Suppose, in the light of this, Sam *had* managed to follow Annie when he first saw her at the airport and felt that tug of attraction. Suppose she had seen, and they had spoken, and realised and so on. We would, of course, feel cheated, because a romantic comedy in which things do not go wrong before they go right, would not be 'proper'.

Implied audience: the implied audience is a very knowing audience. But if what I have said above holds true, it is not just a knowingness that might protect an audience from some 'ideology' of romance contained within the film. It is not that being 'knowing' makes overt something otherwise hidden. Rather, the significance of the film lies in its process, in the way of participating that is necessary if a viewer is to enjoy it. This marks a vital difference from the most usual ways of understanding such films, indeed films in general. In a 1992 essay, Steve Neale addressed then-contemporary romantic comedy.[16] Neale's argument is that structures are already implicitly ideological, in that, for example, 'ideology is always at stake both in the mode and context of the meeting and, among other things, in the gender, age, class, race and sexual orientation of the members of the couple' (p.288). And one rarely if ever gets romantic comedies in which the couple are lesbian, or gay, or Asian or black. Along with this criticism of the film for what it isn't, Neale argues that within such films the establishment of the 'right' person to marry almost always exemplifies and reinforces 'conventional morality'. This account is then tried out on some recent 1990s films. Neale has much that is interesting to say, in particular, pointing out the eccentricity and neuroticism in characters – but also the way these tend to be dropped by the end of the film – and the use of motifs of 'old-style' romance (in the songs, for instance). But as is so common, Neale then jumps from identifying these formal components to claiming a 'dominant ideological tendency: one which, in countering any "threat" of female independence, and in securing most of its female characters for traditional female roles, very much echoes the tendencies of the screwball films' (p.298). However lightly one reads this, Neale must believe that these films might find and harm 'vulnerable' audiences. So, to enjoy such films is to put oneself at risk of adopting conventionalised (Neale even uses the word 'infantilising') attitudes.

My account of *Sleepless in Seattle* points elsewhere. Romantic comedies are built on dilemmas whose resolution *within the film* may be tidy and utopian. But the conditions for finding it funny are that we recognise the dilemmas of *our* world being worked through. It may be oneself – although too much of oneself in a film inviting laughter could be very uncomfortable. It is surely recognising the 'typicality' of the situation – this could happen, people do have daft problems like this – that makes the film funny. But then, on this account, the *ending is the least important part of the film*. It provides, one might say, a guarantee that in our laughing no one will get hurt. Because we know very well that the film will end with the couple re-formed, we can afford to play the game of right and wrong decisions, true and false understandings, as we watch. If such a film were to cheat and end, say, with the couple failing to meet, or parting, or with the death of one character, the right to laugh would have been retrospectively withdrawn.

Proffered modality of viewing: I began by noting that Hollywood's romantic comedies have been relatively ignored, in favour of, for instance, the huge amount of attention given to *film noir* and its treatment of women. I now want to suggest that in part it is because of the difficulty of using notions of 'surface' and 'depth', of embedded meanings and 'subtexts' on a genre that wears its significances on its sleeves. Romantic comedies are *all surface*, and are only really approachable with an analytic method that can address surfaces as such. Perhaps this is why, among such work as there is on this kind of film, some of the most insightful commentary comes from Virginia Wexman who focuses essentially on acting and performance in these films.[17] I offer this as a suggestion as to where one might go next.

9
A Very Deep Impact

(*with Thomas Austin*)

In the summer of 1998, two very different Hollywood blockbusters shared a narrative premise: a huge meteor is hurtling towards earth, a select team is dispatched into space to intercept and blow up the rock, while the planet anxiously awaits the outcome of the mission. *Armageddon*, starring Bruce Willis, combines training scenes familiar from countless war films, a major star presence, and plenty of spectacular action sequences, including the destruction of New York and Paris. By contrast, *Deep Impact* plays down the astronauts' preparations and withholds most of its special effects until the climax, choosing to explore the familial relationships and emotional dilemmas of those on earth faced with impending doom. These reportedly 'female-oriented' concerns (accentuated, perhaps, by a female director, Mimi Leder) along with a narrative structure based on multiple storylines, marked the film as in some ways different from previous disaster movies, and led some reviewers to liken it to a television soap.[1]

In this chapter we aim to investigate how the audience is invited to participate in *Deep Impact*, via a series of interconnected cognitive and emotional processes. The film is clearly about finding out 'what really matters' in life, a realisation arrived at under the threat of imminent death. Its politics valorise family ties, and portray nation and planet as natural extensions of the family. But how exactly is the audience asked to invest in these values? How is the film's emotional resonance for its 'implied audience' produced? And how do the film's value system and its emotional affects interrelate?

It has been argued that the recent spate of disaster movies (*Dante's Peak* (1997), *Volcano* (1997), *Twister* (1996), as well as *Armageddon* and *Deep Impact*) engage with millennial fears about the end of the world, and thus participate in and cash in on the zeitgeist of the late 1990s.[2] It is not hard to read films about volcanoes and tidal waves as displacements of anxiety about climate change and global warming, even if technology – including nuclear weaponry represented as a morally neutral tool[3] – typically triumphs over a restive nature. However, the problem with this kind of analysis is that it is too easy, and too easily transfers analysts' own preoccupations onto a film, like over-loose clothing. It also ignores the industrial contexts of such films, which inevitably refract and complicate their relationship with contemporary society at any particular historical moment. Disaster films, like any other cycle, are shaped by the societies and cultures in which they are produced and consumed,[4] but this connection is mediated by industrial procedures. As Rick Altman has argued, the production of popular film is a process of both imitation and innovation, shaped in part by producers assaying previous successes and recombining their components in new exploitable forms.[5]

Both *Deep Impact* and *Armageddon* return to a highly successful genre which has served film-makers over the twentieth century.[6] In the process, they also incorporate successful elements from a range of media products. In the case of *Armageddon*, Bruce Willis' star persona, familiar from action hits such as the *Die Hard* franchise (1988 onwards), is revitalised by its location in a new diegetic frame which offers not just a large-scale natural disaster but also war film and space adventure components.[7] Similarly, seen from a producer's perspective, *Deep Impact* picks up on a trend in action films of the 1980s and 1990s which have gradually been reoriented towards female audiences by the incorporation of women protagonists and new emphases on emotional relationships.[8] The film was a box office success, earning more than $300 million against a budget of $75 million – a fact of some importance to DreamWorks, Spielberg's new studio which up to this point had not had an unqualified hit. What can we conclude from this success? We approach this by asking how audiences are asked to mobilise and activate a range of (often genre-specific) assumptions, competences and allegiances at particular moments in the film.

Analytic Description

A starry night sky, with light orchestral overlay, rising uneasily as the title **DEEP IMPACT** appears alone on the screen. The camera pans down across the Milky Way, to reveal (heard just in advance) a crowd of students sky-watching with telescopes: 'Richmond, Virginia'. Among the crowd, a boy and girl seen in close-up mix making serious notes on the constellations they are seeing, and discussing her possible new boyfriend. Teacher interrupts to check are they working, or something else? He tests them, asking them to name a series of stars. The boy confidently names the first two, then hesitates over the third – he's not sure it *is* a star … The teacher is also unsure, and says casually to take a picture of it to send to the Observatory. The girl quietly (affectionately?) teases that she knows, he doesn't. From a further shot of their sky, cut in opera music, then pan down to reveal the massive structures of 'Adrian Peak Observatory, Tucson Arizona'. An astronomer is alone at work, walking round and singing in time. He sits to look at photos sent to him, in particular one with the boy's name, 'Leo Biederman' with the unidentified bright point. Eating pizza with one hand, he types in the co-ordinates and aligns the huge telescope. On his computer screen, a bright spot with a halo comes into focus: 'Well hello there, little fella – do I know you? … Where are you going in such a hurry?' Contentedly he calls up a calculation of speed and trajectory, the results scroll – and he drops his pizza in shock, and starts typing furiously. In extreme close-up we see his face, then his saving the results onto a disk and writing his name (Wolf) and the boy's on it. Running to his car he heads off along a darkened road, distractedly trying to call ahead. His phone won't work. Coming the other way we see a lorry, its driver also distracted by dropping his cigarette. Inevitably they crash, and the astronomer's jeep explodes into ripping flames. Fade to black.

'Washington, DC. One year later.' A news broadcast, then backing out onto a news team's meeting. News just received that Secretary Rittenhouse is resigning 'because his wife is sick …'. They don't believe it. They run round a series of political reasons why he should be unpopular, only pausing when a figure we've hardly seen – a young woman – contributes that the wife isn't sick, she's become a drunk after her husband had a series of affairs. The camera focuses in on her. Jenny is a junior researcher, eyeing promotion to anchorwoman. Her boss (Beth) coolly blocks her, sends her out to do more research on Rittenhouse. As the meeting breaks up, Beth lectures her on the realities of the promotion process – then breaks off to pick up her small daughter. End of conversation. Bridge in the sound of a new conversation, then cut to an older woman drinking repeated cocktails and talking with near-bitterness (to Jenny, we now see) about a wedding happening right then. 'Jason Lerner' is taking a new young wife. We gradually fill in the details: it is Jenny's father, this woman's former husband. Telling her mother she loves her, Jenny has to leave. Cut to Jenny walking in front of the White House with a smart woman who is telling her about being Rittenhouse's secretary, about his private calls and one woman in particular. Bitterly she says that because he 'couldn't keep his hands off women', she's lost her job. The name of the woman? 'Ellie … I think the President knows about it too.' New scene: a car and van arriving at a quayside: Jenny and cameraman looking for someone. As they try to pump a small girl, and take note of the piles of provisions ready for a long trip, a man appears: Rittenhouse, insisting his wife is sick, unwilling to be interviewed. Jenny drops in 'Ellie', and he goes very still. Jenny plays the professional reporter, bluffs about the amount they know and waits for an answer. Turning, he mock-congratulates her on having 'the greatest story in history'. 'Look – I know you're just a reporter, but you used to be a person ... right? ... I wanted to be with my family – can you understand that?' and he leaves a coolly frustrated Jenny standing there.

Cut to Jenny, seen first in long shot, driving over a bridge talking ideas into a dictaphone. It doesn't make sense to her, to think his resignation over an affair is the 'biggest story in history – what an ego!' As she makes up ever-more wild theories, we are looking at her face on, and see a car coming up behind her. It rams her. Jenny startles, terrified as she sees what is happening. Three big black cars force her off the road into an incomplete section of freeway. FBI. She is taken away under escort to a basement. High nervous strings overlay as she begins to sense she has stumbled on something even bigger than her theories. Cut to suited men's legs approaching, pan up to reveal an authoritative black man (actor: Morgan Freeman). Introducing himself as 'Tom Beck', he asks her about her information. Stunned, she hesitates ... 'Mr President, I'm not interested in using "Ellie" to further my career.' 'What do you know about this "Ellie"?' he asks. Increasingly confused and uncertain, Jenny covers her ignorance by hinting at things. The President confuses her further by saying that they would have had to make an announcement when the budget was published, since too much money has been spent to be hidden. He and an associate discuss what to do about her, as Jenny looks round – and sees packs of provisions as at Rittenhouse's. The scene ends as he makes a bargain with her, two days silence and she gets centre of the second row at the press conference – a real boost for her career, he believes. Faced down when she tries to push for more, she *just* manages to beg first question, and the President turns and leaves her without direct answer. [See below, **Zooming In (1)** ..., for a detailed examination of this scene.]

At the office, close-up of her typing in 'E.L.E.' (moody orchestral music over). She looks tired and concerned. A series of 'hits' take her through palaeontology, to 'Extinction of Life Event', to a picture of an asteroid, the camera cutting faster and into extreme close-up as the music climaxes, then cuts dead as she jumps at Beth speaking behind her. Discombobulated, she only just keeps her end of the conversation until Beth leaves. Cut from Jenny's bewilderment to a hotel lobby (via small sound-bridge of live piano music), Jenny being greeted by an older man – her father – with his new bride Chloe. A scene full of awkwardness. They offer Jenny a present but she can hardly bring herself to open it. When her father proposes a toast, she downs her Martini in one, and then bursts into near-hysterical laughter when Chloe says that hating her won't help because 'life goes on'. They don't, can't understand. Jenny tells her father he ought to get back with her mother because she is lonely, then walks away, all sides hurting.

Cut via a brief shot of a melee of reporters outside the White House, to Jenny arriving for the press conference, and shown to her favoured 'Reserved' seat, to Beth's confused annoyance. 'Ladies and Gentlemen, the President of the United States.' He enters. In a controlled, yet quite informal manner he tells the story – which he has just told to the heads of all other governments in the world – of the discovery, by 'two astronomers, Marcus Wolf and Leo Biederman' (cut in Leo at home with his family, jerking upright to the TV) of a comet with 'well, a remote possibility' of a collision with the earth. The comet is the size of Mount Everest. Cut in shots of journalists' – including Jenny's – reactions; the newsroom going into overdrive, the President's speech continuing over loudspeaker; graphics of astronomical movements. The President announces Project Messiah, a spaceship constructed jointly with the Russians to stop the comet. Cue in live shot of the astronauts waiting to be introduced. President makes a point of speaking to 'Captain Tanner' (known as 'Fish'), the oldest of the astronauts and last man to walk on the moon. 'God speed to you all – we're counting on you.' More newsroom mayhem, then back to hearing the President making firm, humane announcements that life will go on, all prices and wages frozen, 'what a bottle of water costs you today, it will cost you tomorrow'.

Jenny gets to ask first question and almost fluffs it. Given leeway, she asks a second, and a third – and only the third is the one she wanted to dare to ask: given Rittenhouse's resignation, doesn't this mean that not everyone believes we can survive the impact? The question bites, but the President pauses then gives a declaration, ending: 'I can promise you this – life will go on. We will prevail.' While this has gone on, we have seen the reactions to her getting to ask the questions from her office, her mother, her father and Chloe; and a reminder of Leo watching. The press conference ends in a melee of questions. At the Biedermans' house, neighbours and friends are already gathering to talk to the now-famous Leo (whom the President thought was killed in the car crash). Cut to Leo addressing his school about the events, with the girl, Sarah, watching admiringly. Questions to him: one of his friends asks how he feels now he will 'get to have more sex than anyone else in the school – that's the whole point to being famous, isn't it?' Cheers round the school, and Sarah looking abashed/excited.

Cut to a casual party/barbecue for the astronauts and their families, discussing their futures (one getting married, one giving 'instructions' to the unborn baby in his wife's stomach, Tanner advising his sons on their futures). Tanner is weighing up the crew. Then, in reverse shot, we see him overhearing the rest of the crew discussing whether he is too old to go, or is there just for public relations. He joins their conversation, looking for honesty and the possibility of acceptance of what he can contribute. A friendly but awkward stand-off results.

'Messiah Mission – Day One.' Scenes at flight control. A perfect takeoff, docking and launch to the comet are shown in dramatic close-ups, accompanied by uplifting music and an explaining TV news commentary. Clean, smart technology smoothly moving into action, seen from good angles. Inside their cabin, the crew experience G-force, uncomplaining. Cut to '5 Months Later', the newsroom preparing for 'the most important story of our lives – let's not muck it up'. Jenny gets to anchor it, Beth looking put out. In flight, weightless crew inspect the comet as they rendezvous. Arming the missiles (smart, beautiful technologies), to powerful orchestral accompaniment, as we 'participate' in their descent. Mix in Jenny's very professional news commentary, seen live then as watched by her father, then by the Biederman family with Sarah whose hand Leo takes as the difficult descent begins. Visual contact with earth is lost. With wise words about limits of knowledge, Tanner takes command and goes to manual. For a long scene, we are mainly with the mission team, in an action sequence but mixed with plenty of facial reaction shots. Occasional intercuts bring explanatory or predictive fragments of news broadcast. Through hurtling debris, they make it to the fractured surface. Four crew leave the ship to plant the bombs, but one of their drills jams and in freeing it they run out of time (we are constantly reminded via instrumentation of the approach of the horizon when the sun will melt the gases on the comet's surface). Fish risks flying the landing craft nearer them, though it runs them dangerously short of fuel. As the sun strikes, one of the crew, Monash, is blinded, and another, Portenza, blown off the comet by one of the spectacular blasts of gas. They just make it off, with Fish having to calm one distraught crew member who wants them to go back for Portenza. Camerawork is shaky, visuals breaking up, all shot at awkward angles and incomplete, added to at crucial moments by subjective in-helmet shots and sounds. The cut back to earth is a harsh return to still silence. Jenny reports on the mission and awaits its outcome. From here on, there is a period of cutting back and forth between Messiah, studio and various listeners. The bombs explode, but only fracture the comet in two, and earth loses touch with Messiah.

The President makes a second speech, with the bad news, plus the backup plans for a Titan missile strike. This speech is even more human than his first. Reaction shots as he says: 'Now we have to make some decisions together. What do we do? You have a choice … *we* have a choice.' And he spells out the 'ark' programme whereby a million people – and animals, seeds, etc. – can be saved in underground caves for two years. His speech ends powerfully: 'I wish … No, wishing is wrong. … It's the wrong word right now, that's not what I mean. What I mean is, I believe in God … I know a lot of you don't, but I still want to offer a prayer … for our survival, mine included. Because I believe that God, whomever you hold that to be, hears all our prayers, even if sometimes the answer is no. So may the Lord bless you, may the Lord keep you …' This is done in a wholly unaffected, non-sermonic way, as if humanity has here reached its apex. Details of the lottery and evacuation plans – Jenny showing her reactions to having to read out that no one over 50 (i.e. her parents) will be selected. The Biedermans are selected, but Sarah's family isn't. On board Messiah, they decide to try for home, and hope to re-establish communications at close range.

'Time to Impact: 4 Weeks, 2 Days': Jenny and her mother discuss how they feel about what's coming. Jenny feels it's unfair that she has been picked. Leo goes to see Sarah, to ask her to marry him so that she and – using his influence as 'Biederman' – her family can be saved. There follows a collage of scenes of a contemplative President, news reports of rioting, Leo and Sarah's marriage ceremony, and Jenny's mother preparing herself to die. [See below, **Zooming In (2)** …, for a detailed examination of this scene.]

Cut to ominous comet shot, then the Messiah. Fish, finding the blinded Monash awaking, talks with him about reading, and life, and what they had wanted to be, and – with rich laughter between them – Fish begins to read *Moby Dick* to him.

The evacuation. It's gone wrong, and Sarah's family don't get to go, so – desperate but helpless – Leo and Sarah get separated. Jenny learns about her mother's death and – broken-spirited – goes silently to collect the items from her body. All these scenes are overlaid with quiet, thoughtful music. To silence, then just the sound of rain and traffic, we see Jenny sitting in the pouring rain as her father (whom Chloe has left) finds her and tries to 'reach' her. She refuses and walks away: 'How does it feel? I feel like an orphan.'

'Five Days to Impact': the ark, thousands arriving to take their places, thousands more being shut out, pleading. Leo can't go in – he has to go back for Sarah. Diegetic sounds only until the moment of parting from his parents, then an orchestral accompaniment over this and subsequent scenes. Jenny's father comes to see her at the studio. He brings her photos to prove she is not an orphan: photos of her childhood and happiness at the beach. Jenny denies any memory of them, but he leaves them with her, tears forming in her eyes. Leo, returning on the back of a lorry, is accompanied by broadcast reports of the Titans heading for the comet. Back to Jenny reporting: 'one more time we have to wait'. Cut to the President's fingers tapping tensely as he waits to announce that this second attempt has failed. Now he is no longer formal at all – he tells raw truths to everyone about the coming devastation. The sun sets behind the earth.

'Time to Impact: Ten Hours.' On Messiah, Fish realises there is one last chance to blow up the main comet, if they go with it. We realise this is suicidal before other members of the crew. Says Andy, wryly: 'Look on the bright side – we'll all have High Schools named after us.' The decision made, stirring music accompanies and links all scenes which use action-style (fast-moving, point-of-view, ever-active) camerawork, with fast editing. The crew arm the remaining missiles. Intercut the studio, and Jenny deciding to give up her place on the escape helicopter to Beth and her child, with Leo arriving back and not finding Sarah and taking her father's prize motorbike to chase after them. [See below, **Zooming In (3)** ..., for a detailed examination of this scene.] Leo finds Sarah and her parents make her leave them, taking her baby sister on the motorbike. Stillness begins to return as Sarah's parents ready themselves to face coming death, and Jenny joins her father on the beach where the photographs were taken. They are reconciled and recall her childhood in peace. He looks up – and the camera locks onto the fragment of the comet coming down. Its strike becomes a vast, god-like effect, raising a tsunami that strikes the pair on the beach, then overwhelms all the icons of New York before it roars inland. In the traffic queue, most run futilely, but Sarah's parents don't need to. Leo and Sarah race ahead of the wave.

Cut to space, and the crew have time to say longing farewells to their families. 'We'll never be closer to home than we are right now', says Fish, as they approach the comet. A last desperate rush brings Monash's wife and child to the screen and the crew help him to conceal his blindness as he says his emotional farewell. Countdown ... Explosion. On earth, scrambling to the top of a hill above the flood waters, Leo and Sarah turn to see the sky filled with the fireworks of the destroyed comet.

Over a high shot of them the President's voice begins, telling of the scale of the disaster. 'But the waters receded. Cities fall, but they are rebuilt. And heroes die, but they are remembered. We honour them with every brick we lay, and every field we sow.' As the speech progresses, a slow dissolve takes us to a makeshift podium as he speaks of a new beginning: 'In every child we comfort and then teach to rejoice at what we have been re-given. Our planet. Our home.' A final shot of the crowd listening and responding, and the end.

Preliminary Analysis

What patterns and processes does this bring into view, and what preliminary questions do these provoke? The first thing – both obvious yet necessary – is the inevitability of the coming disaster. The narrative's primary event – the comet's collision with earth – was rendered unsurprising by publicity materials in circulation around the film. These both positioned *Deep Impact* within the disaster genre in general, and promised the prospective audience just such an event, along with the possibility of survival. For instance, the poster tag line ran: 'Oceans rise. Cities fall. Hope survives.' It is hard to conceive an audience attending the cinema to see *Deep Impact* not knowing at all that the film will deal with a comet's threat. More than that, they must know that in some way, at some point, there will be an impact. A disaster movie with no disaster is a no-no. But that doesn't do away with the point of the film. *Deep Impact* has to set in motion a *way of attending* that will introduce tension, uncertainty, caring, and some sense of a morality. Any disaster movie has to do this, but *Deep Impact* does it in a most striking way, as we can see in the following close-up.

Zooming In (1) …

The sequence immediately follows Jenny's ambiguous interview with Rittenhouse. It amplifies and extends that scene's play with anxieties about American government, but also starts a process of allaying such fears. Audience knowledges and expectations are recognised, cued, but then contradicted.

As Jenny drives away from Rittenhouse's boat, the rhetoric of the conspiracy thriller is suddenly deployed. Her car is forced off the road by black saloons driven by men in dark suits. Threatening synthesiser music on the soundtrack and canted framing add to the feeling of danger. The camera tracks through a gloomy, underlit room and spies from behind a pillar and the backs of the FBI men as Jenny is frog-marched up to their boss. However, having cued its audience to mobilise assumptions about a government cover-up, the film begins to complicate these inferences, and finally to soothe suspicions. How is this effected? First, by the introduction of Morgan Freeman as President Beck, the man to whom the FBI are answerable. Freeman's star persona is of a wise, care-worn but unimpeachably reasonable and humane authority figure.[9] *Deep Impact* thus stages a collision between this persona – familiar to some audiences – and the generic codings of the conspiracy thriller. The audience who can recognise both, is invited to weigh each against the other – to ask: has Freeman been cast against type as a villain? If not, how will his familiar persona be allowed to sit comfortably in such a narrative setting? One way to resolve the question is to radically revise previous inferences about a conspiracy, jettisoning this generically identifiable viewing strategy for one which takes Freeman's star persona as a guide. Audiences familiar with the persona may begin to entertain the idea that this will override their knowledge so far (a knowledge which, due to hitherto restricted narration, we have been dependent upon Jenny to find out for us). Freeman's entrance into the room thus opens up – for some star-aware viewers – a temporary knowledge gap over Jenny who still fears the worst – a way to bypass reliance upon her as a source of information. For viewers who remain uncertain (the most likely position, even if one has identified a tension between star and his present generic setting), dialogue gradually clarifies the situation, in this scene and the subsequent one.

Freeman as President Beck bargains with Jenny, promising to hold a press conference in 48 hours on the (still mysterious) subject of E.L.E., and to grant her the first question, if she sits on the story until then. The subsequent press conference assures Jenny and the audience of the President's good intentions. The institutions of state are legitimated, and its methods justified – the gagging of the media is a reasonable tactic to avoid widespread panic while measures are put into place to counter the threat.[10] The casting of Freeman as the President is crucial to this validation of government as trustworthy. It effectively advises the audience that cynicism about politics will not be an appropriate response to this narrative. Contrary to the speculation of journalists and Rittenhouse's secretary, Washington is not 'sick' after all. Unlike the reporters played by Warren Beatty in *The Parallax View* (1974) or Robert Redford and Dustin Hoffman in *All the President's Men* (1976), Jenny discovers neither private sector nor state-endorsed abuses of power.

Thus the film calls for audiences to draw upon their knowledges of the stylistic conventions of the conspiracy thriller and of Freeman's star persona, and to evaluate the relative strength of each at this particular moment. To grasp with ease what is going on in the scene a familiarity with both is required. But because the process of revelation to us (and to Jenny) is a gradual one, the film can accommodate a range of levels of knowledge. Imagine a viewer lacking the filmic experience to identify either the thriller conventions hinting at state corruption, or Freeman's subsequent recuperation of the idea of good government. How would s/he manage this episode? First, s/he will have to make the move of identifying the agents who ram Jenny's car, and threaten her, as government agents – not a given, by any means. Then at some point s/he will have to manage the transition to seeing

Freeman as a caring, careful man – otherwise his first television speech will make no sense. In that case, Freeman/Beck (with the emphasis on the latter, since Freeman's star persona is not operating for such a viewer) must be understood to behave as he does *because he is a good man*. From such generic unpreparedness would come a *doubling* of the emotional intensity of Freeman's symbolic capacity: as a good man, as an increasingly tortured man, and as a black President carrying the feelings of *all* America, *all* humanity.

Freeman is revealed as the nation's *pater familias*. His approachability, decency and humanity are signalled by the increasing informality of his speech and of his clothing in televised broadcasts to the nation. As the news gets bleaker, so his humanity (implicitly linking him with the watching multitudes) is emphasised over the trappings of state power. His gravitas and moral rectitude are even reinforced by the biblical nomenclature of his emergency procedures: a 'Messiah' spaceship sent to intercept the asteroid; an ark from which the chosen few will emerge to rebuild civilisation; the intimation of America's Edenic foundation myth in the presidential speech which closes the film. The last is an emphatic assertion of continuity: a restatement of manifest destiny, a celebration of a new world issued from a new Capitol, a recognition of sacrifice and a thanksgiving for 'what we have been re-given. Our planet. Our home.' Yet even his religiosity is inclusive, as in his final speech before impact he declares his own belief in God but acknowledges and includes all those who don't share that belief. And the star's blackness confirms that in *this* filmic future, all are welcomed. 'Race' has become a redundant category, via this embodiment of caring humanity.

But this is at the level of overt ideology. How does the film try to get us to care about it all? We suggest that the film does so by showing us characters *making mistakes* and learning to correct them – just in time to die, having recovered their 'full humanity'. Consider the progress through the film of three characters:

1 *Leo Biederman:* the meteor is discovered by 14-year-old schoolboy astronomer Leo Biederman (Elijah Wood). Leo's part in the subsequent narrative is to be part of an initially 'typical' middle-class American family, which functions as representative of the national (and global) population – as members of a television audience horrified by the scale of the impending disaster. But the family becomes atypical when Leo and thus his parents are selected for the Missouri Caves sanctuary. Leo is forced to choose: family or girlfriend? His initial choice of family is not wrong, indeed proves him virtuous. But it isn't enough, and Leo ultimately changes his mind and opts for the ad hoc constitution of a new family

with his sweetheart Sarah and her baby sister, staging his own rescue mission by leading them to high land out of reach of the tidal wave.

2   *Captain 'Fish' Tanner:* the mission is led by veteran astronaut 'Fish' (Robert Duvall) who, like President Beck, is a substitute father figure. Fish is positioned as a 'rustic' specialist rather than a bureaucratic one. He equates himself with Mark Twain's riverboat pilot, and is a successor to the two heroes in *The Towering Inferno* (Paul Newman and Steve McQueen) who combine expert knowledge with practical skills.[11] Fish is initially doubted by his younger crew, who think he is only there for the sake of public appearances. But they have to learn differently. Fish proves his worth in piloting the Messiah and finally by leading them in their self-sacrifice. In a reworking of the 1986 Challenger disaster as a triumphant, worthwhile and *premeditated* act, the Messiah crew has time before the end for a series of farewells transmitted to loved ones back on earth. They cannot be allowed to die unblessed.

3   *Jenny Lerner:* Jenny Lerner (Tea Leoni) appears for a while to be the audience's surrogate, trying to solve the narrative enigma: what is going on? Jenny also relays vital narrative information to the diegetic television audience and, of course, to the film's spectators, via her job as a reporter and later as anchor at the heart of the benign televisual network which spans and unites the nation.[12] But Jenny also commutes between public and private spheres, and plays a crucial function in resolving a conflict between domestic obligations and public duties. And she herself has to learn (rediscover) the importance of her emotional bond with her father before the final impact. How is this brought about, and how are we, in our audience-role, led to agree?

The moral education of characters is developed and amplified across intercut narrative strands. Shifts from one scene to another in a single storyline also develop the structural parallels between family and nation/planet. What is particularly interesting, to us, is how often the links between these strands are effected via a TV link: Jenny announcing a development to viewers watching her, for instance. What is the function of this manoeuvre?

Zooming In (2) …

Consider one short montage sequence which comes almost two thirds of the way through the film. The first strike has failed, and the fallback is being readied. The lottery is in process, and Jenny has just met with her mother who has declared that she is not afraid to die if she knows Jenny will live. Leo arrives by bike at Sarah's house – his plan: to marry her and thus save her and her family. He finds her sitting alone under an old tree, and offers her the ring he's bought. The $2\frac{1}{2}$ minute scene that follows is constructed almost entirely through smooth camera movements and slow dissolves, in warm browns highlighted by other complementary colours:

'This is the only chance to survive', says Leo as they look long at each other. A light, thoughtful piano theme begins which gains sonorous texture as strings join it. Cut to slow rising shot of the President standing behind his desk gazing out of his window, then to side-on close-up of him standing very still and 'inward'. Over the end of this shot, introduce distant voice of Jenny reporting what's happening 'All across the country ...', and cut in shots of burning buildings as her commentary continues and what's seen becomes a TV screen in a long almost-empty apartment revealed by a slowly swinging camera. Slow dissolve to a close-up of a tray of makeup and brushes, and moving across a woman's hand picking up a brush. Cut to extreme close-up of Jenny's mother's mouth, and the brush beginning to apply makeup. Slow dissolve to studio shot of Jenny facing away from us reporting on riots in Moscow, seen on a large screen behind her. Fade out her voice, slowly dissolve in the President sitting, resting head in hand. Camera moves round him, first in midshot, then in close-up as he moves minimally. Cut to a hand moving, lifting out a beautiful grey gown. Slow dissolve to hands – Leo's and Sarah's – clasping as we hear the voice of a man speaking the ritual words: 'When I was a child, I thought as a child. But when I became a man, I gave up childish things.' As he speaks, the camera moves up from their hands to Leo's face, then gently across to Sarah's who turns to look at her father as the camera glides to him. Slow dissolve to extreme close-up of Jenny's mother carefully putting on eye-liner, then lifting a pendant to her neck. Slow dissolve to man (shown) asking: '... you take this woman to be your wife?' Dissolve to Sarah's mother, the camera already moving down her face to reveal her baby daughter, looking around and up. Slow dissolve to Jenny's mother lifting up black and white photos of a man (Jenny's father) with little girl on his shoulders on a beach. Slow dissolve to corona shot of Sarah looking at, then moving across to kiss, Leo. Slow dissolve to long shot, then midshot of Jenny's mother lying quietly back, dressed in the grey gown, in a chair – as the orchestral theme resolves and returns to the quiet piano with which it had begun.

This is a mood piece. Although there are fragments of dialogue, they are framed and subordinate to the non-narrative continuities established by music, camerawork, dissolves and colour-continuities. It is elegiac: a combination of thoughtful, sad and hopeful. The riot scenes, though shown, are an anonymous backdrop to a series of transitions and completions: Jenny, continuing her job, and present in the rooms of the world; her mother (we presume, and will shortly have confirmed) readying herself to die; Leo and Sarah marrying – but for more than survival's sake; the President, carrying the weight of the world. What interests us is how this elegiac tone is made possible. Here is a disaster movie where disaster is accepted and in some way *proves our fullest humanity*. We have to 'read' the sadness but also the rightness of each action. It is not possible that Sarah should be marrying just for a 'green card' to the ark – such a cynical reading would undo the smooth integration of the parts. Equally, we haven't a single clue as to what the President is thinking, but there is no doubt but that we 'read' him as carrying the burden of the impending disaster, fully, humanly … And Jenny's mother's suicide – for that is what it is – is not only not morally damnable, it is an *achievement*. She readies herself, and goes out in the best way imaginable. It is hard to see how we wouldn't approve, if we have participated in the logic of this film. And because of the linkages via the TV, all the fragments belong together.

But *Jenny* is not yet 'saved' …

In an early scene, a structuring opposition between work and family is expressed by Rittenhouse to the ambitious Jenny: 'I know you're just a reporter, but you used to be a person. I wanted to be with my family – can you understand that?' Jenny's initial misreading of Rittenhouse's resignation, which the audience at first has little reason to challenge, draws on a standard model of moral misdemeanour familiar from both politics and previous movies.[13] But Jenny's reading is revealed as an overly cynical misinterpretation which inverts the politician's honourable motives: putting his family first. Jenny has to learn better – and we watch her learn. What she learns is the value of *home*. As the meteor threatens people and planet, so something unnamed threatens family and home. Indeed the word 'home' comes to summarise them all. When the Messiah's commander intones, 'We'll never be closer to home than we are right now', shortly before crashing into the comet, the term stands for the crew's families – linked by satellite for their final farewells – for America and planet earth, which they are about to save, but also for heaven, the celestial 'home' and final resting place of Christian heroes. When Freeman announces the rebuilding after impact, it is the rebuilding of that which has been given back: our planet, our 'home'. So, Jenny has to learn the values of 'home'. Why? So that she can face death, secure in her sense of belonging.

Zooming In (3) …

The third scene we want to look at is the moment of Jenny's decision. At just under 2 minutes, the scene comes very near the end. Her father has visited her and given her those same photographs we first saw in Jenny's mother's hand as she prepared to die. Leo is racing to find Sarah. At the studio, a helicopter is due to collect the lucky ones – who will not include Beth or her daughter Katie.

Cut to the studio, the camera running behind Jenny and a colleague, Aaron. She turns aside, and hunts quickly in a drawer for something – the photographs – while Aaron yells: 'We don't have time!' Running again. A pacy orchestral theme accompanies all that follows. Again, Jenny swings aside as she sees (and then we see) Beth sitting with Katie on her lap in a room of toys. Beth starts talking in distraught, barely coherent sentences: 'The road was so crowded so we obviously wouldn't make it so I thought the place to be was here because she likes it here and we're on the fifteenth floor so maybe we'll be OK ... Katie will you say goodbye to Je ...' Jenny reaches forward and grabs Katie and runs with Aaron to the stairs to the roof, Beth behind her calling out desperately. External perfect shot of a helicopter landing on the roof. Shot from above, they race in confusion onto the roof and towards the helicopter. Jenny swings round and pushes Katie back into Beth's arms as the wind from the blades whips their hair and clothes: 'You're taking my seat. I'm not going', she yells. Those going are forced on board, and look out in astonishment at Jenny standing still as the helicopter rises, and the camera swings to show a phalanx of helicopters heading away past the Lincoln Memorial, leaving Jenny alone on the roof. Cut to close-up of Jenny's hands lifting the two photographs into view; the camera swings round to show her face as a muted trumpet theme enters.

How do we understand Jenny's actions? Up to this point we have had two contrary pulls in interpreting her. On the one hand we have seen the career woman, a tough journalist prepared to face out politicians, cope with the FBI, pose hard questions, go for promotion, even if it hurts those around her. On the other hand we have had a woman who cares for her mother, is angry with her father for deserting her mother, is full of tensions over her own childhood. The photographs – indexing what she felt was taken from her ('I feel like an orphan') – make their third appearance just before she encounters the distraught and helpless Beth. Why does she snatch the child? We don't know – but there is a rightness about the outcome when we realise that she has chosen to do something we have yet to see: to go to her father and find reconciliation and peace. We are tracking a transformation into full humanity that is tested at a key moment, and forgives itself as it forgives others.

This emotional and ideological logic is confirmed in an uncharacteristically flamboyant camera movement as Jenny stands alone atop the skyscraper. The camera lifts from the family photographs she carries and circles her until it frames the familiar dome of the Capitol over her right shoulder. The uninterrupted sweep from images of family intimacy to a powerful icon of nationhood conflates public and private allegiances and duties in the context of Jenny's decision, at once an assertion of love and an act of self-sacrifice. *Now* she can go to her father.

The melodramatic effect of impending disaster and narrow escape, or (as we shall see) the mature acceptance of death, is to foreground the lesson learned – the value of loved ones.[14] This moral is not just stated in dialogue but played out in the structural connections established between family, nation and planet, and in the emotional effect of events on both characters and audience. The film's 'deep impact' comes from its recurrent theme of characters preparing themselves to face death. This gradual achievement of emotional maturity and recognition of what matters in life – 'home' values (including emotional bonds to family members and the duty to save the planet) – grants featured characters a dignity which transcends death. The astronauts who sacrifice themselves to destroy one comet; Jenny and her estranged father who overcome their differences to face the final tidal wave together on the beach outside the family home; Sarah's parents who pass on their new baby to Sarah and Leo, have all had time to say their farewells and to die secure in an emotional bond. Lesser (anonymous) characters who die in the panic of the tidal wave do not have the time to get ready for (and so transcend) death in this way. *Deep Impact* thus traces a process of transformation and reaffirmation through disaster, and the recovery of true family bonds, so that death can be accepted and meaningful – as an expression of love for one's family, nation and planet.

The Moral Meanings of Effects

This allows us to rethink the meaning of the special effects in *Deep Impact*. Reserved until almost the end, they can now be seen to be much more than a technological spectacle. We've seen the importance of the idea that FX have a dual character, demanding a doubled attention of us.[15] We are asked simultaneously to see the effect and to see it *as* an effect. But the tricky thing is to understand how, in any particular film, the relation between these is posited.[16] This can only be considered by looking both at the point where they occur in the narrative and what role they play at that point, and at what signals them *as* special effects and how their specialness itself contributes to the narrative process. This is where we would disagree with those who have argued that the growth of special effects industries has meant the death of narrative – FX are only special to the extent that they momentarily alter the manner in which narrative is to be perceived and understood. In this sense, we agree very much with Warren Buckland's way of approaching such recent movies.[17] The key effect comes very near the end of the film – a mere 9 minutes from the end, in fact – in the climactic impact of the 'Biederman' comet fragment on the earth and the ensuing tidal wave.

The major effects are precisely those which were signalled in the film's poster and in much pre-film publicity. In that sense, importantly, the audience is waiting for them to occur.[18] By the time the comet strikes earth, it has already defeated two attempts to destroy or deflect it, and the film's central characters have been seen undergoing a series of tests through which they are being variously transformed. They have each learnt something about their own limits and failings, and about their dependence on each other. The impact comes, for each of them, on the heels of a desperate rush to complete that transformation, followed by a moment of pause, even peace, as they ready themselves for death. The double nature of the impact, then, turns it into an *implement of completion*. We, as audience, adopt an astronomical eye to observe the scale of the impact, and then switch back and forth between impossible all-knowing perspectives (above and under the water as the Statue of Liberty is first toppled and then crashes to the floor of the ocean; directly over the rise of the tsunami as it sucks the beach in front of Jenny and her father bare of water) and participative perspectives (seeing the god-like scale of the wave as it forms over their heads, then seeing their faces as they ready to brave it). Knowing its scale, then, to see Jenny and her father, and Sarah's parents, turn and face it is to watch them transcend. The impact, through its ultimate testing of these people, *is as it ought to be*. If we were to take it only as an event happening to occur here in the narrative process, and did not experience it as something special, these people would simply be crushed, defeated, destroyed. In the other direction, to take it only as a special effect would distance us from the emotions which come to fruition here. To take it in its combination (seeing the disaster, experiencing it as a *special* disaster) means that Jenny has done more than sacrifice herself to save Beth and her child – she has also, in a very human sense, saved herself.[19] This is not religious, except in the sense of being as human as it is possible to be. She has, as so many of them say it, 'come home'. If audiences manage to enter that combination role, they can experience the emotional fulfilment of hope through despair, uplift through pain, a future achieved through self-sacrifice.

Special effects have to be both narratively integrated and convincing as representations of a realistic fictional world here for the audience to believe in them sufficiently, and so to engage with the resulting dilemmas posed for the film's characters. On the other hand, the simultaneous self-reflexivity of effects solicits attention in a more direct fashion, inviting the audience to see them *as* effects, and to react with awe and wonder at the capacity of the cinematic apparatus. (This second viewing strategy is encouraged by discussions of how special effects are achieved in film promotion and journalistic coverage.) Thus, in the case of *Deep Impact*, the audience sees both a frightening and credible tidal wave hitting New York, and a manifestation of the latest computer-generated imagery produced by Industrial Light and Magic. But an audience which devotes too much attention to the latter in and for itself in a very real sense departs from the movie. What *Deep Impact* proffers is an invitation to experience its effects *as fully human, emotional beings*, in which case their 'wizardry' becomes something else and more: a god-like force testing the characters and measuring us in our responses.

Jenny's actions have been read by some commentators as a combination of masochism and passivity.[20] However, on the film's own terms, she achieves transcendence and grace by making her peace with her father. The assertion of the father–daughter bond occurs on the beach outside the family home, site of the last image of the happy pair, united more than 20 years earlier in a photo taken by her mother. Once again functioning as an invisible author, the mother now presides symbolically over the recreation of that bond. Why is this scene, which shifts from the pair's reconciliation to their death in each others' arms, so moving? Partly because they finally grab enough time to say what they need to. The film has tracked the comet's implacable trajectory towards earth, and mapped the time wasted – in arguments and misunderstandings – by characters whose lives are running out. In this scene, Jenny and Jason have just enough time to reunite, and so to revive all their shared past (memories represented by the photos). This feeling of asserting love and saying goodbye just in time[21] (and its concomitant emotional power and feelings of release) transfers to the serial farewells of Fish and crew to each other and to families and loved ones (with the added charge of heroic sacrifice to save others). All these deaths are rendered meaningful as assertions of care, love and allegiance – to family, nation, planet.

Deep Impact and the Disaster Tradition

It may be helpful to look on this film as asking a series of questions: what will the disaster look like? How will different characters cope? Who (and what) will survive, and how? Who deserves to survive? How does this make *Deep Impact* compare with other disaster movies, say, from the 1970s cycle? In earlier disaster films, a character's selfishness is most likely to advance the narrative and lead to disaster. This is apparent in *The Towering Inferno*, where corner-cutting contractor Richard Chamberlain's greed (which causes the fire) is supplemented by his on screen cowardice and ultimately punished by his death. The escalation of the disaster amplifies his crime but delivers to the generically aware audience a number of anticipated pleasures. The disaster provides the motivation for spectacular display, tension, star performances (the heroics of Newman and McQueen) and ultimately Chamberlain's 'punishment' and an affirmative 'moral' conclusion.

Unlike *The Towering Inferno*, where characters essentially stay the same – either good or evil – in *Deep Impact* characters are more complicated, making choices and often not getting them right first time, but getting them right, just in time, in the end (Leo, Sarah, Jenny, Jason, Fish). Characters' wrong choices do add to tension in the film – by frittering away valuable time before the predicted impact, and building up emotional crises which need to be resolved in time, so that death can be faced (Jenny and Jason), sacrifices correctly made (Fish and the astronauts), or survival feel right and justified (Sarah and Leo). And, as we've shown, there are powerful invitations to respond empathetically to characters. From this perspective, the audience is encouraged to invest in characters' re-education, their faltering attempts to get it right. Characters' misunderstandings and wrong or selfish actions thus pave the way to the final disaster – a disaster which is inevitable since without it the film has no *raison d'être*. The 'spectator's itinerary' (Rick Altman's useful phrase) thus includes an investment in the *failure* of the various missions to destroy the comet, otherwise all that learning process will remain incomplete.

10
Showing That It Is What It Is

What do I hope that this book has achieved? I hope that it will convince my readers that the approach I have developed is useful and productive, and respectful towards individual films. My approach emphasises the individuality of films, as opposed to common or generic formulae, structures, themes or broad ideological meanings. But it is still compatible with *subsequently* looking for common ground between films. I want to say a bit more about this in a moment. But in this last chapter I want to return to the question with which I began the book: what can academic analysis of films claim to show that other kinds of analysis can't?

It should be clear from my critique of certain dominant tendencies within film studies that there are a number of things that I believe it can't and shouldn't claim. We can't deduce 'harm' (or 'good' for that matter) from analysis of films. We can't place films along some supposed dimension of political or ideological acceptability, from conservative/reactionary to radical/subversive. Most importantly, we cannot read off possible influences upon an unnamed, 'vulnerable' audience. And part of the reason for that is that films don't contain 'messages' plus message-launching devices in the way that much analysis has supposed.

These are the negatives. What I have proposed instead is a way of looking at films which still gives analysis an important role. Film analysis matters, in at least the following ways:

- Film analysis is capable of challenging the claims of those who attack particular films as 'dangerous' or 'harmful', and who find threats to the moral order in films they dislike. Simply by demonstrating how parts interconnect, how themes are addressed, and the ways in which audiences are invited by the characteristic organisation of the film to play a role opposite a film, we can challenge a wide range of moralising stupidities about film. It is a failing of the field that this too rarely happens.

- Film analysis is capable of revealing the conditions under which a film can involve and be important to an audience. It can show what an audience is invited to do and – through that – what interests, motives and cultural capacities they must have to be able to match that invitation. In other words, it can be a significant, if not necessary, precursor to audience research, marking out the dimensions to which real audiences, with their different patterns of acceptance or rejection, involvement or detachment, commitment or disinterest, are responding.

- Film analysis can contribute to other related fields of study. For instance, it can disclose how, over time, films 'train' their viewers. This notion of films training their viewers is lifted directly from David Bordwell, who argues that it is a necessary feature of all films.[1] But he means something quite specific: not that films train us to accept particular ideas, or to incorporate aspects of films into our identities, etc. Rather, films train us in how to watch films. They have to provide us with sufficient information and motivation, so that we will take part in their imaginative worlds. But the skills we practise on films are not so medium-specific that we could not carry them over into other areas of cultural and social life. Therefore film analysis can, eventually, contribute to our historical knowledge of the shapings of human frames for perceiving and conceiving their world.[2]

Although I may not have spelled these out until now, they were, I believe, implicit within all that I have said up to this point. But except for the first, which is essentially negative, film analysis cannot be an answer in itself. And always the contribution it can make to our knowledge and understanding depends on the confidence we can have in the claims analyses make. That is tricky.

Testing, Testing

How do we go about deciding on the validity or otherwise of an analysis of a film? When an author claims that s/he is demonstrating the presence and operation of significant 'meanings' within a film or films, when should we allow ourselves to be convinced by them? There are some people who would immediately object to the way I put these questions, saying that it reveals an implicit positivism: do I really believe that there are 'facts' about a film independent of interpretative position? To offset this (to me, mischievously avoiding) objection, I will reword my question: under what circumstances should we find one analysis or interpretation of a film more convincing than another? There are good reasons to insist on our right to an answer this question:

- If we don't have some measures for validity/convincingness, then the harshest elements of David Bordwell's critique of film analysis must surely apply. Those that persuade are simply those which play the game best. Bordwell argues that the rules of academic advance must dictate a need for 'novelty', for showing that one has something different to say from other people – first, of course, extensively referencing them and showing in some way that one has 'gone further' and seen things they 'failed to see'.[3]

- Unless there are some criteria for confidence, then in truth we have no grounds for rejecting – on grounds other than just personal dislike – the worst of the moral campaigners' claims about the films they revile. When, for instance, a campaigner howls that the 'message' of *Natural Born Killers* is that it's OK to go out and kill people and expect to get away with it, how do we query the way this 'message' is found if there are no checkable criteria? When Tory MP Gerald Howarth argued that the 'message' of *Romance* (1999) was such that it was no surprise that 12-year-old girls are getting pregnant if we allow such things to be distributed, what right have we got to argue back? When Christopher Tookey of the *Daily Mail* asserted that *Crash* was the ultimate in degradation because of the way it presented gratuitous sex, who is to say he was wrong?

- It also seems right that our *students* insist on a clear answer to this question. They are often required either to evaluate approaches and analyses, and indeed to carry out exercises in film analysis. How can they know if they are doing the job well if there aren't explicit criteria? The alternative will be that, like religious acolytes, they have to demonstrate their right to admission by guessing or by feeling the right ways to do it.

- Given the centrality of ideas of 'meaning' to filmic analysis (whether or not all studies use this precise word), the absence of criteria for determining the strength of the claim for the presence of structures of significance will mean that 'meaning' will surely reduce to no more than 'what it means to me'. But in that case the juggernauts of theory and technical terminology contribute nothing more than the person who simply says, 'I liked it because it made me think about …'

How, then, might we actually measure analyses, to decide which convince us, and which don't?

Some Criteria for Evaluating Textual Analyses

One of the big gains of the cultural studies tradition was its recognition that what the media of all kinds produce are complex symbolic objects, and that we cannot understand their social significance unless we attend seriously to this. Hence the search for ways of analysing media 'texts'. But we lose all the benefits of this important truth if there are no means of submitting our claims in our analyses to testing. In the spirit of inviting challenge, correction and clarification, I offer for consideration the following ways of querying the validity of textual analyses of films. In each case I offer an example, to make as clear as I can how a test would work. It would be easy to choose examples of analyses which, in my view, fail when measured against one or more of these criteria. I've deliberately gone in the other direction, for several reasons. First, I want to be positive about the possibilities offered by film analysis. The obscurantism and anti-empirical tendencies in much textual analysis has caused a growing number of critics to turn away from the idea of such analysis altogether. I offer this book, and these criteria, in part as a defence of formal analysis. Second, I hope to elucidate where these criteria can take us, and good examples do more to bring this into view. If I can show what a good analysis achieves, I can hopefully generalise. Third, I hope that these criteria are not biased towards my own way of approaching films. Instead, some of the examples I give below are analyses with which, in important respects, I disagree. But they do still meet one or more of the criteria I am proposing.

I suggest, then, that analysts of film or any other symbolic materials should be willing to submit their claims to the following five tests: *adequacy to the object*; *theoretical transparency*; *acknowledging implicit claims*; *overcoming idiosyncrasy*; and *research productivity*.

1 *Adequacy to the object*: any analysis of a film has to have a limit, which means that there must come a point when the analyst can say that s/he has examined enough features to draw a conclusion. In choosing some features for attention, the grounds must be clear for finding these more significant than others. My first test therefore proposes that after we have read an analysis, we should be convinced that we understand the processes, patterns and principles of a film better than we could without the analysis. Put baldly like that, it seems to invite all kinds of mental flattery. But despite this, the criterion can be helpful, if we insist that it must expand and enrich our perception of the particular film, rather than dissolving it into external generalities. As a positive example of this, consider Rick Altman's remarks on *Top Hat* (1935). The comments come

in the midst of Altman's discussion of the ways in which an audience's generic classification interacts with the potentialities of a film. By exploring the transaction between these, he shows that the film takes risks with propriety:

> [A] musical, as the genre's critics regularly remind us, cannot exist without its three constitutive moments: boy meets girl, boy dances with girl, boy gets girl. But in *Top Hat*, from the very start, this process runs into trouble. When Astaire awakens Rogers with his nocturnal tap dancing, she does what any proper young lady would do in the 1930s: rather than complaining directly to the offending noise-maker, she complains to the management. According to this scenario, the manager would silence Astaire, report back to Rogers, and the incident would be closed. But there would be no musical, because the boy would never meet the girl. The spectator's allegiances are already being tested. Should Rogers obey proper etiquette? Or should she shun society's notion of acceptable behaviour in favour of conduct becoming the musical?[4]

Altman proceeds to show how pleasure might be gained from the succession of such risk-takings, based on it *appearing* that Rogers may be tempted to adultery. What does this reveal? Altman puts it thus: 'When we are in the world, we follow its rules. When we enter into the world of genres, we reveal tastes and make decisions of an entirely different nature, to the point where familiar norms directly conflict with another kind of satisfaction that looks nothing short of "dirty" when seen from a cultural viewpoint' (pp.147–8). So what his analysis reveals is a set of rules which the film enacts, rules which draw attention to a society's rules by hinting at breaking them. Although brief, Altman's account has to my eyes the virtue of revealing something otherwise non-obvious about the way this individual film works: its internal pattern and to what rules that pattern is a response. And in the process, it opens a door to further exploration of the relations between the rules operative in the *film* and the external referents of those rules in the social world.

On its own, this test could not carry much weight, because of the risk that I might find something 'insightful' that others just wouldn't see as such. But even if its use is only to make us spell out more what we claim an analysis has achieved, it may still be worthwhile.

2   *Theoretical transparency*: by this I mean that analyses of films should be regarded as persuasive to the extent that, through them, the concepts deployed are made clearer and more precise. Ignoring my promise for

a moment that I would use good examples, I must comment that many recent film analyses using the concept of 'identification' have ended by making that concept *less* clear and *less* operationally distinct. If, as such analyses conclude, our 'identifications' with characters must be seen as mobile (rather than fixed), and multiple (not singular) because of the nature of the films, we ought to be wondering what is left of the concept, and – most interestingly to me – whether anything at all is disallowed or impossible.

For a positive example I return to David Bordwell's analysis of *Rear Window*, which I touched on in my first chapter.[5] This analysis comes at the end of a chapter in which Bordwell has set out his case that films work by cueing audiences through narrational devices, such that we are required to make inferences and form hypotheses about the course of events. His analysis of *Rear Window* tries to demonstrate exactly how this will work. He points to two kinds of requirement: moment to moment, the ways we are required to accumulate evidence, sometimes in parallel with Jeff, sometimes observing things he misses; but at another level, structurally, we experience these accumulating into overall dilemmas which press towards resolutions, although what exactly these might be is hard to predict since we are also learning about the unreliability of much apparent information and the hypotheses we (and Jeff) have acquired.

The strength of this lies in the way it fills out the meaning of Bordwell's central concepts: 'narration', 'cueing' and 'viewer activity'. And thus it allows Bordwell to prepare for both similarities and differences between *Rear Window* and other films he will examine:

> Every fiction film does what *Rear Window* does: it asks us to tune our sensory capacities to certain informational wavelengths and then translate given data into story. … Of course, not every film reinforces such conventional ideological categories (nagging wife, society model, adventurous photographer, lusty newlyweds, old maid) and places such trust in the relationship between seeing and understanding. Some films … undermine our conviction in our acquired schemata, open us up to improbable hypotheses, and cheat us of satisfying inferences. But no matter how much a film arouses expectations only to frustrate them, or creates implausible alternatives that turn out to be valid, it still assumes that the spectator will initially act upon those assumptions which we use to construct a coherent everyday world.[6]

This seems to me an admirable clarification of the implications and operational force of his central concepts.

3 *Acknowledging implicit claims*: it should be a normal part of analytical practice to bring into open view claims that take the form: 'If I am right, then the following ought also to hold true.' Since a good part of my opening chapter addressed the problems in the way film analysis does this as it applies to audiences, I want to stress here that such implications can also run to ideas about production, and the relations of cinema and politics, for example. Consider, in this light, an intriguing essay by Warren Buckland, designed to challenge the current conventional wisdom what 'blockbusters' amount to a dilution of narrative complexity in films, and its replacement by spectacle for its own sake.[7] Using the case of *Raiders of the Lost Ark* (1981), Buckland examines in detail a series of moments in which a conflict emerges between apparent omniscient narration and actual management by characters – to enjoy this, we have to have been paying close attention to its cinematic operation. For example:

> Jones and Marion have an argument, and Jones leaves – or appears to leave – the bar. As he walks away, he leaves the camera's field of vision, while the camera itself remains in the bar in order to show us what happens next. We are thus led to believe that Jones has left, and that the narration itself is omniscient. ... As Marion closes the bar, Toht ... arrives and threatens her when she refuses to relinquish the headpiece. However, at the moment at which he is about to scar her with a red hot poker, we hear Jones' whip as it knocks the poker to the floor. ... Jones' sudden reappearance makes the spectator retrospectively reinterpret the scene, negating its previously omniscient nature. ... [T]he spectator assumes that he has been privileged by the narration and thus more than Jones does, whereas in fact Jones knows as much as the spectator.[8]

Buckland's analysis clearly has implications for thinking about audiences, but could also go in other directions. There is a clear statement of the requirements for the spectator if s/he is to follow the film. There is also an implication that this becomes a mode of enjoyment, in which we welcome being deceived by films. But this depends on various kinds of 'training' of audiences in handling this kind of filmic material, or they might respond with confusion or irritation, rather than delight. Addressing this would take us into a range of related operations: the ways films are marketed; how advertising and publicity build up expectations; and how those expectations play into the actual watching of the film. In the case of *Raiders of the Lost Ark*, for example, the name 'Spielberg' surely has come to guarantee a certain kind of film. In a very different case,

The Blair Witch Project (1999) promised real life – even to the extent of releasing a spoof documentary on the deaths of the film's characters. Without such training, it is very doubtful that the film could have sold the audience role it proffered.

The implications of this would take us beyond the audience role that Buckland explicitly considers into a wide range of associated production and distribution practices, from the operation of publicity regimes to the new meanings surrounding director superstars. I regard this as one of the attractive aspects of film analysis, that it must drive us outwards to such a range of other questions.

4   *Overcoming idiosyncrasy*: this is not about writing style, although sometimes it feels as though it is. It is about reproducibility – can someone other than this author follow the procedures, arrive at the same conclusions, and apply the procedures to a different film? That means that the procedures used ought to be transparent, and not dependent on the private insights of an analyst. I have to admit that I am not entirely happy with my own practices in this respect. While the means of producing analytic descriptions are pretty clear, it isn't so clear how I moved to my second stage: finding preliminary patterns and posing preliminary questions. How does one do this, other than by insight? I am, if I am frank, not quite sure.

In the other direction, an example of very good practice is Mike Cormack's analysis of cinematographic practices during the 1930s, from which he develops an argument about the ideological signification of his films.[9] Cormack demarcates and discusses a series of aspects of cinematography, such as lighting, angle of filming, distance and movement. And with these he offers an account of their ideological significance. This informs his examination of individual films. For example, he investigates *All Quiet on the Western Front* (1930), and shows that, along with a great many shots which are motivated by the position and actions of characters, it contains a series of distant shots whose 'motivation' is not clear. These, he argues, 'suggest a narrator's subject position – someone outside the diegesis who is addressing the viewer in a particular way' (p.42). And from this, he draws conclusions about the ideological meaning of the film and its capacity to 'interpellate' viewers.

It happens that I disagree substantially with the theorisation that Cormack adopts: an Althusserian notion that audiences are 'hailed' via the constitution of a systematic 'point of view' in a film. But that is separate from my welcome for his detailed and reproducible filmic analysis. In fact, better than that: the very clarity of the analysis makes evident the point at which I have to part company. For at the end of his account, Cormack appears to compromise on his own theory, extemporising another explanation *separate* from the ideological. Aware that his own analysis shows the presence of some camerawork not entirely consonant with his 'ideological' reading, Cormack introduces another idea to account for this remainder, the idea of an 'authorial position': 'the appearance of an authorial subject position can function, like the unconventional structuring, as another "proof" (perhaps the ultimate one) of the film's quality. The film becomes linked, however tenuously, to the values of high art and to the seriousness of artistic (that is, authorial) statement. Thus the film's ideological unity is not threatened' (p.42). I believe that if we closely examine this move it will show an arbitrary distinction and solution, which would throw doubt on his analysis' 'adequacy to the object'. But that does not detract from the exemplary explicitness of his analysis; rather, it confirms it.

5   *Research productivity*: by this criterion I mean that we consider how far any textual analysis brings into view characteristics which, without blurring and overwriting differences, points us on to consider or perhaps reconsider similar aspects in other films. The rider in that sentence is crucial. One bane of film studies has been a rush to those kinds of generalisation which do away with historical specifics and drown differences. One essay which illustrates what I intend by a criterion of productivity is Charles Wolfe's examination of the shorts produced by Vitaphone in the period running up to the full introduction of sound in 1927.[10] Wolfe questions the popular wisdom that has generally marginalised the shorts as uncinematic and stagey because of the way characters directly address the camera. On this approach, the shorts were the last gasp of the theatrical tradition in which live performers appeared alongside silent films. Their dependence on this is signalled by the way events are filmed as though there were a proscenium arch between characters and audience. This approach has therefore seen the introduction of sound in the studios as a major break. Wolfe shows, rather, that shorts such as *Old San Francisco* (1927), *Tenderloin* (1928) and *Show of Shows* (1929) share many characteristics with *The Jazz Singer* (1927), the first accredited 'sound picture'. They introduced a series of ways in which sound could be dissociated from visual image. Songs would remain continuous while cameras zoomed, roamed, refocused. And links were suggested between the *recorded* audience and the *live cinema* audience. Wolfe shows how these characteristics carry over into *The Jazz Singer*, and indeed are arguably present in a large number of subsequent films, such as musicals.

This seems to me a very productive account. It not only draws attention to some 'lost' connections between silent and sound eras, but also reopens from different angles the debates about visual and auditory point of view. The tradition Wolfe is questioning has privileged visuals over sound, under the term 'spectatorship'. His query can easily be broadened to raise awkward questions about the relations between sound and image in other periods. For example, how does the demotion of sound cater for the fact that a series of classical Hollywood films were almost simultaneously broadcast on the radio, often with the same actors?[11] The problem, I suspect, is an overhomogenising account of what 'Classical Hollywood' was. But outside that period, even a film such as *Reds* (1981) could profitably be revisited, with Wolfe's account to hand, to consider the density of demand made on audiences by the opening sequence in which real survivors from the time of the Russian Revolution recall, often with dislike and hostility, the film's central character John Reed.

These five evaluative grounds can't be entirely independent of each other. Indeed, a number of the above examples could well have featured under another heading (Bordwell on *Rear Window* under 'research productivity', for example, or Buckland under 'adequacy to the object'). But equally I believe that particular analyses may prove their worth on one or more grounds while causing worries on others. I offer these five as a first bid. The examples I have chosen are just that: examples. They weren't designed to favour my own account, though I doubt they are as independent of that as I would wish. But I welcome other people challenging these – providing they are willing to propose other criteria for evaluating textual analyses, which can in turn be debated.

Staging *Stagecoach*

I want to show how these various criteria might work together, for their interest must surely lie in how easily we can move between them in evaluating any particular analysis. I have chosen as my example a piece of work which I admire and simultaneously disagree with: Nick Browne's analysis of *Stagecoach* (1939).[12]

Stagecoach was John Wayne's first major hit as a star. Directed by John Ford, the film shows a stagecoach ride through dangerous American Indian territory. A heterogeneous group of travellers have to learn to rely on each other, and each is tested in the process: among them an eastern banker on the run with his bank's money; a pregnant middle-class woman (Lucy) going to join her husband; a prostitute, Dallas, who has been kicked out of town by local puritans; Wayne's Ringo Kid, escaped from jail to seek revenge for his murdered brother; and a marshal who puts Ringo under arrest. Nick Browne focuses on one scene, quite early in the film, when they are stopped for a meal. The scene depicts Lucy reacting to the presence of Dallas, an 'indecent' woman, with whom she doesn't want to sit at table. Ringo takes Dallas' side. Browne is interested in how it can be that, although the film clearly invites our sympathy with Dallas, the camerawork seems to favour Lucy's point of view. Since, according to conventional theory, motivated camera angles signify an invitation to identification with a character, it seems that the cinematography is approving Lucy's attitude.

Browne shows a conflict: on the one hand, there is no doubt that Dallas is presented as the sympathetic figure, excluded and hurt; but the camerawork insistently shifts between showing us Dallas from Lucy's point of view, and showing us Lucy's reactions. This leads Browne to propose a distinction within the meaning of the 'position of the spectator': between the *optical* position of the person watching (in the cinema, centred in relation to the presented image) and his or her *figured* position – the latter being a combination of 'two places at once, where the camera is and "with" the depicted person' (p.111). Otherwise, he asks, how can we explain the complex reactions he believes the film works to elicit?

> [H]ow can I describe my 'position' as spectator in identifying with the humiliated position of one of the depicted characters, Dallas, when my views of her belong to those of another, fictional character, Lucy, who is in the act of rejecting her? What is the spectator's 'position' in identifying with Dallas in the role of the passive character? Dallas in averting her eyes from Lucy's ... accepts a view of herself in this encounter as 'prostitute' and is shamed. However, in identifying with Dallas in the role of outcast, presumably the basis for the evocation of our sympathy and pity, our response as spectator is not one of shame, or anything even analogous. We do not suffer or repeat the humiliation. I understand Dallas' feeling but I am not so identified with her that I re-enact it.[13]

The impressive density of consideration here well meets my criterion for 'adequacy to the object'. Browne is revealing important processes at work in the film. And his careful procedures certainly render his account non-idiosyncratic.

However, there is a price to be paid, in theoretical consistency and clarity. It arises because Browne, in concert with much film theory then and now, insists on giving primacy to the *visual* aspect of film. Thence he links the visual to the idea of 'identification'. At the end of his essay he writes:

> Though the spectator may be placed in the 'center' of things by the formal function Lucy performs, he is not committed to her view of things. On the contrary, in the context of the film, that view is instantly regarded as insupportable. Our response to Dallas supports the sense that the spectator's figurative position is not stated by a description of where the camera is in the geography of the scene. On the contrary, though the spectator's position is closely tied to the fortunes and views of the characters, our analysis suggests that identification, in the original sense of an emotional bond, need not be with the character whose view he shares, even less with the disembodied camera. Evidently, a spectator is in several places at once – with the fictional viewer, with the viewed, and at the same time in a position to evaluate and respond to the claims of each. This fact suggests that like the dreamer, the filmic spectator is a plural subject: in his reading he is and is not himself.[14]

Several moves here seem to me insupportable. First, he has slipped through as a judgement independent of the analysis of the scene that 'of course' we are on Dallas' side – that is something we apparently know from the 'context of the film'. But what is that *apart* from the very features he is analysing? Why should we not argue that this is an *inconsistency* in *Stagecoach*? Browne cannot do this, because he needs that peg to be secure so that he can then resist the notion of 'identification' via camerawork. But then, if the spectator *can* be in several places at once, what is to stop him or her sharing sympathy with *Lucy*? While seeming to resolve the problem, his notion of the viewer-as-dreamer instead opens up the film to an indefinite number of possible responses. And ultimately it does this because of his insistence on that concept of 'identification'. If normally we are tied to films via such an 'emotional bond' evoked in us through the force of cinematic technique, then for this to fail, we have to suppose a kind of self-destructive camerawork – that in the very act of involving us, the film somehow also says: 'Don't trust me … this is not my view, it is just Lucy's.' How on earth might that be done? Because Browne is so sold on the visual aspect of films – he calls them 'specular texts' – he has to resort to desperate manoeuvres, which he calls 'forgetting' and then 'fading' (p.113). Apparently we experience Lucy's 'affront' at the presence of a prostitute at her dinner table, but then we 'forget' it and it 'fades' because Lucy seems to turn her attention elsewhere. This somehow allows us to reach back to Dallas, and sympathise despite the camerawork. This is a patchwork solution. Browne is right that there is a problem, but his adherence to those standard film analytic concepts undoes his solution. Adequacy to the object is bought at the price of theoretical confusion. It is thus in the combination of applied criteria that we are able to evaluate such an analysis in full.

In fact, a solution is relatively easy, on my approach. From its earliest scenes, *Stagecoach* offers a series of clues and cues about the kind of world it is offering us. And a recurrent feature of this is a disjunction between characters who are direct and plain-speaking, and those who use formalities, who insist on rules, and use these as masks over other motives. From the beginning, we are encouraged to look at each character in this light: for example, the drunk doctor, who will clearly come good since he is a plain-speaker; versus the southern gentleman who may have all the manners, but that precisely makes him untrustworthy; and the prurient townswomen, who pretend morality, but can't be trusted because they are hypocritical. The banker may bluster about his 'rights' and other people's 'duties', but we have seen enough to know that he is cheating. Dallas meanwhile hardly speaks, indeed makes clear that she doesn't think she has the right to speak on whether they should continue with their journey, in the face of the danger of Geronimo. By the time Ringo appears, his instant directness, and his inability to hide his feelings about his murdered brother, mark him as the right kind. So, when we come to the meal, the camerawork functions to show us a contrast: on the one hand the formal silences and accusatory looks of Lucy, backed by the known-to-be-untrustworthy gentleman/gambler; and the silenced Dallas. But the moment Ringo starts talking to her, man to woman, she speaks back in the same honest, direct way that marks her as a good 'un. Rethink the film in terms of cues, and it appears that the camerawork is functioning *evidentially* in this section. Who would *you* respect, it asks?

Post-analysis

I hope I have by now established several things. First, that evaluation of textual analyses is necessary. Second, that it is possible, and that my five criteria are a useful step down this road. Third, that those five criteria work best when used together. Perhaps most important is where they take us. If you look at the marks of a good analysis, on these criteria, they have the effect of pushing us beyond the film in itself. My proposal amounts to this: *a film analysis is valuable to the extent that it raises and clarifies questions, concepts, approaches, which indicate how that film might be researched in other, wider contexts*. This is the sense in which film analyses are of necessity preliminary. And they ought to be most persuasive when they signal clearly *how* that further, wider investigation might be undertaken.

Taking a risk, I offer an example. Take, once more, the example of *Titanic*. Through my analysis of the film I have claimed that this film embodies a call upon audiences to feel responsibility for the past, to reconnect themselves with where they come from, to learn about themselves from what the past has left to us. How might that be tested? It certainly isn't possible to do this by some simple survey of people who went to see the film. For a start, a survey would lose all differences between those who engaged strongly with the film, and those who went for the ride, to see what all the fuss was about, to be able to say to friends that they had seen it – a more important motivation than a lot of research allows. But also, people would not necessarily be able to put into words this aspect of the film, since we have a culture that in many discourages articulation of what popular films do to people.[15]

But although it might not be possible to do it simply and directly, it is still possible to conceive research that would bring into view dimensions of response that would confirm or challenge my account of *Titanic*. Take the simple fact that, whatever role this film may have invited people to play opposite it, many young women will have gone to see *Titanic* because of the promise of screens-full of Leonardo diCaprio.[16] Imagine some research which explored how satisfied or dissatisfied these audiences were with the way they got to see diCaprio. In our research on *Judge Dredd*, Kate Brooks and I discovered how much disappointment can bring to the surface two things: people's ideal expectations of a film and what the film is perceived to do instead.[17] It should then be possible to explore the relations between the following elements among young women who were fans of diCaprio: using, as a differentiating factor, how they felt about the fact that his character sacrifices himself before the end of the film in order to save Rose – how is this related to (connected with? separated from?) how far they perceived this character as an embodiment of what they are attracted to in diCaprio; to the 'rightness' or otherwise of his dying; to Rose/Kate as the recipient of his affections; and to the meaning of his death for them? My hypothesis would be that the more such young women (a) wanted to fantasise Leo as *their* potential lover, and (b) saw him as quintessentially a 'modern' boy/ man, the more they would be disappointed by *Titanic*, and decline the role that the film proffered. But in their declining it, we might well see the traces of recognition of what they would not do. And we now have, in the developed procedures of discourse analysis, an array of methods for drawing out those traces, and from them learn much about the social orientations of their speakers.

I don't pretend this has a perfect fit with my analysis of the film – audience research rarely has. But it would be relevant to my claims. And a large part of me says to those who might criticise my research outline: do better.

But the attractions of the safety of textual analysis mean that few are likely to respond. It is a real problem that the community of those committed to audience research is so small, so scattered, and so intermittent that the kinds of detailed development of research strategies that are needed just don't occur.[18] But the interesting thing, beyond this, is that the demand for criteria of adequacy for film analyses is so often taken to mean its virtual replacement by audience research. And that is not what I am saying at all, as I hope the following makes clear.

One real danger currently facing cultural studies approaches to film and other media is the opening of a breach between analysis of symbolic organisation and other kinds of enquiry. This has arisen in part because of the regular failure of predictions. From David Morley's honest self-critique onwards, it has seemed that either we determinedly carry on with textual analyses or we study audiences – but the chances of finding any real link between the two are minimal. This has led many commentators to pose a dilemma – a wholly false one, in my view. For example, Linda Williams says: 'The issue that now faces the once influential subfield of spectatorship within cinema – and indeed all visual – studies is whether it is still possible to maintain a theoretical grasp of the relations between moving images and viewers without succumbing to anything-goes pluralism.'[19] Or again, Elizabeth Traube writes: 'To recognise the active role of audiences in constructing textual meanings is not to ignore the influences exerted by texts.'[20] The problems in these very typical statements are many, and deeply ingrained, and can't be dealt with adequately here. They include those notions of 'texts' as message-missiles, seeking out unprotected viewers. I am arguing that this privileging of meanings over processes of participation is the start of a whole series of consequent problems. They also work with a model of 'influence' which requires 'passivity', whereas I would argue that such things as *passionate, thinking involvement* are far more apt grounds for thinking about how people can be changed by the media.

This brings me right round to a question which was implicit in the opening of this book. I hope I have made clear my answer to the question: what can academic analysis of a film achieve? But that leaves the subsidiary question: what is the relation between academic and other kinds of analysis? There are, I believe, several answers.

First, we should just be increasing the attention we pay to other kinds of analysis. And the first thing which would happen would be the undermining of that stubborn tendency to assume 'effects' on audiences. What in fact appear are *responses*: that is, real people combining their understanding of a film, their degree and kind of emotional involvement in it, their (aesthetic, moral, cultural) evaluation of it, and their weighing of its significance (which often includes having all kinds of ideas about who it is for and, oddly, what kinds of 'effect' it might have!). Real audiences retell the stories of films (see Chapter 2). For this purpose, a press reviewer is not especially different from any ordinary cinema-goer who tells partner, friends, whoever what they thought of a film. And in their retellings they reveal much about *how* they watched the film.

A small number of studies have used reviews and other published responses to films as a resource for considering the reception of films.[21] These have made a significant contribution to what has become known as reception studies. But curiously, they end up having little to say about the *films themselves*. It is as if we are posed a choice: either analyse a film (and be tempted to make various imputations to 'the audience') or examine empirical responses to it (in which case, 'the audience' dissolves into heterogeneous responses). Either study *The Birth of a Nation* as a 'text', with a possible meaning; or examine the varied history of responses which seem to suggest multiple, indeed changing meanings.[22] Either deconstruct the Disney corpus for its ideological operations – which is only worth doing if someone somewhere might be conceived to be in receipt of the thus-discovered plague of reactionary forms;[23] or undertake the difficult task, not yet even started as far as I know, of looking at why and how people *enjoy* Disney films, theme parks, merchandising, etc. This separation has become an opposition. How might we overcome it and meaningfully reconnect analysis of films with analysis of responses to films?

My proposal is a radical one. I believe we have to learn to investigate a particular kind of response to films. My idea is derived from something we learnt in our research into the audiences of *Judge Dredd*: the significance of disappointment. Disappointment was a strong feature of many people's responses to *Dredd*, and it told us much.[24] It told us about people's expectations, and had the real advantage of making people put them into words which could be analysed. People revealed their filmic ideals through their anger. They revealed that they felt their rights had been invaded, that something had been stolen from them. But that shows the results of prior cultural training in Bordwell's sense – that a 'proper' action film behaves in this and such ways. In a subsequent piece of research with two colleagues into responses to David Cronenberg's *Crash*,[25] however, we were able to discover the dimensions of untrained enthusiasm for a film. Among our audiences for *Crash* were many who were surprised and delighted by it. Through an investigation of their responses, it was possible to see in considerable detail the filmic role into which they realised they had been inducted, which they had accepted with enthusiasm, and which they were delighted to have the chance to talk about.

This, then, is my proposal: that research needs to focus on *enthusiasts* for particular films. Enthusiasts *care* about their films, by definition. What we need to explore are the links between the kind of importance they attach to their preferred films and how they watched them. In this way, the role they entered, and what it meant to fill that role, may become transparent, and may then provide a pivot for examining those who reject the film or temporise over its demands on them. This will not be some easy or mechanically manageable research process, but the value of the possible outcomes make it worth the effort, I am convinced.

In this way, I believe we can overcome that division between texts and audiences, and develop checkable ways of using our own analyses of the audience roles a film generates, and the kinds of involvement achieved by enthusiastic viewers.

Susan Sontag's Critique

There is one approach that seriously challenges my proposal. In a justly famous essay, Susan Sontag has challenged the whole emphasis on 'interpretation'.[26] Sontag's target is an attitude towards art which insists on asking about its 'content'. By this she means a determined will to search for the intentions of the artist, or the meaning of the text, what it is really 'saying'. Originally art had primarily ritual significance, which preserved it from the attentions of theory. But from Plato onwards, art has been the topic of 'justifications', and in Western cultures, Sontag argues, those 'justifications' have been dominated by a criterion of 'mimesis'. Art in some way copies or represents the world around it, and therefore is to be measured by criteria of truth, or usefulness, or in some way by the adequacy of its relation to that world. This means that art is not experienced, but examined, 'interpreted'. She believes that this has taken a new characteristic form in recent years:

> The old style of interpretation was insistent, but respectful; it erected another meaning on top of the literal one. The modern style of interpretation excavates, and as it excavates, destroys; it digs 'behind' the text, to find a subtext which is the true one.[27]

In this way, art ceases to *be* art, stripped of its capacities to outrun the world we live in. 'It is the revenge of the intellect upon the world. To interpret is to impoverish, to deplete the world – in order to set up a shadow world of "meanings".'[28] Sontag is not rejecting all forms of analysis, but stating the case for a different kind of analysis. This is how she states this, at the close of her essay-cum-manifesto:

> The aim of all commentary on art now should be to make works of art –
> and, by analogy, our own experience – more, rather than less, real to us.
> The function of criticism should be to show *how it is what it is*, even *that
> it is what it is*, rather than to show us *what it means*.[29]

Sontag is reclaiming the sensuality of artistic experience, or as she says,
she wants to 'recover our senses'. She talks of the 'sensuous surface of art',
the 'luminousness of the thing in itself'. This I share, completely. Films are
experienced. An important part of their importance to audiences is their
visual power, and their wash of sound. Special effects, for example, are
pointless if they don't evoke at least a component of the reaction that fireworks can catch from us: 'Wow!' But equally, like a good firework display,
their presentation is timed.[30] Yet the *process* of film-watching has hardly
been addressed by academic analysts. Sontag's reassertion of the experiential is vital. But in her argument it is linked with something else, an appeal
to a lost innocence which, if it could be recaptured, would be *only* experiential, *purely* responsive. She writes with more than a hint of sadness that
'[n]one of us can ever retrieve that innocence before all theory when art
knew no need to justify itself, when one did not ask of a work of art what
it *said* because one knew (or thought one knew) what it *did*' (p.5).

It seems to me that Sontag here conflates two things. In their day-to-day
encounters with works of art (from family photographs, through public
art, to television and films) people share their responses through talking
about them. This is not an incidental extra. It is an essential circulatory
medium for art. It enables people to share languages for responding to
things, to know how to seek them out, to be ready to respond to them. It
also provides the normal, day-to-day food for the upkeep of communities
of response, through which people recognise that their way of responding
to the world is not theirs alone, but is filled and enriched and confirmed
by being joined with other people's. And the more they care, the more they
have to share.

But alongside this shared atmosphere there exist various worlds of professional judgement, some of which have developed rules of interpretation
which pass judgement on the responses of others. Interpretations here are
never simply articulations of 'what this has come to mean to me'; rather
they become judgements on the acceptability of other people's responses.

I want to separate these components. It is right that we should attend
more to artistic form, as something experienced and lived. And it is right
that we should attend to what a film *is*, rather than reducing it to a delivery
vehicle for something else: representations, themes, meanings, sub-texts
or ideologies.[31] It is also right that this includes close attention to the sphere

of the sensual, in wide senses. But films are talked about – and, yes, analysed – by ordinary cinema-goers and video-viewers because talking is what people do. To ignore this is to privilege very private acts of response, typified by reading alone. Yet, even there, the many kinds of inner speech in which we address ourselves, sort out our reactions and prepare for shared talk, marks our persistent membership of social groups.[32] Meaning-seeking is not the problem, despite Sontag. It is only a problem when it is done in ways that (a) deny the essential filmicness of its objects – turning them into implements of cultural corruption, for instance, or vehicles for ideology, and (b) in and through our analyses, pass judgement on ordinary viewers – usually even without the courtesy of wondering how these might be checked.

Film analysis without judgements, then. Film analysis without 'pants'.

Naming and Shamaning

What to call the approach I am advocating? To achieve intellectual respectability, an approach has to become a named account. Then it can be regarded, and taught, as a distinct 'entity'. So, debates can be staged among students between 'formalist', 'neo-formalist', 'psychoanalytic' (be that (subcategorising) 'Freudian', 'Jungian', 'Lacanian'), 'feminist' (now sundering into so many fragments, that only the name coalesces them), 'postmodern', 'postcolonial', 'deconstructive' and … what? How will dictionaries of film studies ever grant a heading to the approach if there is no name? My approach owes a great deal to Kristin Thompson's Neo-Formalist account, but I am disinclined to accept that name. It still hangs too much on that notion of 'defamiliarisation' and has too little space for all the sensuous, emotional and social aspects of the audience-role. And I am not tempted at all by the idea of 'post'-ing the name, as in 'post-formalist'. Ugh.

Yet there is a politics to naming. Names have a surprising power to normalise. Conceptual tags supposedly crop up naturally, but in fact come to seem so obvious (in a virtually Barthesian fashion) that all the following appear to have evident referents: 'dominant discourse', 'representation', 'spectator', 'encoding/decoding', 'unconscious'. Pardon the pun, but these have come to equate to a dominant discourse in our field. Expressions that stand outside this dominant tradition look made up – as Kate Brooks and I learnt to our cost when, in *Knowing Audiences*, we offered – with quite precise definitions, let it be said, and based on some concrete and extensive research – some new concepts. With smiles to acknowledge a semi-joke involved, we coined expressions to capture processes we felt we'd discovered. With not a smile in sight, we were chided in *Sight and Sound* for these. It was all pointless, too, since our research just didn't get very far. After all, these people we had researched didn't even seem to have an 'unconscious'.[33] Well, there you go. The fact that our research had something to say about the temporal, cognitive, emotional, sensory, cultural and social processes of going to see an action-adventure movie made no difference. A hypothetical entity whose usefulness has been subjected to nothing resembling a validating test has priority. 'It' decides the value of research. That which does not measure up to the claims of this name, does not measure up. Research that won't use the right terms hits a handicap.

Names matter, then, so there'd better be one. I propose to call the approach I am advocating 'pro-filmic'. 'Pro-filmic' collects up three possible meanings. My approach is about being 'in front of' films, and the way that the role of implied audience is constituted as a 'space' between film and audience. I am also borrowing from Susan Sontag that need to emphasise the simple force of retelling: to show that it is what it is, is important. And in this case this means reminding ourselves that this is what films are: they are *films*. Not as tautologous as it sounds, this may remind us that films are not, without damned good reason, to be regarded as 'expressions of dominant ideology', or 'cultural expressions of unconscious tendencies', or etc. In this sense, I am being pro-*film*ic. Finally, and I admit more riskily, I offer it as another acronym: *P*roffering a *R*ole *O*pposite a *F*ilm, and thus referring to a central concept of this book. 'Pro-filmic', then. Who knows? If the ideas catch on, and a second edition becomes possible, maybe it can then carry that in its title.

Pro-filmic theory, then, is that aggregate of concepts through which we can address films as constituting imaginative universes. These generate possible (sensuous, emotional, aesthetic, cognitive, social) roles for audiences to occupy. Through inhabiting these, they can construct an engagement with the film's process. In and through this process, films proffer proposals for how the imaginative universe might be brought into relation with other aspects of its audiences' lives. Pro-filmic theory therefore always reaches out beyond films themselves to the surrounding worlds of film production and distribution, to the histories of cinema and its role in people's lives, to different communities of response, and so on. A *pro-filmic analysis* is an account of any film which seeks to understand it in ways consonant with the theory and its concepts. And *pro-filmic methodology* is an appropriate range of tools and techniques for approaching individual films, and investigating the way they structure an audience participative role.

I have to say that the last still bothers me. While I am confident with my general case, I am acutely aware of several things in the seven analyses. First, because of the generally blighted state of research into audiences' affective relations with films, I know of few if any procedures for exploring how emotional responses to films might be structured. I have been very aware of inventing ways to deal with this issue, and I am certain that it will be important to refine and advance these. I made up my test for the mental operations involved in getting Kint's breakdown in *The Usual Suspects*. I simply invented the notion of three kinds of caring against which to measure the possibilities of responses to *The Lion King*. I do not think this matters in itself, since I believe that the outcome is a gain in understanding the logic of possible relationships to these films. But the tool is crude. In both cases, they need sharpening, and the principle behind them needs to be made transparent.

Second, I am starkly aware that, having said that an understanding of films must encompass not just cognitive, but also affective, sensuous, social, in fact as I proceed down that line of adjectives my achievements become fewer and less. Since I believe seriously in the idea of a community of researchers, I hope very much that others will find material of worth in this book and will attempt to replicate, extend and develop its currently limited box of tools.

Notes

Chapter 1. Films, Audiences and Analyses

1. See in particular Richard Dyer, *Heavenly Bodies: Film Stars and Society*, London: Macmillan 1987; and for a good introduction to studies of stars, see Paul McDonald, 'Star studies', in Joanne Hollows & Mark Jancovich (eds), *Approaches to Popular Film*, Manchester: Manchester University Press 1995.

2. This is an approach just now advocated by a government-established Working Party. See Film Education Working Group, *Making Movies Matter*, London: BFI 1999.

3. Janey Place, 'Women in film noir', in E. Ann Kaplan, *Women in Film Noir*, London: BFI 1980, pp.35–67. These words are from p.41.

4. Place, 'Women in film noir', p.36.

5. Laura Mulvey, 'Visual pleasure and narrative cinema', *Screen*, Vol.16, No.3, 1975, pp.6–18.

6. Douglas Kellner, *Media Culture: Cultural Studies, Identity and Politics and the Postmodern*, London: Routledge 1995, p.76.

7. Ibid., p.77.

8. The book I co-edited with Julian Petley offers such an overview: see Martin Barker & Julian Petley (eds), *Ill Effects: The Media/Violence Debate*, London: Routledge 1997.

9. Kevin Browne, 'Violence in the media causes crime: myth or reality', Inaugural Lecture, University of Birmingham, 3 June 1999.

10. Ibid.

11. For a fuller critique of Browne on just these grounds, see David Gauntlett, 'The worrying influence of useless "media effects" studies', in Martin Barker & Julian Petley (eds), *Ill Effects: The Media/Violence Debate* (2nd edition), London: Routledge 2000.

12. It's also worth noting that a film being much-vaunted as I write this – *The Blair Witch Project* – shares a very high proportion of its plot with another registered 'video nasty', *Cannibal Holocaust* (1979).

13. David Bordwell, *Narration in the Fiction Film*, London: Methuen 1985, p.30.

14. See ibid., pp.40–7.

15. Ibid., pp.29–30. In fact Bordwell does have something more to say than this, when (p.39) he mentions briefly the possibility that our relationship to the *narration itself* (puzzling out, expectation, finding hypotheses confirmed or defeated) can arouse emotions. Though important, this does not yet include the kinds of relations with characters films evoke.

16. David Bordwell, *Making Meaning: Rhetoric and Inference in the Interpretation of Cinema*, Cambridge, MA: Harvard University Press 1989.

17. Elizabeth Traube, *Dreaming Identities: Class, Gender & Generation in 1980s Hollywood Movies*, Boulder, CO: Westview Press 1992, p. 36.

18. Ibid., p.37.

19. Ibid., p.36.

20. Bordwell, *Making Meaning*. Having said that the book can't be ignored, I have to say that in my experience it largely is – perhaps because its challenges are a 'scandal' to the field it examines, and make life just too uncomfortable.

21. This distinction is one he has used before, in earlier work with Kristin Thompson. See David Bordwell & Kristin Thompson, *Film Art: An Introduction*, New York: McGraw Hill 1993, pp.49–52.
22. George Wilson, 'On film narrative and narrative meaning', in Richard Allen & Murray Smith (eds), *Film Theory and Philosophy*, Oxford: Oxford University Press 1997, pp.221–38.
23. Interestingly, Wilson himself invokes a 'figure' to make his case: the figure of the 'reasonable viewer' (see pp.234–5). A 'reasonable viewer', it seems, is someone who is careful, pays attention to a film sufficiently that s/he is concerned to make good sense of it, establish continuities, discover operative principles, and so on. I am curious about the way this privileges both a certain kind of viewer (intellectual, investigative) and a particular kind of movie (intellectually stimulating etc.). It is hard indeed to see how such a 'viewer' could ever account for the invited or actual responses to a film such as *Star Wars: The Phantom Menace*. It is odd in the extreme to think that someone watching *Sleepless in Seattle* 'reasonably' accounts for the 'look' that passes between Sam (Tom Hanks) and Annie (Meg Ryan) when they first glimpse each other. To 'get' either the spectacle of FX in *Star Wars* or the 'logic of romance' in *Sleepless in Seattle*, you have to suppose a viewer who not only knows the *kind* of movie s/he is watching, but also is *motivated to join in appropriately*. This substantially outruns Wilson's notion of 'reasonableness'.
24. Kaja Silverman, *Male Subjectivity at the Margins*, London: Routledge 1992, pp.90–106.
25. Ibid., pp.92–3.
26. Poague also remarks that, contra Silverman's account, George doesn't seem to take on any of the religious discourses that supposedly underpin Clarence's intervention. He gains no religious faith. All he does is ask to get his life back. The religion is very much 'sufficient unto the needs of the film'. This game could go on for ever ...
27. Robert Ray, *A Certain Tendency in Hollywood Cinema, 1930–1980*, Princeton, NJ: Princeton University Press 1985, pp.179–214.
28. Ibid., p.200.
29. Leland Poague, *Another Frank Capra*, Cambridge: Cambridge University Press 1994.
30. Ibid., p.202.
31. Sam B. Girgus, *Hollywood Renaissance: The Cinema of Democracy in the Time of Ford, Capra and Kazan*, Cambridge: Cambridge University Press 1998, pp.86–107. In what follows, I have done my best to extract the implicit pattern of Girgus' argument. If anyone doubts the toughness of the task, or wants to check how far I have been, I recommend reading the original.
32. Ibid., p.96.
33. Ibid., p.97.
34. Ibid., p.105. My emphasis.
35. Martin Barker & Kate Brooks, *Knowing Audiences:* Judge Dredd*, its Friends, Fans and Foes*, Luton: University of Luton Press 1998. See esp. Chapters 6–7.
36. James Kavanagh, 'Feminism, humanism and science in *Alien*', in Annette Kuhn (ed.), *Alien Zone: Cultural Theory and Contemporary Cinema*, London: Verso 1990, pp.73–81. This quote, p.75. As a small test, try substituting 'I', or 'you',

or 'cinema-goers in Nuneaton in 1982', or any other concrete film-watcher for Kavanagh's generic 'viewer'.
37. Ray, *A Certain Tendency*, p.357.

Chapter 2. Formalism and the Implied Audience

1. Kristin Thompson, *Breaking the Glass Armor: Neo-Formalist Film Analysis*, Princeton, NJ: Princeton University Press 1988.
2. There is a long tradition of claims, spanning large amounts of cultural theory and sociology, that people need help to escape the trap of uncritical acceptance. Its implicit elitism – that artists escape routinism as no others ordinarily can – is clear. Apart from Formalism, this strain of thinking is also to be found in much of the writings of the Frankfurt School, in the long tradition of ethnomethodological sociology (typified by Alfred Schutz) which then resurfaces in the popular work of Peter Berger in the 1960s, and in the tradition led by Roland Barthes of analysing for 'myths' whose discovery led the way to the educational practices of 'demythologisation', especially around the mass media. I await the evidence that the rest of us are trapped in routinism.
3. Thompson, *Breaking the Glass Armor*, p.26.
4. Ian Christie, 'Formalism and neo-formalism', in John Hill & Pamela Church Gibson (eds), *The Oxford Guide to Film Studies*, Oxford: Oxford University Press 1998, pp.58–64. Although clear and succinct, I have to note that Christie perpetuates a common misunderstanding of Vladimir Propp and his relationship with later structuralist film theory, via Claude Levi-Strauss.
5. Ibid., p.60.
6. This research was funded by the Economic and Social Research Council (Award No. 000222491). We plan to publish the findings of this in full in the near future.
7. Wayne Booth, *The Rhetoric of Fiction*, Chicago: University of Chicago Press 1961, p.4.
8. Ibid., pp.83–4.
9. Susan Suleiman, 'Introduction: varieties of audience-oriented criticism', in Susan Suleiman & Inge Crosman (eds), *The Reader in the Text: Essays on Audience and Interpretation*, Princeton, NJ: Princeton University Press 1980, p.9.
10. Peter J. Rabinowitz, 'Audience's experience of literary borrowing', in Suleiman & Crosman, *The Reader in the Text*, pp.241–63. This quotation, pp.243–4.
11. Jonathan Culler, *On Deconstruction: Theory and Criticism after Structuralism*, London: Routledge 1983, pp.34–5.
12. Wolfgang Iser, *The Implied Reader*, Baltimore: Johns Hopkins University Press 1974, p.xvii.
13. Horst Ruthrof, *The Reader's Construction of Narrative*, London: Routledge 1981, pp.48–9. Notice in this quote the necessary balancing act indicated in the last sentence. After an account which seems to talk entirely of the *reader*, Ruthrof calls the outcome the *narrative*'s work-ideology.
14. See, for instance, Wolfgang Iser, 'Interaction between text and reader', in Suleiman & Crosman, *The Reader in the Text*, pp.106–19.
15. A rare but very useful essay on this concept in media studies is John Corner's 'Meaning, genre, context', in James Curran & Michael Gurevitch (eds), *Mass*

Media and Society, London: Edward Arnold 1996, pp.267–84. But Corner's essay contains a major lacuna, in fostering a hard distinction between 'factual'
and 'fictional' media, which I have addressed in my 'Taking the extreme case:
understanding a fascist fan of Judge Dredd', in Deborah Cartmell *et al.* (eds),
Trash Aesthetics: Popular Culture and its Audience, London: Pluto Press 1997,
pp.14–30.

16. For an example of the latter, let me cite my own reaction to *The Matrix* (1999).
The premise, as the film gradually untangles, is that the human race, bar a
very few who have managed to break free, are held in foetus-like positions
coupled to machines which feed them dreams of reality. Keanu Reeves' hero
has the task of invading the central computer and beating it at its own game,
so that humans can be free to choose. My struggle set in when I put together
the above, with the state of the earth as we are shown it: a shattered, post-
nuclear lifeless crust. If Reeves at the end appears to break the computer and
free humanity, what on earth are they going to live on?

17. John Berger, *Another Way of Telling*, London: Writers and Readers 1992,
pp.284–5.

18. Paul Ricoeur, 'Between the text and its readers', in his *A Ricoeur Reader*,
New York: Harvester Wheatsheaf 1991. This quote, p.403.

19. How about: '*The Usual Suspects* contains at least thirty deaths, most of them
horribly violent. Guns play a large part of this, and are sometimes shown
almost fetishistically. This is a film which celebrates the underworld of criminals, and tries to make you even like them. The police are shown as corrupt,
an attitude hardly designed to encourage respect for law and order. Only one
character has any good motives, and he is shown at the end of the film to be
a fool'? It is interesting to play this game with a film which, so far as I know,
did not receive any such treatment. Michael Rogin interestingly does this with
Independence Day (1996), a film which, on its release, received celebratory
responses from American politicians who took it as an instance of positivity
to be set against such awful things as *Natural Born Killers*. As Rogin points out,
mischievously, they were vying to welcome a film which 'wipes out a hundred
million humans' before its happy end. (Michael Rogin, *Independence Day, or
How I Learned to Stop Worrying and Love the Enola Gay*, London: BFI 1998, p.10.)

20. The Formalists' terms for these, 'fabula' and 'syuzhet', are easily confused with
apparently equivalent distinctions drawn by other, especially literary, theorists.
But they function differently from, for example, 'story' and 'discourse' (Seymour
Chatman's pairing), or 'presented world' and 'presentational process' (Horst
Ruthrof's).

Chapter 3. Usual Suspects, Unusual Devices

1. A number of instances were shown in the television documentary 'Nothing Is
What It Seems: The Making of *The Usual Suspects*' – itself an unusual achievement, since such documentaries are usually made as promotional materials *in
advance* of a film's release. This was made and released *after* the film gained its
unexpected popularity – hence its ability to include honorific responses. See in
addition *The Face*, January 1996, which used the poster, significantly, to compose a set of grunge images of young bodies displaying bruises, like victims of

police violence, each tagged with a line from the film. I owe my knowledge of these to a student at Sussex University, Athena Kalkopoulou. As late as 1999 at least one such 'borrow' occurred, in an advertisement for ITV's *Daylight Robbery*, with the linking caption 'the unusual suspects'. (See *The Guardian*, 9 September 1999, p.17.)

2. See for example Todd McCarthy, film critic of *Variety*, cited in 'Nothing Is What It Seems'.

3. 'Introduction: Christopher McQuarrie interviewed by Todd Lippy', in Chris McQuarrie, *The Usual Suspects* (script of the film), London: Faber & Faber 1996.

4. J. P. Tellotte, 'Rounding up *The Usual Suspects*: the comforts of character and neo-noir', *Film Quarterly*, Vol.51, No.4, 1998, pp.12–20. Another issue lurks in Tellotte's essay. He borrows from David Bordwell the notion that classical Hollywood cinema is characterised by giving 'realistic' motivation to its characters. Too large an issue to deal with here, still, I want at least to raise the idea that what counts as 'realistic' is a function of *shared repertoires* of recognisable behaviours – a great number of which would not seem *at all* realistic outside films.

5. Kristin Thompson, *Breaking the Glass Armor: Neo-Formalist Film Analysis*, Princeton, NJ: Princeton University Press 1988. See in particular Chapter 5 'Duplicitous narration and *Stage Fright*'. For an opposite view of the significance of this process, see Claire Johnston, '*Double Indemnity*', in E. Ann Kaplan, *Women in Film Noir*, London: BFI 1980, pp.100–111. Johnston is led to her conclusion – that films such as *Double Indemnity* are an embodiment of patriarchal law, resolving away the male fear of 'castration' – by dint of 'knowing in advance' that, faced with a choice between the evidence from narration and evidence from diegetic developments, the 'spectator can do no other than identify with the camera' (p.101). Why? And who? Evidently she didn't – so who does she know who did?

6. This sub-head is borrowed, purposefully, from an essay by Trevor Pateman, 'How is understanding an advertisement possible?' (in Howard Davis & Paul Walton (eds), *Language, Image, Media*, Oxford: Basil Blackwell 1983, pp.187–204). Largely forgotten, Pateman's essay argues that to understand an advertisement is only possible *once a person has identified and taken note* that it is indeed an advertisement. This assertion ran counter to the claims implicit in the then-dominant semiotic approach to materials such as advertisements. This claim, that understanding materials such as advertisements or films requires shared cultural knowledges and repertoires, is in principle more widely acknowledged now, but in practice has had little impact on the way researchers approach such a topic. A related point is made in Justin Lewis' *The Ideological Octopus* (New York: Routledge 1991) when he picks up on the absurdity of those analyses of music videos which fail to take account of the fact that they are made as 'promos' (pp.45–8). Such is the hold of certain styles of analysing films that while Pateman's and Lewis' point might be conceded for their materials, it does not seem so obvious if we seek to emphasise, when asking about possible relations to audiences, that something is a 'film'.

Chapter 4. 'An Ant With Ideas …'

1. Although *Antz* must count as a financial success, its takings do not compare favourably with those achieved by Disney's *A Bug's Life* which earned more

than double *Antz*' income from the box office and will assuredly have out-stripped its video performance.

2. Something of this 'adulthood' was expressed in publicity around the film which stressed the difference that *Antz* had from Disney's productions. See for instance David Elmer, 'Disney makes cartoons. DreamWorks make animated movies', *The Guardian*, 4 December 1998, G2, p.10.

3. *Antz* is not alone in containing within itself such paradoxical politics. A recently screened episode of *The Simpsons* had Rupert Murdoch as a guest character, having him speak of himself as a 'tyrant'. *The Simpsons* was produced by one of Murdoch's own companies.

4. Not my association alone. The Internet Movie DataBase lists *ID4* as one of the movie references (among a dozen others) contained in *Antz*.

5. It's worth noting a small point here. In the production notes supplied to press and cinemas, it says:

> Microphotography books also gave them insight to the perspective of an ant. 'The central challenge for us on this film was to get down to a scale where the most imperceptible details on the smallest natural elements revealed totally new and fantastic worlds of textures and forms', says Bell. 'Once we were able to visualise that perspective, we knew we had something unique.' Producer Aron Warner adds, 'Most people don't spend a lot of time wondering what a blade of grass would look if you were very, very tiny. So we spent a lot of time with cameras down at ant level looking at the world and examining textures close up'. (*Antz* Production Notes, UIP & DreamWorks 1997, p.14)

What is missing from this is any recognition of the *as if* quality they have introduced. Ants' eyes are configured very differently from humans (therefore without our distance resolution); and human motion to an ant would seem impossibly *fast*, not slow motion. But these qualities are necessary for the *as if almost-human* quality of this special scene.

6. What I argue here amends in important ways the account I proposed, with Kate Brooks, in *Knowing Audiences: Judge Dredd, its Friends, Fans and Foes*, Luton: University of Luton Press 1998 (Chapter 10).

7. Albert J. LaValley, 'Traditions of trickery: the role of special effects in the science fiction film', in George Slusser & Eric S. Rabkin (eds), *Shadows of the Magic Lamp: Fantasy and Science Fiction in Film*, Carbondale: Southern Illinois University Press 1985, p.144.

8. Ibid.

9. Steve Neale, 'Hollywood strikes back: special effects in recent American cinema', *Screen*, Vol.21, No.3, 1980, pp.101–5.

10. Robin Baker, 'Computer technology and special effects in contemporary cinema', in Philip Hayward & Tana Wollen (eds), *Future Visions: New Technologies of the Screen*, London: BFI 1993, pp.31–45.

11. Scott Bukatman, 'Zooming out: the end of off-screen space', in Jon Lewis (ed.), *The New American Cinema*, Durham, NC: Duke University Press 1998, pp.248–72.

12. Michael Rogin, *Independence Day or How I Learned to Stop Worrying and Love the Enola Gay*, London: BFI 1998.

13. Brooks Landon, *The Aesthetics of Ambivalence: Rethinking Science Fiction Film in the Age of Electronic (Re)production*, Westport, CT: Greenwood Press 1992.

14. See *The Aesthetics of Ambivalence* pp.95–100 for Landon's statement of this.
15. See for instance Warren Buckland, 'Between science fact and science fiction: Spielberg's digital dinosaurs, possible worlds and the new aesthetic realism' (pp.158–76), and Michele Pierson, 'CGI effects in Hollywood science-fiction cinema 1989–95: the wonder years' (pp.177–92), both in *Screen*, Vol.40, No.2, 1999.

Chapter 5. *Titanic*: A Knight to Remember

1. Richard Howells, *The Myth of the Titanic*, Basingstoke: Macmillan 1999.
2. See Stephen J. Spignesi, *The Complete Titanic: From the Ship's Earliest Blueprints to the Epic Film*, Secaucus, NJ: Birch Lane Press 1998. The story in question is Morgan Robertson's 'The wreck of the Titan', originally published in 1898, and reprinted in full in Spignesi's collection.
3. For an excellent account of Cameron's life and work up to *Titanic*, see Christopher Heard, *Dreaming Aloud: The Life and Films of James Cameron*, Toronto: Doubleday 1997.
4. For useful accounts of the making and distribution of the film, see Paula Parisi, *Titanic and the Making of James Cameron*, London: Orion Paperbacks 1998; and Kevin S. Sandler & Gaylyn Studlar (eds), *Titanic: Anatomy of a Blockbuster*, New Brunswick, NJ: Rutgers University Press 1999.
5. Indeed when the film was running late and over-budget, the title's associations became a resource for sneering press predictions.
6. I have to note that these words exactly repeat a crucial exchange in *Blade Runner* (1982), when Deckard, near the end of the film, finds the replicant Rachel asleep and, choosing to save rather than kill her, wakes her to flee together.
7. A 1998 documentary 'The computer that ate Hollywood' (*Horizon*, BBC2 31 April 1998) includes an interview with *Titanic*'s special effects designers, one of whom remarks specifically that unlike most other films the FX in this film were *designed* to be invisible.
8. This is part of a larger retheorisation of special effects in which I have been engaged. The principles of it are that special effects, in so far as audiences engage with them, amount to shifts in the *modality of viewing* or, in other words, alterations at that point in audiences' relationships to the narrative process. But the implication, if this is at all useful, is that beyond a certain point there cannot be a *general* theory of special effects since the 'special' can only be defined by its difference from the ordinary modality of viewing proposed by the particular film within which FX occur.
9. 'The epic form transforms the accomplishments of the past into an inspirational entertainment for the present, trading on received ideas of a continuing national or cultural consciousness, Myth – the projection of a people's beliefs into a fictional past – allows scope for allegory based on moral, religious, or political qualities pertinent to the audience'. Derek Elley, *The Epic Film: Myth and History*, London: Routledge & Kegan Paul 1984, p.13. See also J. B. Hainsworth, *The Idea of Epic*, Berkeley: University of California Press 1991, who proposes that epics 'must be more than storytelling' (p.7), and that one indication of this is that their names usually refer to wider meanings. His examples are *Paradise Lost* and *The Odyssey*, but *Titanic* works just as well.

Chapter 6. In the Jungle, the Mighty Jungle

1. The story of *The Lion King*'s success is well told in Peter Kramer's 'Entering the magic kingdom: the Walt Disney company, *The Lion King* and the limitations of criticism', given as a paper to the annual conference of the British Association for American Studies, Birmingham in April 1997, to be published in *Film Studies*, No.2, 2000. I owe most of my detailed information on its earnings to this.
2. I propose this expression 'contracted semioticians' to summarise what I sense (although my suggestion is tentative) is a new situation in Hollywood, under which stars are employed on actors' contracts (earning no points, having no script or editorial rights) but whose presence is important for the way they contribute to the overall package of meanings in a film. Particularly relevant to voiced characters in animated films, such semioticians authenticate movie characters and broaden their dimensions. A very clear example of this relationship was Robin Williams as the genie in Disney's *Aladdin* (1992).
3. On the family audience, see again Peter Kramer, 'Would you take your child to see this film? The cultural and social work of the family-adventure movie', in Steve Neale and Murray Smith, *Contemporary Hollywood Cinema*, London: Routledge 1997, pp.294–311.
4. Jack Zipes, *Fairy Tale as Myth, Myth as Fairy Tale*, Lexington: University Press of Kentucky 1994, esp. Chapter 3 'Breaking the Disney spell'.
5. Janet Wasko, *Hollywood in the Information Age: Beyond the Silver Screen*, Cambridge: Polity Press 1994.
6. Kramer, 'Would you take your child to see this film?'
7. Alan Bryman, 'The Disneyisation of society', *Sociological Review*, 1999, pp.25–47. On 'McDonaldization', see George Ritzer, *The McDonaldization of Society*, London: Sage 1995; *The McDonaldization Thesis: Explorations and Extensions*, London: Sage 1997; and Barry Smart (ed.), *Resisting McDonaldization*, London: Sage 1999.
8. Robin Wood, ''80s cinema: dominant tendencies', *CineAction!*, Vol.1, Spring 1985, pp.2–5. See also his *Hollywood from Reagan to Vietnam*, New York: Columbia University Press 1986, esp. Chapter 8 'Papering the cracks: fantasy and ideology'.
9. Their problem here would parallel that to which Tania Modleski draws attention, in her *Loving with a Vengeance: Mass-Produced Fantasies for Women*, New York: Methuen 1984. She notes that in many romances identification is a real problem given the tendency of the heroine to be asleep, or unconscious, at the moment when the male manages to come to terms with his mixed emotions.
10. For an excellent introduction to the way animals have been made to 'represent', see Steve Baker, *Picturing the Beast: Animals, Identity and Representation*, Manchester: Manchester University Press 1993.
11. The temptations to find 'masked blackness' overwhelm some authors. Eleanor Byrne & Martin McQuillan's *Deconstructing Disney* (London: Pluto Press 1999, Chapter 5: 'Racing Disney') reads *The Lion King* as winding itself into a knot on this issue, in their deconstructionist determination to do away with any empirical tests, or even referents. A recent newspaper article claimed a similar problem in the new *Star Wars: The Phantom Menace* (1999). John Sutherland discussed why the character Jar Jar Binks – ostensibly a cheerful alien ally – has

become sufficiently controversial as to have a website dedicated to his death (www.jarjarmustdie.com). Analogising with Raymond Williams' suggestion that *Animal Farm* owes some of its 'charm' to making the working class allegorically into animals, Sutherland argues that Jar Jar's problem is that he is 'miscegenated'. 'New technologies allow Lucas a divine power. He can "create" species. What, at a level between subtext, disturbs the thoughtful observer of *Phantom Menace* most is not the "racism" of the representation of Jar Jar, but the fact that he can't be categorised. When the fuss dies down, and audience come to terms with that, Jar Jar may well be seen as the first post-modern black face.' John Sutherland, 'Phantom menace or post-modernist?', *The Guardian*, 31 May 1999, G2, p.7. Actually, a visit to the 'jarjarmustdie' website doesn't really support Sutherland's account – its objection to Binks is more that he just isn't *funny*.

12. On *Falling Down*, see the excellent essay by John Gabriel, 'What do you do when minority means you? *Falling Down* and the construction of "whiteness"', *Screen*, Vol.37, No.2, 1996, pp.129–51.

13. Richard Dyer, *Only Entertainment*, London: Routledge 1992, Chapter 2.

Chapter 7. 'Like Food Processors, But Nasty'

1. This phrase is lifted from a very funny review in the *San Francisco Chronicle*, 7 November 1997, accessed through the Internet.

2. For a good account of Paul Verhoeven's life and work, see Rob van Scheers, *Paul Verhoeven*, (trans. Aletta Stevens), London: Faber and Faber 1997.

3. See *Screen International*, 23 April 1999: '*Starship Troopers* remake creates digital depth.'

4. On this period of American intellectual and cultural life, see James Gilbert's *A Cycle of Outrage: America's Reaction to the Juvenile Delinquent in the 1950s*, New York: Oxford University Press 1986.

5. See Robert Heinlein, *Stranger in a Strange Land*, Sevenoaks: New English Library 1965.

6. On this, see my (with Kate Brooks) *Knowing Audiences: Judge Dredd, its Friends, Fans and Foes*, Luton: University of Luton Press 1998, esp. Chapter 9.

7. Paul M. Sammon, *The Making of Starship Troopers*, London: Little, Brown & Co. 1997: 'Through the character of Johnny Rico, Heinlein espouses certain ethical and moral issues which have been variously described as reactionary, libertarian, or right-wing. Moreover, *Starship Troopers*' planet-wide values of discipline, personal responsibility, and sacrifice of the individual for the good of the group – characteristics heartily endorsed by the futuristic, militaristic culture under which Rico lives – have resulted in a "society that works", a not-so-subtle slam against the more "liberal" attitudes of the twentieth century (which, at least in Heinlein's view, resulted in a society that didn't work). Additionally, what little crime is left on *Starship Troopers*' Earth is dealt with swiftly and ruthlessly – sometimes by public floggings and hangings.' (p.4)

8. Interview with Ed Neumeier, *Dreamwatch*, No.42, February 1998, p.41. Neumeier put it well also in *The Making of Starship Troopers*: '[T]he message of the original book was pretty straightforward: Democracy is failing, and we need some strict controls on our culture. I retained that outlook in the *ST* scripts. But I

also wanted to play with it. To me, the whole spin of the movie is this: You want a world that works? Okay, we'll show you one. And it really *does* work. It happens to be a military dictatorship, but it works. That was the original rhythm I was trying to play with, just to sort of mess with the audience. It'll be interesting to see if it works.' (p.12)

9. In Sammon, *The Making of Starship Troopers*, pp.11–12.
10. John Berger, *Ways of Seeing*, Harmondsworth: Penguin 1972.
11. 'We purposely sabotaged your sense of the movie. You can cheer one moment because the big Bug has been blown up and then you lose your favourite character.' Ed Neumeier, interviewed in *Starburst*, No.223, January 1998, p.26.
12. Review, *Metro Pulse*, 17 November 1997, found at www.weeklywire.com/filmvault/knox/s/starshiptroopers1.html

Chapter 8. Dear Meg, Dearest Tom

1. On the re-emergence of the 'woman's film', see Peter Kramer, '"Women first": *Titanic*, action-adventure films and Hollywood's female audience', *Historical Journal of Film, Radio and Television*, Vol.18, No.4, Winter 1998, pp.599–618.
2. See, for instance, Tania Modleski, *Loving with a Vengeance: Mass-Produced Fantasies for Women*, New York: Methuen 1984; and Ann Snitow, 'Mass-market romance: pornography for women is different', in Ann Snitow *et al.* (eds), *Desire: The Politics of Sexuality*, London: Virago 1984, pp.258–75.
3. See, for instance, Ien Ang, *Watching Dallas: Soap Opera and the Melodramatic Imagination*, London: Methuen 1985; and Janice Radway, *Reading the Romance: Women, Patriarchy and Popular Literature*, Chapel Hill: University Press of North Carolina 1984.
4. Not my judgement alone: 'the dearth of theory and criticism about comedy in general and the "unbearable lightness" (in Andrew Horton's words) of what does exist'. Kathleen Rowe, 'Comedy, melodrama and gender: theorising the genres of laughter', in Kristine Brunowska Karnick & Henry Jenkins, *Classical Hollywood Comedy*, New York: Routledge 1995, p.43.
5. See my review of the different ways of 'reading' humour in the Disney comic books, in my *Comics: Ideology, Power and the Critics*, Manchester: Manchester University Press 1989, Chapter 13. For one of the most famous examples of seeing humour as a form of disguise, see Ariel Dorfman & Armand Mattelart, *How To Read Donald Duck: Imperialist Ideology in the Disney Comics*, New York: International General 1973.
6. But see the recent studies by Bruce Babington & Peter Williams Evans, *Affairs to Remember: Comedy of the Sexes*, Manchester: Manchester University Press 1989, and Peter Williams Evans & Celestino Deleyto (eds), *Terms of Endearment: Hollywood Romantic Comedy of the 1980s and 1990s*, Edinburgh: Edinburgh University Press 1998.
7. See for instance Susan Purdie, *Comedy: The Mastery of Discourse*, Hassocks: Harvester Wheatsheaf 1993.
8. Steve Neale & Frank Krutnik, *Popular Film and Television Comedy*, London: Routledge 1990.
9. Ibid., p.149.
10. Ibid., p.150.

11. Kristine Brunovska Karnick, 'Commitment and reaffirmation in Hollywood romantic comedy', in Karnick & Jenkins, *Classical Hollywood Comedy*, pp.123–46.
12. Peter Evans' essay on Meg Ryan makes much of this moment, in a way that to me reveals the bizarreness of deconstructive modes of enquiry:

> When Walter discovers her hidden in the kitchen broom cupboard in the middle of the night ..., she screams at him, 'Walter, you scared me. Don't ever do that again!' The remark is as significant as Walter's own *Cluedo*-inspired accusation: 'Miss Scarlett, in the broom closet, with the radio!' Both the accusation and the reaction it provokes are given a comic mode and setting, but their aim is higher than farce. There is an unconscious level at which the remark belongs to a pattern of dramatised frustrations and tensions surrounding the Meg Ryan persona which sometimes seems in spite of itself to wish to free it from its American sweetheart packaging. Read deconstructively, the remark represents an unconscious desire for the cynical, darker, more sexualised Meg Ryan to come out, if not from the closet, then from the domestic broom cupboard of ideological fantasy. (Peter William Evans, 'Meg Ryan, superstar', in Evans & Deleyto (eds), *Terms of Endearment*, pp.188–208. This quote, pp.195–6.)

This weird interpretation seems to have nothing to do with the film, its narrative process or the role of this moment with them, and everything to do with an analyst's need to say 'something different'.
13. See for instance Christine Gledhill (ed.), *Stardom: Industry of Desire*, London: Routledge 1991; and Richard Dyer, *Heavenly Bodies: Film Stars and Society*, Basingstoke: Macmillan 1987.
14. See for instance Yvonne Tasker, *Spectacular Bodies: Gender, Genre and the Action Cinema*, London: Routledge 1993; and Susan Jeffords, *Hard Bodies: Hollywood Masculinity in the Reagan Era*, New Brunswick, NJ: Rutgers University Press 1994.
15. Barry King, 'Stardom as an occupation', in Paul Kerr (ed.), *The Hollywood Film Industry*, London: Routledge & Kegan Paul 1986, and 'The star and the commodity: notes towards a performance theory of stardom', *Cultural Studies*, Vol.1, No.2, 1987, pp.145–61.
16. Steve Neale, 'The *Big* romance or *Something Wild*?: romantic comedy today', *Screen*, Vol.33, No.3, Autumn 1992, pp.284–99.
17. Virginia Wright Wexman, *Creating the Couple: Love, Marriage and Hollywood Performance*, Princeton, NJ: Princeton University Press 1993.

Chapter 9. A Very Deep Impact

1. Mike Goodridge, Review of *Deep Impact*, *Screen International*, 15–21 May 1998, p.24.
2. See Kim Newman, *Millennium Movies: End of the World Cinema*, London: Titan Books 1999, especially pp.256–7. See also Diane Negra, '*Titanic*, survivalism, and the millennial myth', in Kevin S. Sandler & Gaylyn Studlar (eds), *Titanic: Anatomy of a Blockbuster*, New Brunswick, NJ: Rutgers University Press 1999, pp.220–38.
3. Newman, *Millennium Movies*, p.135.
4. In a fascinating examination of the 'social construction' of natural disasters in Southern California, Mike Davis has argued that rampant urbanisation and

unrealistic expectations fed by boosterism have combined with a volatile yet predictable 'Mediterranean' climate to produce a highly destructive cycle of floods, earthquakes and fires. One implication of Davis' work – which remains relatively underdeveloped – is that such 'local' conditions have inflected filmic and literary representations of disaster. Mike Davis, *Ecology of Fear: Los Angeles and the Imagination of Disaster*, New York: Metropolitan Books, London: Picador 1998.

5. Rick Altman, *Film/Genre*, London: BFI 1999, pp.41–7.

6. Howard Rabinowitz has suggested that the late 1990s disaster movie production cycle was initiated by the successful relocation of spectacular special effects from science fiction to earth-bound disaster scenarios in three major box office hits: *Independence Day* (1996), *The Lost World* (1997) and *Twister* (1997). Rabinowitz, 'The End Is Near! Why disaster movies make sense (and dollars) in the '90s', *Washington Monthly* April 1997, pp.38–41. Thanks to Dan Chappell for pointing me to this article.

7. *Armageddon* producer Jerry Bruckheimer described the film as 'a *Dirty Dozen* in outer space'. Cited in Charles Fleming, *High Concept: Don Simpson and the Hollywood Culture of Excess*, London: Bloomsbury 1998, p.263.

8. This trend is most apparent in the work of director superstar James Cameron, from *Aliens* (1986) to *Titanic* (1997). See Peter Kramer, '"Women first": *Titanic*, action-adventure films and Hollywood's female audience', *Historical Journal of Film, Radio and Television*, Vol.18, No.4, Winter 1998, pp.599–618.

9. Cf. Richard Dyer's comments on Freeman as 'the site of wisdom' in *Seven*. Dyer, *Seven*, London: BFI Modern Classics 1999, p.9.

10. Unlike *The Towering Inferno* (1974), *Titanic*, *Jaws* (1975) and countless other disaster/horror movies, those in positions of authority in *Deep Impact* are never complacent in the face of danger.

11. For a more exaggerated version of this character function, see Bruce Willis' oil driller in *Armageddon*. Unlike *Deep Impact*, that film borrows the war film template of an initially inept bureaucracy (NASA) disrupted and ultimately revitalised by a maverick hero who mediates between top brass and lower ranks, and whose expertise is grounded in action rather than theory. What both films share, despite their differences, is an ultimately affirmative message of trust in authority and reliance on those in uniform. Cf. Nick Roddick on this tendency in 1970s disaster films, in his excellent 'Only the stars survive', in D. Bradby *et al.* (eds), *Performance and Politics in Popular Drama: Aspects of Popular Entertainment in Theatre, Film and Television, 1800–1976*, Cambridge: Cambridge University Press 1980, p.261.

12. An internet review by Steve Kong (1998) notes the film's affiliations with NBC and Microsoft. Leoni previously starred in NBC's *The Naked Truth*, and director Leder and two supporting actors have worked on the network's hit show *ER*, which shares an executive producer with the film in Steven Spielberg. In the film, Lerner works for MSNBC, and uses Microsoft's software to search for the meaning of E.L.E.

13. Roddick, 'Only the stars survive'.

14. Compare Ib Bondebjerg's comments about 'real life rescue' television shows: 'Everyday life is given a much stronger dimension and meaning, often expressed in the final statement of the people involved: they have come closer to each other, they have learned to value life and to take care of what they have.'

Bondebjerg, 'Public discourse/private fascination: hybridization in "true-life-story" genres', *Media, Culture and Society*, Vol.8, 1996, pp.27–45.

15. See Chapter 4 of this book for further discussion of this.

16. For an instance where this relationship is not worked through, see Michele Pierson's interesting essay on the role of FX in contemporary science fiction films ('CGI effects in Hollywood science-fiction cinema 1989–95: The wonder years', *Screen*, Vol.40, No.2, 1999, pp.177–92). Pierson argues that the meaning of FX was heavily mediated in this period such that primary attention inevitably focused on the accumulation of technical prowess. The problem is that her argument draws heavily, for its evidence, on magazines such as *Starlog* and *SFX* which tend to celebrate FX *as* effects – in other words, the second aspect only of the dual nature of effects. In so doing, it misses out precisely what seems most interesting, and what emerged in Barker & Brooks' study of audiences for such action/sci fi movies, that these movies proffer through their use of FX ways of conceiving the future in relation to the present.

17. Warren Buckland, 'A close encounter with *Raiders of the Lost Ark*: notes on narrative aspects of the New Hollywood blockbuster', in Steve Neale & Murray Smith (eds), *Contemporary Hollywood Cinema*, London: Routledge 1997, pp.166–77.

18. Noel Carroll has argued that suspense is produced when an audience expects an event to occur, but wishes for a less likely outcome (Carroll, 'Towards a theory of film suspense', *Persistence of Vision* 1, Summer 1984, pp.65–89, quoted in David Bordwell, *Narration in the Fiction Film*, London: Methuen 1985, p.46). But as we argue below, there are important senses in which we *do* want the impact to occur – not just to witness the glorious FX but because the *characters are ready for it*.

19. Compare this with the earlier death of one of the space crew, Portenza. It comes after we have been given 'perfect vision' sequences of the wondrous technology of 'Messiah': a sleek clean spaceship, viewed at the very best angles to emphasise its marvels. But as they prepare to attempt the landing on the comet, two things change. (1) Technology is no longer adequate: Fish switches to manual, and uses raw human skills out of honed experience to get them down. (2) The manner of filming becomes experiential. Shaky camerawork, images breaking up, inserts of information from instruments, broken sound. At its height, as we approach the moment of Portenza's death, a sudden and without warning switch positions us within the soundscape of a helmet outside the ship (alone, echoey, without clear location). This dislocation prepares us for the *uselessness* and *pointless horror* of Portenza's death. He does not simply die, his life is wasted. To die in this way is just scary and awful, with no redeeming transcendence.

20. See, for example, Philip Strick's review in *Sight and Sound*, Vol.8, No.7, July 1998, p.40.

21. Our approach here shares an idea interestingly proposed by Linda Williams, who has suggested that the three 'body' genres of horror, pornography and melodrama work with different presumptions about how audiences will relate to the *time* within the films. So, horror encourages us to relate to its stricken characters by feeling that they will face death *too soon*; pornography arouses its viewers to hope to parallel the film's arrival at orgasm with their own *just in time*; while melodrama encourages us to weep at characters arriving (at

realisation, or whatever) *just too late* (see Linda Williams, 'Film bodies: gender, genre and excess', *Film Quarterly*, Vol.44, No.4, 1991, pp.2–13). The similarity of ideas is striking, I think – but with this difference. Williams feels obliged to ground her argument in a deal of psychoanalytic claims which, to me, look not only unnecessary but positively inconsistent with this insight. Williams' own work in other areas has been enormously fruitful, when she has attended to specific histories, for example, of the management of the launch of Hitchcock's *Psycho*. The powerful suction towards (quintessentially anti-historical) psychoanalysis still so evident in film studies, I am arguing, undoes the possibility of pursuing such insights in concrete researches.

Chapter 10. Showing That It Is What It Is

1. David Bordwell, *Narration in the Fiction Film*, London: Methuen 1985, in particular Chapter 1.
2. This is a difficult task even to explain, and I am not seriously attempting it here. The best example I can point to of an attempt to research the history of perceiving and conceiving in this way is Robert Darnton's remarkable examination of how readers learned to read Jean-Jacques Rousseau. See his *The Great Cat Massacre, and Other Episodes in French Cultural History*, New York: Vintage Books 1985.
3. David Bordwell, *Making Meaning: Rhetoric and Inference in the Interpretation of Cinema*, Cambridge, MA: Harvard University Press 1989.
4. Rick Altman, *Film/Genre*, London: BFI 1999. This quote, p.147.
5. Bordwell, *Narration in the Fiction Film*, pp.40–7.
6. Ibid., p.47.
7. Warren Buckland, 'A close encounter with *Raiders of the Lost Ark*: notes on narrative aspects of the New Hollywood blockbuster', in Steve Neale & Murray Smith (eds), *Contemporary Hollywood Cinema*, London: Routledge 1997, pp.166–77.
8. Ibid., p.173.
9. Mike Cormack, *Ideology and Cinematography in Hollywood, 1930–39*, New York: St. Martin's Press 1994.
10. Charles Wolfe, 'Vitaphone shorts and *The Jazz Singer*', *Wide Angle*, Vol.12, No.3, 1990, pp.59–78.
11. Among the films broadcast on the radio were *Casablanca* (1942), *The Maltese Falcon* (1943), and *It's a Wonderful Life* (1947). I have not come across any discussion of the significance of these radio versions in any literature on classical Hollywood.
12. Nick Browne, 'The spectator-in-the-text: the rhetoric of *Stagecoach*', in Philip Rosen (ed.), *Narrative, Apparatus, Ideology: A Film Theory Reader*, New York: Columbia University Press 1986, pp.102–19.
13. Ibid., p.106.
14. Ibid., p.115.
15. The predominance of a very small number of ways of thinking it is possible to talk about popular films has hit me directly through two bodies of film audience research I have conducted, on *Judge Dredd* and action-adventure movies, and on Cronenberg's *Crash*. In the first case we found powerful evidence that

people assumed that if we were researching a film like this, we *must* be enquiring into whether/how far people might be made 'violent' by watching such films. In the second case, even though *Crash* does not have a single scene in it involving any interpersonal violence, people who disliked it had repeated recourse to the same language to categorise why they rejected the film: it was 'violent' without being violent.

16. There are some interesting reflections on this fact in Melanie Nash & Susan Hunt, '"Almost ashamed to say I am one of those girls": *Titanic*, Leonardo DiCaprio, and the paradoxes of girls' fandom', in Kevin S. Sandler & Gaylyn Studlar (eds) *Titanic: Anatomy of a Blockbuster*, New Brunswick, NJ: Rutgers University Press 1999, pp.64–88.

17. See Barker & Brooks, *Knowing Audiences:* Judge Dredd, *its Friends, Fans and Foes*, Luton: Luton University Press 1998, especially Chapters 6, 7 & 10.

18. For the record, how many people reading this book have ever seriously looked at the research strategies developed either by the Glasgow University Media Group or the University of Leeds Communications Group? This isn't a matter of right or wrong – it is probably well known that I have had serious disagreements with the former – but of lack of serious consideration.

19. Linda Williams, 'Introduction' to her (ed.) *Viewing Positions: Ways of Seeing Film*, New Brunswick, NJ: Rutgers University Press 1994, p.4.

20. Elizabeth Traube, *Dreaming Identities: Class, Gender & Generation in 1980s Hollywood Movies*, Boulder, CO: Westview Press 1992, p.5.

21. See most notably Janet Staiger's very valuable *Interpreting Films: Studies in the Historical Reception of American Cinema*, Princeton, NJ: Princeton University Press 1992; and see, for instance, a number of the essays in Melvyn Stokes & Richard Maltby (eds), *American Movie Audiences: From the Turn of the Century to the Early Sound Era*, London: BFI 1999.

22. Compare and contrast John Hope Franklin, '*The Birth of a Nation* – propaganda as history', in Steven Mintz & Randy Roberts (eds), *Hollywood's America: United States History through its Films*, New York: Brandywine Press 1993, or Michael Rogin, '"The sword became a flashing vision": D W Griffith's *The Birth of a Nation*', in Robert Lang (ed.), *The Birth of a Nation*, New Brunswick, NJ: Rutgers University Press 1994, pp.250–95, with Janet Staiger, *Interpreting Films*.

23. I have in mind, as an example, Eleanor Byrne & Martin McQuillan, *Deconstructing Disney*, London: Pluto Press 1999.

24. See in particular Martin Barker & Kate Brooks, 'On looking into Bourdieu's black box', in Roger Dickinson, Olga Linné & Ramaswami Harindranath (eds), *Approaches to Audiences*, London: Arnold 1998, pp.218–32.

25. This research, funded by the Economic and Social Research Council, was carried out with two colleagues, Jane Arthurs and Ramaswami Harindranath. The findings are currently being written up for publication.

26. Susan Sontag, *Against Interpretation, and Other Essays*, New York: Octagon Books 1978. My particular interest here is in the title essay.

27. Ibid., p.6.

28. Ibid., p.7.

29. Ibid., p.14.

30. Fireworks do have a typical narrative: opening show, with crescendo almost as a promise of what is to come, a series of more localised intense sets, then gradually building up to a climactic final burst.

31. I run a risk here of being misunderstood. I am not denying that films may utilise representations and that this can matter, for example, nor am I rejecting the possibility of films playing ideological roles. I am arguing that these cannot be understood and assessed except through their *functioning within particular films*. If we wish, for instance, to claim that a film may have a particular 'ideological effect', it must be through its operation *as a film*, not through some notion of social 'side-effects'.

32. On inner speech, see Valentin Volosinov, *Marxism and the Philosophy of Language*, New York: Seminar Press 1973.

33. See the review of our book by Roger Silverstone, 'So who are these people?', *Sight and Sound*, Vol.9, No.5, May 1999, pp.28–9.

Bibliography

Allen, Richard & Murray Smith (eds), *Film Theory and Philosophy*, Oxford: Oxford University Press 1997

Altman, Rick, *Film/Genre*, London: BFI 1999

Ang, Ien, *Watching Dallas: Soap Opera and the Melodramatic Imagination*, London: Methuen 1985

Babington, Bruce & Peter Williams Evans, *Affairs to Remember: Comedy of the Sexes*, Manchester: Manchester University Press 1989

Baker, Steve, *Picturing the Beast: Animals, Identity and Representation*, Manchester: Manchester University Press 1993

Barker, Martin, *Comics: Ideology, Power and the Critics*, Manchester: Manchester University Press 1989

— & Kate Brooks, *Knowing Audiences: Judge Dredd, its Friends, Fans and Foes*, Luton: University of Luton Press 1998

— & Julian Petley (eds), *Ill Effects: The Media/Violence Debate*, London: Routledge 2000

Berger, John, *Ways of Seeing*, Harmondsworth: Penguin 1972

—, *Another Way of Telling*, London: Writers and Readers 1992

Bondebjerg, Ib, 'Public discourse/private fascination: hybridization in "true-life-story" genres', *Media, Culture and Society*, Vol.8, 1996, pp.27–45

Booth, Wayne, *The Rhetoric of Fiction*, Chicago: University of Chicago Press 1961

Bordwell, David, *Narration in the Fiction Film*, London: Methuen 1985

—, *Making Meaning: Rhetoric and Inference in the Interpretation of Cinema*, Cambridge, MA: Harvard University Press 1989

— & Kristin Thompson, *Film Art: An Introduction*, New York: McGraw Hill 1993

Bradby, D. *et al.* (eds), *Performance and Politics in Popular Drama: Aspects of Popular Entertainment in Theatre, Film and Television, 1800–1976*, Cambridge: Cambridge University Press 1980

Browne, Kevin, 'Violence in the media causes crime: myth or reality', Inaugural Lecture, University of Birmingham, 3 June 1999

Bryman, Alan, 'The Disneyisation of society', *Sociological Review*, 1999, pp.25–47

Buckland, Warren, 'Between science fact and science fiction: Spielberg's digital dinosaurs, possible worlds and the new aesthetic realism', *Screen*, Vol.40, No.2, 1999, pp.158–76

Byrne, Eleanor & Martin McQuillan, *Deconstructing Disney*, London: Pluto Press 1999

Carroll, Noel, 'Towards a theory of film suspense', *Persistence of Vision* 1, Summer 1984, pp.65–89

Cartmell, Deborah *et al.* (eds), *Trash Aesthetics: Popular Culture and its Audience*, London: Pluto Press 1997

Cormack, Mike, *Ideology and Cinematography in Hollywood, 1930–39*, New York: St. Martin's Press 1994

Culler, Jonathan, *On Deconstruction: Theory and Criticism after Structuralism*, London: Routledge 1983

Curran, James & Michael Gurevitch (eds), *Mass Media and Society*, London: Edward Arnold 1996

Darnton, Robert, *The Great Cat Massacre, and Other Episodes in French Cultural History*, New York: Vintage Books 1985

Davis, Mike, *Ecology of Fear: Los Angeles and the Imagination of Disaster*, New York: Metropolitan Books, London: Picador 1998

Davis, Howard & Paul Walton (eds), *Language, Image, Media*, Oxford: Basil Blackwell 1983

Dickinson, Roger, Olga Linné & Ramaswami Harindranath (eds), *Approaches to Audiences*, London: Arnold 1998

Dorfman, Ariel & Armand Mattelart, *How to Read Donald Duck: Imperialist Ideology in the Disney Comics*, New York: International General 1973

Dyer, Richard, *Heavenly Bodies: Film Stars and Society*, Basingstoke: Macmillan 1987

—, *Only Entertainment*, London: Routledge 1992

—, *Seven*, London: BFI Modern Classics 1999

Elley, Derek, *The Epic Film: Myth and History*, London: Routledge & Kegan Paul 1984

Elmer, David, 'Disney makes cartoons. DreamWorks make animated movies', *The Guardian*, 4 December 1998, G2, p.10

Evans, Peter Williams & Celestino Deleyto (eds), *Terms of Endearment: Hollywood Romantic Comedy of the 1980s and 1990s*, Edinburgh: Edinburgh University Press 1998

Film Education Working Group, *Making Movies Matter*, London: BFI 1999

Fleming, Charles, *High Concept: Don Simpson and the Hollywood Culture of Excess*, London: Bloomsbury 1998

Gabriel, John, 'What do you do when minority means you? *Falling Down* and the construction of "whiteness"', *Screen*, Vol.37, No.2, 1996, pp.129–51

Gilbert, James, *A Cycle of Outrage: America's Reaction to the Juvenile Delinquent in the 1950s*, New York: Oxford University Press 1986

Girgus, Sam B., *Hollywood Renaissance: The Cinema of Democracy in the Time of Ford, Capra and Kazan*, Cambridge: Cambridge University Press 1998

Gledhill, Christine (ed.), *Stardom: Industry of Desire*, London: Routledge 1991

Goodridge, Mike, Review of *Deep Impact*, *Screen International*, 15–21 May 1998, p.24

Hainsworth, J. B., *The Idea of Epic*, Berkeley: University of California Press 1991

Hayward, Philip & Tana Wollen (eds), *Future Visions: New Technologies of the Screen*, London: BFI 1993

Heard, Christopher, *Dreaming Aloud: The Life and Films of James Cameron*, Toronto: Doubleday 1997

Heinlein, Robert, *Stranger in a Strange Land*, Sevenoaks: New English Library 1965

Hill, John & Pamela Church Gibson (eds), *The Oxford Guide to Film Studies*, Oxford: Oxford University Press 1998

Hollows, Joanne & Mark Jancovich (eds), *Approaches to Popular Film*, Manchester: Manchester University Press 1995

Howells, Richard, *The Myth of the Titanic*, Basingstoke: Macmillan 1999

Iser, Wolfgang, *The Implied Reader*, Baltimore: Johns Hopkins University Press 1974

Jeffords, Susan, *Hard Bodies: Hollywood Masculinity in the Reagan Era*, New Brunswick, NJ: Rutgers University Press 1994

Kaplan, E. Ann, *Women in Film Noir*, London: BFI 1980

Karnick, Kristine Brunowska & Henry Jenkins, *Classical Hollywood Comedy*, New York: Routledge 1995

Kellner, Douglas, *Media Culture: Cultural Studies, Identity and Politics and the Post-modern*, London: Routledge 1995

Kerr, Paul (ed.), *The Hollywood Film Industry*, London: Routledge & Kegan Paul 1986

King, Barry, 'The star and the commodity: notes towards a performance theory of stardom', *Cultural Studies*, Vol.1, No.2, 1987, pp.145–61

Kramer, Peter, '"Women first": *Titanic*, action-adventure films and Hollywood's female audience', *Historical Journal of Film, Radio and Television*, Vol.18, No.4, Winter 1998, pp.599–618

—, 'Entering the magic kingdom: the Walt Disney company, *The Lion King* and the limitations of criticism', *Film Studies*, No.2, 2000

Kuhn, Annette (ed.), *Alien Zone: Cultural Theory and Contemporary Cinema*, London: Verso 1990

Landon, Brooks, *The Aesthetics of Ambivalence: Rethinking Science Fiction Film in the Age of Electronic (Re)production*, Westport, CT: Greenwood Press 1992

Lang, Robert (ed.), *The Birth of a Nation*, New Brunswick, NJ: Rutgers University Press 1994

Lewis, Jon (ed.), *The New American Cinema*, Durham, NC: Duke University Press 1998

Lewis, Justin, *The Ideological Octopus*, New York: Routledge 1991

McQuarrie, Chris, *The Usual Suspects* (script of the film), London: Faber & Faber 1996

Mintz, Steven & Randy Roberts (eds), *Hollywood's America: United States History through its Films*, New York: Brandywine Press 1993

Modleski, Tania, *Loving with a Vengeance: Mass-Produced Fantasies for Women*, New York: Methuen 1984

Mulvey, Laura, 'Visual pleasure and narrative cinema', *Screen*, Vol.16, No.3, 1975, pp.6–18

Neale, Steve, 'Hollywood strikes back: special effects in recent American cinema', *Screen*, Vol.21, No.3, 1980, pp.101–5

—, 'The *Big* romance or *Something Wild*?: romantic comedy today', *Screen*, Vol.33, No.3, Autumn 1992, pp.284–99

— & Frank Krutnik, *Popular Film and Television Comedy*, London: Routledge 1990

— & Murray Smith (eds), *Contemporary Hollywood Cinema*, London: Routledge 1997

Newman, Kim, *Millennium Movies: End of the World Cinema*, London: Titan Books 1999

Neumeier, Ed, Interview, *Starburst*, No.223, January 1998, p.26

—, Interview, *Dreamwatch*, No.42, February 1998, p.41

Parisi, Paula, *Titanic and the Making of James Cameron*, London: Orion Paperbacks 1998

Pierson, Michele, 'CGI effects in Hollywood science-fiction cinema 1989–95: the wonder years', *Screen*, Vol.40, No.2, 1999, pp.177–92

Poague, Leland, *Another Frank Capra*, Cambridge: Cambridge University Press 1994

Purdie, Susan, *Comedy: The Mastery of Discourse*, Hassocks: Harvester Wheatsheaf 1993

Rabinowitz, Howard, 'The End Is Near! Why disaster movies make sense (and dollars) in the '90s', *Washington Monthly* April 1997, pp.38–41

Radway, Janice, *Reading the Romance: Women, Patriarchy and Popular Literature*, Chapel Hill: University Press of North Carolina 1984

Ray, Robert, *A Certain Tendency in Hollywood Cinema, 1930–1980*, Princeton, NJ: Princeton University Press 1985

Review of *Starship Troopers*, *Metro Pulse*, 17 November 1997

Ricoeur, Paul, *A Ricoeur Reader*, New York: Harvester Wheatsheaf 1991

Ritzer, George, *The McDonaldization of Society*, London: Sage 1995

—, *The McDonaldization Thesis: Explorations and Extensions*, London: Sage 1997

Rogin, Michael, *Independence Day, or How I Learned to Stop Worrying and Love the Enola Gay*, London: BFI 1998

Rosen, Philip (ed.), *Narrative, Apparatus, Ideology: A Film Theory Reader*, New York: Columbia University Press 1986

Ruthrof, Horst, *The Reader's Construction of Narrative*, London: Routledge 1981

Sammon, Paul M., *The Making of Starship Troopers*, London: Little, Brown & Co. 1997

Sandler, Kevin S. & Gaylyn Studlar (eds), *Titanic: Anatomy of a Blockbuster*, New Brunswick, NJ: Rutgers University Press 1999

Scheers, Rob van, *Paul Verhoeven* (trans. Aletta Stevens), London: Faber and Faber 1997

Silverman, Kaja, *Male Subjectivity at the Margins*, London: Routledge 1992

Silverstone, Roger, 'So who are these people?', *Sight and Sound*, Vol.9, No.5, May 1999, pp.28–9

Slusser, George & Eric S. Rabkin (eds), *Shadows of the Magic Lamp: Fantasy and Science Fiction in Film*, Carbondale: Southern Illinois University Press 1985

Smart, Barry (ed.), *Resisting McDonaldization*, London: Sage 1999

Snitow, Ann *et al.* (eds), *Desire: The Politics of Sexuality*, London: Virago 1984

Sontag, Susan, *Against Interpretation, and Other Essays*, New York: Octagon Books 1978

Spignesi, Stephen J., *The Complete Titanic: From the Ship's Earliest Blueprints to the Epic Film*, Secaucus, NJ: Birch Lane Press 1998

Staiger, Janet, *Interpreting Films: Studies in the Historical Reception of American Cinema*, Princeton, NJ: Princeton University Press 1992

Stokes, Melvyn & Richard Maltby (eds), *American Movie Audiences: From the Turn of the Century to the Early Sound Era*, London: BFI 1999

Strick, Philip, Review of *Deep Impact*, *Sight and Sound*, Vol.8, No.7, July 1998, p.40

Suleiman, Susan & Inge Crosman (eds), *The Reader in the Text: Essays on Audience and Interpretation*, Princeton, NJ: Princeton University Press 1980

Sutherland, John, 'Phantom menace or post-modernist?', *The Guardian*, 31 May 1999, G2, p.7

Tasker, Yvonne, *Spectacular Bodies: Gender, Genre and the Action Cinema*, London: Routledge 1993

Tellotte, J. P., 'Rounding up *The Usual Suspects*: the comforts of character and neo-noir', *Film Quarterly*, Vol.51, No.4, 1998, pp.12–20

Thompson, Kristin, *Breaking the Glass Armor: Neo-Formalist Film Analysis*, Princeton, NJ: Princeton University Press 1988

Traube, Elizabeth, *Dreaming Identities: Class, Gender & Generation in 1980s Hollywood Movies*, Boulder, CO: Westview Press 1992

Volosinov, Valentin, *Marxism and the Philosophy of Language*, New York: Seminar Press 1973

Wasko, Janet, *Hollywood in the Information Age: Beyond the Silver Screen*, Cambridge: Polity Press 1994

Wexman, Virginia Wright, *Creating the Couple: Love, Marriage and Hollywood Performance*, Princeton, NJ: Princeton University Press 1993

Williams, Linda (ed.), 'Film bodies: gender, genre and excess', *Film Quarterly*, Vol.44, No.4, 1991, pp.2–13

—, *Viewing Positions: Ways of Seeing Films*, New Brunswick, NJ: Rutgers University Press 1994

Wolfe, Charles, 'Vitaphone shorts and *The Jazz Singer*', *Wide Angle*, Vol.12, No.3, 1990, pp.59–78

Wood, Robin, ''80s cinema: dominant tendencies', *CineAction!*, Vol.1, Spring 1985, pp.2–5

—, *Hollywood from Reagan to Vietnam*, New York: Columbia University Press 1986

Zipes, Jack, *Fairy Tale as Myth, Myth as Fairy Tale*, Lexington: University Press of Kentucky 1994

Filmography

Affair to Remember, An (Leo McCarey, 1957)
Aladdin (Ron Clements & John Musker, 1992)
Alien (Ridley Scott, 1979)
All the President's Men (Alan Pakula, 1976)
All Quiet on the Western Front (Lewis Milestone, 1930)
Antz (Eric Darnell & Lawrence Guterman, 1998).
Armageddon (Michael Bay, 1998)
Awful Truth, The (Leo McCarey, 1937)
Basic Instinct (Paul Verhoeven, 1992)
Birth of a Nation, The (D W Griffith, 1915)
Blade Runner (Ridley Scott, 1982)
Blair Witch Project, The (Daniel Myrick & Eduardo Sánchez, 1999)
Breathless (Jean-Luc Godard, 1960)
Bug's Life, A (John Lasseter & Andrew Stanton 1998)
Cannibal Holocaust (Ruggero Deodato, 1979)
Casablanca (Michael Curtiz, 1942)
Crash (David Cronenberg, 1996)
Dante's Peak (Roger Donaldson, 1997)
Deep Impact (Mimi Leder, 1998)
Devil's Island, The (Frank O'Connor, 1926)
Die Hard franchise (John McTiernan, 1988)
Die Hard II (Renny Harlin, 1990)
Die Hard with a Vengeance (John McTiernan, 1995)
Dirty Dozen, The (Robert Aldrich, 1967)
Double Indemnity (Billy Wilder, 1944)
Driller Killer (Abel Ferrara, 1979)
ET (Steven Spielberg, 1982)
Falling Down (Joel Schumacher, 1993)
Fatal Attraction (Adrian Lyne, 1987)
Few Good Men, A (Rob Reiner, 1992)
First Blood (Ted Kotcheff, 1982)
Forrest Gump (Robert Zemeckis, 1994)
From Dusk Till Dawn (Robert Rodriguez, 1996)
Gone with the Wind (Victor Fleming, 1939)
Horse Whisperer, The (Robert Redford, 1998)
Independence Day (Roland Emmerich, 1996)
Indiana Jones and the Temple of Doom (Steven Spielberg, 1984)
It Started with a Kiss (George Marshall, 1959)
It's a Wonderful Life (Frank Capra, 1946)
Jaws (Steven Spielberg, 1975)
Jazz Singer, The (Alan Crosland, 1927)
Judge Dredd (Danny Cannon, 1996)

Jurassic Park (Steven Spielberg, 1993)
Laura (Otto Preminger, 1944)
Lion King, The (Roger Allers & Rob Minkoff, 1994)
Lion King II: Simba's Pride, The (Rob DaLuca & Darrell Rooney, 1998)
Little Big Man (Arthur Penn, 1970)
Lost World: Jurassic Park, The (Steven Spielberg, 1997)
Maltese Falcon, The (John Huston, 1941)
Matrix, The (Andy Wachowski & Larry Wachowski, 1999)
Modern Times (Charles Chaplin, 1936)
Natural Born Killers (Oliver Stone, 1994)
Old San Francisco (Alan Crosland, 1927)
Out for Justice (John Flynn, 1991)
Parallax View, The (Alan Pakula, 1974)
Patton (Franklin Schaffner, 1970)
Peacemaker, The (Mimi Leder, 1997)
Psycho (Alfred Hitchcock, 1960)
Public Access (Bryan Singer, 1993)
Pulp Fiction (Quentin Tarantino, 1994)
Raiders of the Lost Ark (Steven Spielberg, 1981)
Rear Window (Alfred Hitchcock, 1954)
Rebel Without a Cause (Nicholas Ray, 1955)
Reds (Warren Beatty, 1981)
Robocop (Paul Verhoeven, 1987)
Rocky (John Avildsen, 1976)
Romance (Catherine Breillat, 1999)
Saved from the Titanic, (Étienne Arnaud, 1912)
Saving Private Ryan (Steven Spielberg, 1998)
Schindler's List (Steven Spielberg, 1993)
Showgirls (Paul Verhoeven, 1995)
Show of Shows, The (John Adolfi, 1929)
Sleepless in Seattle (Nora Ephron, 1993)
Small Soldiers (Joe Dante, 1998)
Sound of Music, The (Robert Wise, 1964)
Stage Fright (Alfred Hitchcock, 1950)
Stagecoach (John Ford, 1939)
Starship Troopers (Paul Verhoeven, 1997)
Star Wars (George Lucas, 1977)
Star Wars: The Phantom Menace (George Lucas, 1999)
Taxi Driver (Martin Scorcese, 1976)
Tenderloin (Michael Curtiz, 1928)
Terminator, The (James Cameron, 1984)
Terminator 2: Judgement Day (James Cameron, 1991)
Terror by Night (Roy William Neill, 1946)
Titanic (James Cameron, 1997)
Top Gun (Tony Scott, 1986)
Top Hat (Mark Sandrich, 1935)
Total Recall (Paul Verhoeven, 1990)
Towering Inferno, The (Irwin Allen & John Guillerman, 1974)
Toy Story (John Lasseter, 1995)

True Lies (James Cameron, 1994)
Twister (Jan de Bont, 1996)
Usual Suspects, The (Bryan Singer, 1995)
Volcano (Mick Jackson, 1997)
When Harry Met Sally (Rob Reiner, 1989)
Who Framed Roger Rabbit? (Robert Zemeckis, 1988)

Index